D. H. LAWRENCE'S
Women in Love

❖ ❖ ❖

A CASEBOOK

Edited by
David Ellis

UNIVERSITY PRESS

2006

OXFORD
UNIVERSITY PRESS

Oxford University Press, Inc., publishes works that further
Oxford University's objective of excellence
in research, scholarship, and education.

Oxford   New York
Auckland   Cape Town   Dar es Salaam   Hong Kong   Karachi
Kuala Lumpur   Madrid   Melbourne   Mexico City   Nairobi
New Delhi   Shanghai   Taipei   Toronto

With offices in
Argentina   Austria   Brazil   Chile   Czech Republic   France   Greece
Guatemala   Hungary   Italy   Japan   Poland   Portugal   Singapore
South Korea   Switzerland   Thailand   Turkey   Ukraine   Vietnam

Copyright © 2006 by Oxford University Press, Inc.

Published by Oxford University Press, Inc.
198 Madison Avenue, New York, New York 10016

www.oup.com

Oxford is a registered trademark of Oxford University Press.

Library of Congress Cataloging-in-Publications Data
D. H. Lawrence's Women in love: a casebook/edited by David Ellis.
p. cm.—(Casebooks in criticism)
Includes bibliographical references and index.
ISBN-13 978-0-19-517026-9; 978-0-19-517027-6 (pbk.)
ISBN 0-19-517026-1; 0-19-517027-X (pbk.)
1. Lawrence, D. H. (David Herbert), 1885–1930. Women in love—
Handbooks, manuals, etc.   I. Ellis, David, 1939–   II. Series.

PR6023.A93W6483 2005
823'.912—dc22   2005040652

9 8 7 6 5 4 3 2 1
Printed in the United States of America
on acid-free paper

Credits

The introduction includes amended and augmented versions of material which first appeared in an edition of *Women in Love* published in Everyman's Library by David Campbell Publishers Ltd. in 1992 and in the introduction to *D. H. Lawrence: Critical Assessments* published by Helm Information, also in 1992. The material is reproduced here by kind permission of both publishers.

"Lawrence's *Götterdämmerung*: The Tragic Vision of *Women in Love*" by Joyce Carol Oates was first published in *Critical Inquiry* in 1978 (vol. 4, no. 3, 559–578) and is reprinted by kind permission of the author.

"Totem, Taboo, and Blutbrüderschaft in D. H. Lawrence's *Women in Love*," copyright © Carola Kaplan, is from *Seeing Double: Revisioning Edwardian and Modernist Literature*, ed. Carola M. Kaplan and Anne B. Simpson, 1996 and is reprinted with permission of Palgrave Macmillan.

"Lawrence in Another Light: *Women in Love* and Existentialism" by John B. Humma first appeared in *Studies in the Novel*, vol. 24, no. 4,

"*Ars Erotica* or *Scientia Sexualis?*: Narrative Vicissitudes in D. H. Lawrence's *Women in Love*" by Gerald Doherty was first published in the *Journal of Narrative Technique,* vol. 26, no. 2 (Spring, 1996), 137–157 and is reprinted by permission of the editors.

"Entrapment and Escape in D. H. Lawrence's *Women in Love*" by Bethan Jones is an amended version of an essay which first appeared in *Lectures d'une oeuvre:* Women in Love: *D. H. Lawrence,* published by the Editions du temps in 2001 and reproduced here with their permission.

"Into the Ideological Unknown: *Women in Love*" by David Parker was first published in the *Melbourne Critical Review* (vol. 30, 3–24) in 1990 and is reprinted by permission of the editors and the author.

"Le dialogue avec les avant-gardes dans *Women in Love"* by Ginette Katz-Roy first appeared in *Etudes Lawrenciennes* (vol. 5, 51–75) in 1990. It has been both revised and translated by the author and is reprinted with her permission.

"The First *Women in Love*" by John Worthen first appeared in the *D. H. Lawrence Review* (vol. 28, nos. 1–2, 3–27) in 1999 and is reprinted with permission of the editors.

"Violence in *Women in Love*" by Mark Kinkead-Weekes is a much amended and augmented version of material that first appeared in the introduction to the 1995 Penguin edition of *Women in Love* and is reprinted with permission of the publishers.

"The Myth of the Fall in *Women in Love*" by Jack F. Stewart first appeared in the *Philological Quarterly,* vol. 74, no. 4, 443–463 and is reprinted with permission of the editors.

Contents

D. H. Lawrence's *Women in Love*

A CASEBOOK

Introduction

DAVID ELLIS

◆　◆　◆

IN 1913 D. H. LAWRENCE WAS TWENTY-EIGHT and living in Italy with Frieda Weekley, the German wife of his former language teacher at Nottingham University. Already the author of two novels, he was waiting to see how his third, *Sons and Lovers*, would be received. That novel had been largely based on his childhood and youth in a small mining community near Nottingham but he was looking now for new subjects, new ways of writing, fresh points of view. In April he began writing about Gudrun and Ella Brangwen and their involvement with two men called Gerald Crich and Rupert Birkin. As he decided to ask himself more questions about the likely family background of the Brangwen sisters, Ella was rechristened Ursula and Lawrence found himself imagining not only her parents but the early life of her grandfather. The consequences would have made a very long novel indeed and by 7 January 1915 he had announced his intention of splitting the Brangwen story into two.[1] The first part, which he called *The Rainbow*, was published at the end of September 1915 and suppressed by court order a few weeks later. The ostensible reason was obscenity but expressions of anti-

3

war feeling in the novel might also have influenced the authorities' decision. With the publication of *Sons and Lovers* Lawrence had emerged as a successful young novelist whose future seemed assured but by the time *The Rainbow* was suppressed, his situation had changed completely. Now married to Frieda, his outspoken opposition to the war that Britain had been fighting against Germany and her allies since August 1914, and the unwelcome official attentions that opposition inevitably provoked, meant that he was being increasingly driven into angry and bitter isolation.

Lawrence completed his first rewriting of the second part of his Brangwen story in 1916 yet, largely because of what had happened to *The Rainbow*, he was not able to see *Women in Love* in print until December 1920 (the date of the first American edition). A month later, and with the war now finally over, he was enthusiastic about a scheme for having *The Rainbow* republished in England as *Women in Love. Vol. I.* Nothing came of this and he had been nearer to indicating how his two novels stood in relation to each other when in May 1916 he predicted that, although *Women in Love* was clearly a sequel to *The Rainbow*, it would be "quite unlike it."[2]

One reason the stress on difference rather than continuity seems right is that, often in *Women in Love,* the world of *The Rainbow* is explicitly repudiated. In a triumphant moment of sour comedy, Birkin goes to Ursula's house in order to propose to her and finds instead that he has to talk with her father. In Birkin's jaundiced eyes, Will Brangwen is a meaningless person, "a strange, inexplicable, almost patternless collection of passions and desires and suppressions and traditions and mechanical ideas" (255). He refuses to accept that the connection between Will and Ursula could be in any way significant. Later in the novel Ursula herself feels that a great chasm separates her from the past and that "the child she had been, playing in Cossethay churchyard, was a little creature of history, not really herself" (390). Memory, she feels, was like "a dirty trick played upon her" (409). But perhaps the most striking example of repudiation occurs in the chapter called "Flitting." The Brangwen sisters have returned momentarily to the house that the other members of their family have just vacated. They sit together in their parents' now empty bedroom and ponder what Will and Anna's marriage has meant. The progress of that marriage had been evoked by Lawrence in *The Rainbow* with an unusually sympathetic inwardness and in great physical as well as psychological detail; but for the Ursula of this novel, "It all seems so *nothing*—their two lives—there's no *meaning* in it. Really, if they had *not* met, and *not* married, and *not* lived together—it wouldn't have mattered, would it?" (373).

To anyone who had never read *Women in Love* these feelings might easily be mistaken for the familiar rebellion of youth against the previous generation; but neither Ursula nor Birkin is particularly young, and what they express is in fact only one aspect of the novel's determined and wholesale rejection of "ordinary" social life—work, marriage, children—in all its forms. It is true that Gudrun is intermittently attracted by the atmosphere in the grimy mining village where the Brangwens live, that Beldover has for her a strange underworld glamor of the dark and secretive; but her occasional yielding to its appeal is clearly portrayed in the novel as perverse (what the French call *nostalgie de la boue*), while the strongly endorsed attitude is of those who like Ursula, Birkin, or the mine owner's wife Mrs. Crich, acknowledge and accept their radical difference from the world and people about them. The accusation that what they really acknowledge and accept is their superiority rather than their mere difference would not unduly disturb any of them, the instinctively aristocratic Mrs. Crich least of all. Even more than Ursula, Gudrun of course also feels this radical difference from her surroundings and aggressively, if not entirely self-consciously, displays it in her clothes. There can be no genuine or lasting solace for her in the world of the miners, nor among members of the middle class such as her father or the electrical engineer who courts her for a while, nor even—as she finally and momentously decides—with a "Napoleon of industry" like Gerald. In the end, her repudiation of conventional society and the wealth-creating processes that sustain it is as decisive as anyone's, and marked by the same violence.

Women in Love is remarkable among novels of its time for the violence of the feelings its characters express. We are prepared for this in the first chapter when the local women jeer at Gudrun's colored stockings and, "A sudden fierce anger swept over the girl, violent and murderous. She would have liked them all to be annihilated, cleared away, so that the world was left clear for her" (13). In this powerfully disconcerting novel, violent feeling is apt to erupt anywhere but it is surprising to find a good deal of it directed against the coal industry—taken here as a paradigm of all industrial systems—when mining had figured uncontroversially in *Sons and Lovers*, more or less as a fact of nature. Chief among the reasons for the change in Lawrence's attitude must have been his justifiable belief that the war with Germany had been brought about by industrial rivalries and his horror at the idea that it could be prosecuted by industrial means. (Too honest about the turbulence of his own nature to be even remotely pacifist, he found the thought of using sophisticated machinery to kill people one couldn't see unbearable.) The First World War is never explicitly mentioned in *Women in Love,* but in a "Foreword" he provided for the first American edition Lawrence wrote that he wanted its bitterness to be "taken for granted in the characters."[3] That people should violently repudiate the society in which they live and be convinced—with apocalyptic certitude (one of Lawrence's working titles for *Women in Love* had been *Dies Irae*)—that it has no future, is possible at any time; but it is easy to understand why there was more temptation to feel these things after 1914 than before.

"Young as she was," Lawrence writes in one of his final chapters, "Gudrun had touched the whole pulse of social England" (418). Although the phrase is too ambitious to be applied unreservedly to *Women in Love*, the range of the novel's social depiction is nonetheless impressively broad. The social composition of Beldover is rapidly evoked but so, too, is the way of life of a leisured elite at Breadalby—centered on Hermione Roddice—and that of a more radical "alternative society" in London's Bohemia. The character of these last two groups is largely conveyed through dialogue (one of the more striking differences between *Women in Love* and *The Rainbow* is the extent of the later novel's reliance on talk), yet Lawrence has many different kinds of writing at his disposal for his panorama of English society. In "The Industrial Magnate" he successfully employs an analytic manner with only occasional moments of illustrative dramatisation, and in the chapter where Birkin and Ursula buy a chair and then decide to give it to a working-class couple they see who are "having to get married," Lawrence demonstrates how easily and distinctively he can move in the area of what is usually known as social realism. Whatever the method, each aspect of his society Lawrence chooses to write about seems thoroughly present, yet the reader is rarely in its company for very long. The narrative tends to "cut" from one grouping to the other in the manner of a film and with a minimum of concern for explanatory transitions, so that the general effect is of both synoptic vision and a fundamental lack of engagement or commitment. For Birkin, at least, none of the ways of life we are shown is possible. When he and Ursula, having finally committed themselves to each other, resign their jobs and thus their social status as teacher and school inspector, it is not because they have any specific alternatives in view. Their position—and the "bitterness of the war" is evident enough in their creator here—is hostile to society in any of its conventional forms.

Women in Love is a complex novel because most of the positions it might be said to advocate are subjected to rigorous and often highly effective challenge. (A genuine work of art, Lawrence claimed, ought always to incorporate its own criticism of itself.[4]) Toward its end, Gudrun suggests to her sister that it might be an illusion to think one can ever escape society—"After all, a cottage in the Abruzzi, or wherever it may be, isn't a new world" (438)—but Ursula replies with a version of Birkin's belief that one must and can. The issues raised in their discussion are the same as those implied in Lawrence's criticism of Tolstoy's treatment of the lovers in *Anna Karenina*. When Anna leaves her husband to live with Vronsky, she has to give up her position in society just as Vronsky has to abandon the self-definition that had been provided for him by his role as an army officer. In remarkably subtle and convincing ways, Tolstoy shows how these two specifically *social* sacrifices contribute to a deterioration in the feeling Anna and Vronsky have for each other and thus to their eventual destruction. Lawrence denied that this outcome was tragic because he felt that, as in Hardy's novels, what the protagonists were shown succumbing to was no more than a social pressure or conditioning which their creator had made them too conventional to resist.[5] In *Women in Love,* his own protagonists are defiantly unconventional. Birkin does not claim that he and Ursula are completely self-sufficient and he is not shown denying social need entirely: he hankers after a further relationship with Gerald and confesses at one point that he would appreciate the company of a few other people. But he sees no salvation in any of the established forms of society with which he is familiar and clearly believes that to escape them entirely will strengthen rather than damage his relationship with Ursula.

THE RESOURCES A COMPLEX MODERN SOCIETY can offer are evoked in *Women in Love* only to be dismissed, and the emphasis consequently falls on what individuals can do to save themselves. The whole of England, and to some degree at least therefore every English person, is conceived as involved in a process of disintegration—a drift down what Birkin refers to at one moment as "the dark river of dissolution (172). In some ways this is a natural and acceptable process, like the excremental functions of the human body or the decay of leaves in autumn; and it is also one which, in several of its manifestations, can have its own fascination and beauty (rotting matter will sometimes emit a phosphorescent glow). In any case, disintegration is both a natural and necessary preliminary to a fresh start. But in a novel where attitudes are never simple, it is also felt to be corrupt and distasteful, especially in those individuals who, like Hermione, try to deny its existence with the force of their egotistical will or, like Gudrun and the German artist Loerke, deliberately and self-consciously choose to participate in and even further the stages of general decay. In their case, Lawrence appears to be making a difficult distinction between a mindless, approved sensuality—which Birkin observes as characteristic of a previous disintegrative process epitomized in the African statuettes he admires—and a modern consciousness which recognizes fully how bad things are and seeks out whatever sensations are available with a cynical, if despairing, relish. Yet he is not content to imply that the only alternative to sensation seeking or denial is passive submission. A feeling slowly emerges in *Women in Love* that there ought to be ways for certain individuals to escape the general winding-down and assert, if only for themselves, more positive, dynamic principles than those which promise eventual renewal through decay. It is the possibility of these that Birkin (well aware of how deeply implicated he himself is in the corruption around him) glimpses in Ursula. The difference between Ursula and her sister is suggested in "Sketch-Book," the first paragraph of which describes Gudrun's appreciation of the beautiful if sinister water-plants as they rise "straight and turgid" out of the mud with their "dark lurid colours, dark green and blotches of black-purple and bronze"; while the second has Ursula watching butterflies "snapping out of nothingness into a jewel-life" or "breathing with . . . soft wings, intoxicatingly, breathing pure ethereal sunshine" (119). This method of differentiating the two women, poetically suggestive rather than sharply defining, is typical of one of the principal ways in which the novel works and suggests immediately why any mere summary of its themes would be misleading.

Ursula represents a possibility of escape for Birkin only if he can establish a lasting relationship with her, but this raises the issue of "love" and, by extension, marriage. In the novel's opening scene, as accomplished in its entirely different way as the opening of "Sketch-Book" and a reminder that Lawrence was a playwright as well as a novelist, the sisters discuss whether marriage could ever be the answer to their feelings of dissatisfaction; and in "Breadalby" Birkin and Gerald also contemplate marriage as a solution to their problems. In the first instance, the women are talking about conventional wedlock but it soon becomes evident that this is a non-starter (Birkin's attacks on "égoïsme à deux" and the "home instinct" as a "habit of cowardliness" are particularly vehement [352]); but marriage in the sense of mutual commitment—something more than an affair—is very much at issue between the four main characters. When Lawrence first told his friend Jessie Chambers back in 1906 that he would try to write a novel, he said, "The usual plan is to take two couples and develop their relationships . . . Most of George Eliot's are on that plan."[6] *Women in Love* is on that plan also, but in ways George Eliot would have found it hard to anticipate.

If relationships are going to survive without the help of an institutional framework, what is it that will draw and then keep people together? What is "love"? Love in its social, humanitarian aspects is effectively dismissed in the account of the life-long effort of Gerald's father to reconcile the egalitarian Christianity of the New Testament with the inevitable and (according to its own lights) necessary injustices of laissez-faire capitalism. Thomas Crich, we are told, wanted the mines "to be run on love" (225). But, as its title suggests, it is with love in its private, more individual sense that this novel is chiefly concerned and on that topic Birkin is its leading theorist. Matters are so arranged that his ideas are frequently subjected to criticism. Ursula often tells him to his face that he doesn't know what he is talking about and when he is driving Gudrun and Gerald into town in "Threshold," they discuss his shortcomings behind his back. Ursula and Hermione have some sharp things to say about him in one of their conversations, as do Ursula and Gudrun or the London Bohemians. The frequency with which Birkin is discussed makes him much more central to the novel than his appearances might indicate and several of the charges against him seem just— that he has a strong desire to feel "safe," for example, or (in what must be music to the ears of many readers) that he is often confusingly inconsistent. Yet Birkin's views are clearly close to his author's heart and by the end of the novel there is a qualified sense of their justification if not triumph. In the later scenes it is not only on the question of whether a couple can live outside society that his strongest critic, the otherwise fiercely independent Ursula, has become for the moment his spokeswoman.

The sense the reader has that Birkin's ideas are only partly vindicated in the unfolding of the novel's action is related to the extreme difficulty of the problems he struggles to resolve. It is perhaps a strength of *Women in Love* that he has no ready-made solutions. The drama of the book is not only in its many striking episodes, such as the wedding of Laura Crich or the death of her father, but in Birkin's not always successful efforts to establish attitudes which will answer to his acute sense of the corruption around or within him and, at the same time, satisfy a perhaps irrational but nevertheless wholly recognisable instinct that, in the truly full life, people ought to be allowed to both have their cake and eat it. For much of the time, he is found striving to reconcile opposites. At one moment, for example, he feels himself caught between Hermione as the "perfect Idea" and Ursula as the "perfect Womb" (309); and he is clearly troubled that others at least would perceive an opposition between the undoubted physical appeal that Ursula has for him and the attraction of Gerald. (In a "Prologue" to the earliest surviving version of *Women in Love* which was later discarded, Birkin is described as someone who can only be aroused by the bodies of men.[7]) He is contemptuous of ordinary marriage ties and, in his very different way, as committed as Ursula to spontaneity—fidelity to the moment of feeling. Like Gudrun, Ursula is recognizably the Edwardian "New Woman," keen to declare at one point that "love is freedom" (152). This is a position with which Birkin could hardly disagree but he is nevertheless no advocate of free love and so attracted by the idea of irrevocable union as to propose to both Ursula and Gerald his own idiosyncratic and secular version of the marriage vows. Yet perhaps the paradox which concerns him most is his need to feel perfectly at one with another person while still retaining his individuality. It is this which gives rise to his notion of "stellar polarity"—the idea that a couple could be like two stars confirmed in their singleness by the electromagnetic forces which hold them in unison. Several critics have succeeded in making better sense of this image than Birkin does, but he is a character in a novel struggling to find his way; it would be dramatically inappropriate and improbable if he were to find it without difficulty. On one relatively early occasion, when he is expounding stellar polarity to Ursula, they are interrupted by the sight of his cat stalking a female intruder around the garden and cuffing her from time to time with his paw. Ursula is not represented in the novel as an intellectual but when Birkin is tempted to offer the cats as an illustration of what he is trying to explain, it does not take such intellect to point out that they are not a particularly good example of "stable equilibrium." Birkin may be the character in the novel closest to Lawrence himself, but that does not protect him from failing to make his point, getting things wrong, or being made to look foolish.

A reason Birkin wants an alternative to the "love" Ursula "freely" offers is his suspicion that, despite the apparent selflessness of its outward form, it would prove devouring. It is partly this fear of being absorbed and made nothing by a woman's love, together with an undoubted physical attraction, which takes him to Gerald (immediately after the fiasco of his proposal to Ursula). To escape the possible claustrophobia of his relation with her, he needs at least one other social and perhaps—interpreting the term in its broadest sense—sexual option. But even after the handclasp that concludes their naked wrestling in "Gladitorial," Gerald remains doubtful. To Birkin's later proposal for an "additional perfect relationship between man and man—additional to marriage," he responds conventionally if (from a heterosexual point of view) understandably, "Nature doesn't provide the basis" (352). In the last lines of *Women in Love*, Birkin is still insisting that such a relationship is possible; but, although in the second half of the novel Ursula gradually comes to adopt and defend several of Birkin's ideas, on the question of love it is he who is shown capitulating to her more straightforward views.

To say Birkin capitulates is to confirm that by no means all the conflicts in *Women in Love* are resolved. The relationship with Ursula may allow him to step aside from tracks all the other main characters appear doomed to follow, but Lawrence's descriptions of its physical aspects suggest how far it is from sentimentality or idealization—the idealization which might be implied, for example, in the account of Ursula observing the butterflies "breathing pure, ethereal sunshine." On two early occasions Ursula imposes passion on Birkin when he wants to be peaceful ("in passion she was at home" [311]); and as they kiss in "Snow," "her lips were taut and quivering and strenuous, his were soft, deep and delicate" (435). When the initiative is represented as being much more Birkin's, as in parts of "Excurse" or his "licentiousness" after the dance in the ski lodge, Ursula finds the forms his passion takes—some critics have felt they detected in one or both episodes references to anal intercourse—initially troubling. "Excurse" establishes the Birkin/Ursula relationship as the one positive value in a deeply pessimistic novel, but as the action continues it can sometimes seem like a flickering light in the dark, or as if Lawrence's belief in it is sustained—in a way highly characteristic of him—less by the evidence he can produce than the will to believe. In an essay Lawrence could have read, William James pointed out that the will to believe can often create the desired result for the believer.[8] It is important that both Birkin and Ursula are shown as having this will—the faith that there ought and therefore must be something better than the life they see around them—

whereas Gudrun especially has reconciled herself to the grimness of things and has a radical cynicism closely associated with the detached, ironic nature of her art. Even in what, for him, were the darkest days of the war—when his failure to find publishers for his major work deprived him of an income, he and Frieda had been expelled from Cornwall by the military authorities, and his refusal to support the allied cause made him a pariah—Lawrence never abandoned himself completely to despair but remained in the last resort, like Ursula and Birkin, a believer. Yet if the hopelessness of Gudrun had not also been a strong temptation for him, it is hard to see how he could have told the story of her and Gerald so effectively.

THE STRUGGLE BETWEEN Gudrun and Gerald is commonly felt to be the most powerful part of *Women in Love* perhaps because, in describing it, Lawrence's energies were not diverted by any obligation to indicate in their situation anything hopeful or positive. A "barren tragedy" is how Gudrun characterises Gerald's death in the sterile Alpine landscape (476), but if he is a tragic figure it is more in the Greek than the Shakespearean manner. His defeat by Gudrun is a foregone conclusion from the moment they become attached to each other. A marked or doomed character who has killed his brother, accidentally on purpose according to Birkin's formula, it might well be felt by readers looking back as typical of Gerald's luck that his first experience of complete relaxation should be interrupted by the drowning of his sister. This is in "Water-Party," a chapter which begins in the mode of a novel of manners before moving on to Gudrun's eerie eurythmic demonstration, in front of the Highland cattle, that maleness in any form will never intimidate her. With darkness beginning to fall, the strange Chinese lanterns are lit. As the four protagonists then row their two boats across the lake to rejoin the main party at Mr. Crich's annual reception for the people of the area, Lawrence creates a weirdly appealing, phantasmagoric atmosphere. In a way representative of how small naturalistic details are continually invested in this novel with an importance beyond themselves, Gerald is in Gudrun's hands because the bandage on one of his own prevents him from rowing. He abandons himself entirely to her direction, "melting into oneness with the whole . . . He had been so insistent, so guarded, all his life. But here was sleep, and peace, and perfect lapsing out" (178). His mood is violently disturbed by the steam launch suddenly reversing its paddles and then Winifred's frenzied cry, "Di–Di– Di– Di– Oh Di. . . ." (179). In a novel often concerned with the destructive power of women, it is important that when Diana's dead body is recovered the next day, she should have her arms tightly clasped round the neck of the young man who had jumped in the water to save her.

The characters in Tolstoy and Hardy were not tragic in Lawrence's view because they allow themselves to be defeated by society, while the genuinely tragic protagonist struggles against the forces of nature with resistent energy which allows him to aim, like Macbeth and Lear, a "great kick at Misery."[9] By these standards, there is more pathos than tragedy in Gerald's situation. The limitations of his self-understanding often make him seem Gudrun's helpless victim. Yet just as, in Birkin's analysis, a murderer needs a murduree (precisely what it might be said Gerald becomes in this novel where the violence is by no means limited to feeling), Gerald is a victim only because of qualities which make him complicit with his eventual victimizer. In the scenes with the London Bohemians, the Pussum is shown exciting in him a strong if unconscious sadism (after they have spent the night together she has the look of a "violated slave" [80]), the same quality he displays in forcing his Arab horse to face up to the clanking trucks in "Coal-Dust" or—less obviously—in subduing Winifred's rabbit. It is the revelation of Gerald's sadism in these two famous episodes which Gudrun finds sexually exciting. A reader's report on a version of the Brangwen story dating from the time Ursula was still called Ella refers to "Gerald Crich raping Gudrun in a boathouse."[10] There are no rape scenes in *Women in Love,* but intimations of violation often accompany the accounts of Gudrun and Gerald's encounters. Thomas Crich discovers that his passion for a wife who is submissive but resentful can never be appeased; his son is similarly unsatisfied by Gudrun whose submissions are, unlike those of Mrs. Crich, often a matter of wilful sexual preference as well as a means of domination. As Gerald holds the rabbit she looks at him "with strange, darkened eyes, strained with underworld knowledge, almost supplicating, like those of a creature which is at his mercy, yet which is his ultimate victor" (241–242). Lawrence had dramatized before how apparent submissiveness can become a form of control through, for example, its appeal to the supposedly stronger party's guilt feelings; but in *Women in Love* there is a translation of this kind of reversal into physical terms. The Pussum and Gudrun (the reader infers) are the paradoxically stronger parties because they understand the nature of their sado-masochistic association with Gerald much better than he does; can consciously excite tendencies in him of which he is barely aware; and more knowingly, or perhaps simply more frequently, take for themselves from the relationship what most suits them. In the case of Gudrun, this difference is not absolute but a question of degree. She is not always shown in control. There are moments when she knows, as does Birkin after the attack from Hermione, that to turn her back would be fatal; and she comes very close to being strangled. But there are too many anticipatory gestures throughout the novel to make a reader doubt that ultimate victory will be hers.

Gudrun is stronger than Gerald because she is self-sufficient as well as more self-aware. It is a simple truth that the more powerful partner in a relationship will always be the one with the lesser degree of need. Sweeping into the church in the first chapter, Hermione is "possessed by a devastating hopelessness" (18) when she realizes Birkin is not yet there; for all her intellectual and social advantages, she has "a lack of robust self . . . no natural sufficiency" (16). When Gerald's father dies, his world collapses and, in another of the novel's remarkable scenes, he is driven blindly into seeking out Gudrun at night in the Brangwen family home. *Women in Love* does not offer its reader simple moral positions but an abundance of different and sometimes conflicting points of view. There is a good deal of authorial animus expressed against Hermione, but also enough sympathetic understanding of her plight to allow certain kinds of readers to feel that Birkin treats her badly. Gerald's night visit might be taken as either an illustration of the culpable folly of self-abandon or his misfortune in fleeing for comfort to the wrong woman. Gudrun does provide comfort, but in the process she is left painfully dissatisfied, resentful of the burden and the risk. The "violent active superconsciousness" (346) she experiences in this episode is similar to the bleak clarity of her review of the meaninglessness of social life when Gerald is sleeping beside her in their room in the ski lodge or, after they have moved to separate rooms, to her reflections on the remorseless passage of time in a Godless world. In this latter passage she complains that she has to comfort Gerald ("Was she his mother?" [466]) when she needs comfort herself; but, in general, there is a certain heroism in the finality of her knowledge of herself and her acceptance of her relation to the world. She can, of course, be more independent than Gerald because she has her art to sustain her. One of the reasons she is attracted to Loerke, in whose eyes she can see a "black look of inorganic misery" (422), is that they both believe only art can relieve the pointlessness of human life.

Gudrun is as genuine an artist in her own, smaller way as Loerke is in his. Like him and her pupil Winifred, she has the "artistic temperament." Readers of Lawrence have met this before in *Sons and Lovers* where Paul Morel angers Baxter Dawes with his "impersonal, deliberate gaze of an artist."[11] What it might mean in ordinary life is suggested in "Coal-Dust" when Gudrun sees Gerald digging his spurs into his horse's already bleeding flanks. For a moment she loses self-control but when she recovers she is "hard and cold and indifferent' and, via the imagined intermediary of the guard staring out from his guard's van as the train rattles past, she can see "the whole scene spectacularly, isolated and momentary" (112). Most people and events are spectacles for Gudrun: she is the Wordsworthian "spectator ab extra," observing and thereby controlling the world from a distance. In "Water-Party" she regrets that whereas she feels "outside of life, an onlooker," Ursula is "a partaker" (165). The latter's capacity to partake is associated with attitudes very different from her sister's, as is shown in her bludgeoning attack on Loerke's insistence that there is an absolute separation between art and life (later he and Gudrun are to agree that art is the only reality). It may also be said to have something to do with Birkin's late declaration of belief in the "eternal creative mystery," the "incorruptible and unsearchable fountain-head" (479). But neither Birkin nor Ursula are themselves artists. As if a trusting participation in life and devotion to art were incompatible, the novel offers nothing to contrast with Loerke's frieze and statuette, Winifred's drawing of her Pekinese, or

Gudrun's sculpture, nothing (that is) other than itself. Constructed in such an original way that it might seem at first sight disorganized, heterogeneous in literary manner, and sometimes giving the impression of only discovering what its interests and attitudes are as it proceeds, *Women in Love* is the kind of work of art one might imagine Birkin could have produced had he not been a school inspector. Yet since Gudrun's ironic, delimiting vision (we are often invited to see characters through her eyes or in her manner), and an interest in the less familiar forms of sexuality implicit in Loerke's statuette, are both part and parcel of the texture and appeal of *Women in Love*, the novel cannot be said merely to oppose their various forms of aestheticism but rather qualify or complement them with a wider, more inclusive vision. Gudrun and Loerke would not have wanted to produce an equivalent of *Women in Love* in their own media, but neither would the narrowness and dogmatism of their principles have allowed them to do so.

Novelists are not always the best critics of their own novels but I think Lawrence was right to believe that *Women in Love* was a great and original work, in spite of all the difficulties he experienced in having it published. "I consider this the best of my books," he wrote in 1917.[12] The first edition was for subscribers only and had the good fortune to attract the attention of the secretary of the New York Society for the Suppression of Vice. His unsuccessful attempt to prosecute the novel boosted American sales considerably and was largely responsible for the fact that in the early 1920s Lawrence became relatively affluent for the first time in his life. When an English edition appeared in June 1921 it attracted as much puzzlement as outrage. Lawrence had spent the war years conceiving things so differently from most of his contemporaries that he had been driven into methods of fictional presentation which they found either disconcerting or simply baffling, all the more so because *Women in Love* is not obviously and frankly avant-garde, like Eliot's *The Waste Land* (published only a year later) or Joyce's *Ulysses*, but has many features easy to relate to the English nineteenth-century novel. As far as the presentation of character is concerned, for example, Gerald's treatment of his horse in "Coal-Dust" might reasonably be compared with

Grandcourt's behaviour towards his dog in George Eliot's *Daniel Deronda* (as well, of course, as Vronsky's handling of his horse during the race in *Anna Karenina*). Many contemporary readers must therefore have had the uncomfortable experience (not unknown today) of feeling that they knew more or less where they were and then, as the novel shifted into a different manner, realizing that their self-confidence had been unfounded.

Although the novel always had its admirers, *Women in Love* was slow to make its way and it was only in the 1950s and 1960s that it came to be widely recognised as a classic. In Britain, a good deal of the credit for that development must go to F. R. Leavis who, in a series of essays which first appeared in book form in 1955, insisted on Lawrence's status as a major twentieth-century writer and described how slow he himself had been to recognise *Women in Love* as the most profound and rewarding of Lawrence's novels. That view became common on both sides of the Atlantic and coincided with the enrollment of Lawrence in movements or campaigns for greater sexual freedom. As early as December 1912, Lawrence had written to Sallie Hopkin, an older woman friend from his home town of Eastwood, "I shall do a novel about Love Triumphant one day. I shall do my work for women, better than the suffrage."[13] The depiction of two young women in *Women in Love* who are indifferent to conventional restrictions and determined to make their own sexual choices, could well have been taken by many in the 1960s as justification of this claim. In *Lady Chatterley's Lover* especially, but also in *Women in Love,* Lawrence could be said to have done his "work for women" by showing them liberated from the traditional restraints.

In retrospect, this view of Lawrence's contribution to the women's movement may well seem bizarre. Not long after his reputation as both a novelist and proponent of sexual liberation had reached its height, Kate Millett claimed in her hugely influential *Sexual Politics* (1970) that Lawrence went "to every length to make the lot of the independent woman repellent"[14] and other feminist critics, examining in some detail his attitudes to women in general, felt that many of them were reprehensible. In the 1980s Cornelia Nixon identified what she called "the turn against women" in precisely the period when *Women in Love* was being composed and complained of an increasingly misogynist strain in his writings thereafter.[15] Meanwhile, there were other ways in which the view of him prevalent in the 1960s was being challenged or qualified.

Leavis had insisted that there was "no profound emotional disorder in Lawrence, no obdurate major disharmony; intelligence in him can be, as is it, the servant of the whole integrated psyche"; and he had gone on to say that a "strong normative preoccupation . . . informs *Women in Love*."[16] Later critics, like Colin Clarke in his *River of Dissolution* (1969), thought that this claim was exaggerated and pointed to what they felt was an almost obsessive concern in the novel with those processes of decay and excremental flow which I have already mentioned and which some of them associated with sexual practices not usually considered normative.[17] Those who had regarded Lawrence as a spokesman for sexual freedom largely belonged to what might be termed the liberal intelligentsia but, at much the same time that his credentials as an advocate of women's rights were being challenged, it was discovered that many of his political views were not at all liberal and that the characters in *Women in Love*—as in most of his novels, but especially the later ones—could often use language which reflected the racial prejudices of his time. Thus from being hailed as the great novelist who, with his emphasis on spontaneity and the life of the body, could help free both his male and female readers from a hide-bound past, Lawrence quickly came to be regarded as someone whose undoubted literary abilities could not save him from the odium which attends those who stand convicted of misogyny and racism, and whose political thinking can be conveniently dismissed as "fascist." It is true that resting easy with a characterization of Lawrence as misogynist, racist, and fascist requires a good deal of reading out of context, attributing to Lawrence himself views expressed by his characters, and ignoring the volatility of his intellectual and emotional nature (spontaneity has its consequences). But mud sticks and that it does so helps to explain the situation recently described by Gary Adelman in *Reclaiming Lawrence* (2002). Through extensive quotation, Adelman shows that—whereas most practising writers still admire Lawrence—his standing in the universities is very low; that there, from once jostling at the front with Woolf and Joyce, he has become an also-ran while, on university courses, *Women in Love* is no longer the quasi-automatic companion to *Ulysses* and *To the Lighthouse* which it once was.

There was a strong *reaction* against Lawrence in the 1970s and 80s but there are now signs that it may be possible to arrive at a more balanced view (although he is such an instinctively provocative and controversial writer that this may be hard). Apart from the classic essay by Joyce Carol Oates with which this collection begins, all the pieces in it were published in the final decade of the last century or the first few years of this. Some of them, like those of Mark Kinkead-Weekes or Jack F. Stewart, demonstrate that the traditional form of literary commentary Oates represents so well has continued to flourish in spite of the revolutionary changes which have taken place in the teaching of English literature in universities over the last twenty years. Those changes have not of course taken away the need for knowledge of the particular cultural context that fosters a literary work. Early twentieth-century art, artists, and ideas about art are clearly very important to *Women in Love* and Ginette Katz-Roy's essay provides a comprehensive guide to all three. As an addendum to her work, I am very pleased to be able to publish an illustration of the statuette that undoubtedly inspired Lawrence's description of Loerke's *Lady Godiva,* with a note by the scholar who only recently announced his discovery of it.

Textual scholarship is another area of inquiry which, although it has certainly not been immune from the effect of the recent changes, has felt their shock waves less that literary criticism *tout court* and has therefore been able to continue its necessary work in ways which represent rather more a development of, than a break with, past practice. Students tend to assume that, because it is arduous, textual scholarship is dull, but John Worthen shows that it can lead to highly pertinent and challenging conclusions. The remaining five essays in the collection illustrate the present imperative to read and interpret literary works in a more specifically defined theoretical context than was usual in the past. John B. Humma, for example, reveals interesting analogies between the principles that could be said to underlie *Women in Love* and the tenets of existentialism and, although Bethan Jones's close and sensitive study of the novel's imagery may look traditional, it is framed within Bakhtin's notion of the dialogic. Gerald Docherty has used ideas from Foucault's work on sexuality to produce a stimulating analysis and, in his essay, David Parker locks horns with Frederic Jameson in order to show that attempts to nail down the ideology of *Women in Love* tend to result in the novel walking away with the nail. One of the merely incidental merits of Carola M. Kaplan's challenging contribution is that it suggests how hard it will always be to approach *Women in Love* via feminism and postcolonial theory and still think highly of it.

Although Lawrence's reputation may still be low in some quarters, the essays in this volume are intended to show that the struggle to read *Women in Love* adequately still goes on and can provide results whose very variety is a part of their usefulness and interest. "Literary criticism," Lawrence once wrote, "can be no more than a reasoned account of the feeling produced upon a critic by the book he is criticising . . . We judge a work of art by its effect on our sincere and vital emotion, and nothing else." Assuming that what was easy for him would present no particular problem for others, he underestimated how difficult most of us find it to know what our real feelings about an important work of art actually are, and how hard it sometimes proves to find appropriate forms in which to express them. As if all this were not enough, Lawrence went on:

A critic must be able to *feel* the impact of a work of art in all its complexity and its force. To do so, he must be a man of force and complexity himself, which few critics are. A man with a paltry, impudent nature will never write anything but paltry, impudent criticism. And a man who is *emotionally* educated is as rare as a phoenix.[18]

This is hardly encouraging, yet, although Lawrence was a man with exacting standards in all aspects of life, he was also someone who—for himself as well as others—understood and accepted the inevitability of continually falling short. The generosity of his spirit in the literary field is evident in the immense trouble he could take in advising writer friends of patently mediocre abilities. He knew very well the type of creative and critical activity he valued most, but was catholic enough to acknowledge that life is impoverished without a recognition that in all spheres of activity "it takes all sorts." On one point, however, he might well have been adamant: that students should not use a collection like this as a repository of models to be copied, but merely as aids to a closer definition of their own individual response. The view that the inexperienced student's genuine opinion can have no value in comparison with that of established figures in the academic world would have struck him as false. To be the perfect critic in the Lawrencian sense is beyond the reach of most of us, but this does not therefore make the honest definition of our own emotional and intellectual engagement with his work a wasted labor and, in striving to achieve that definition, there may be some dubious but nevertheless wholly human comfort to be found in the fact that the phoenix is not merely rare—but a creature of myth.

Note on the text: *The page numbers after my quotations from* Women in Love *refer to the Cambridge edition edited by David Farmer, Lindeth Vasey, and John Worthen (1987). This is now widely regarded as the most authoritative and is the same text, with the same pagination, adopted for the Penguin edition. There are many differences from the early versions but the one that perhaps affects the reading of criticism more than any other is that, in those, Halliday's girl friend in "Crème de Menthe" is called Minette rather than Pussum. The change had been demanded by the man who felt himself to be the prototype of Halliday.*

Notes

1. See *The Letters of D. H. Lawrence*, vol. 2, eds. George J. Zyutaruk and James T. Boulton (Cambridge University Press, 1981), 256.
2. Ibid., 606
3. The "Foreword" is printed in many recent editions, but also in *Phoenix II: Uncollected, Unpublished and Other Prose Works by D. H. Lawrence*, ed. Warren Roberts and Harry T. Moore (London: Heinemann, 1963), 275.
4. See the *"Study of Hardy"* in *Study of Hardy and Other Essays*, ed. Bruce Steele. (Cambridge University Press, 1985), 89.
5. Lawrence wrote about Tolstoy on several occasions but most extensively in "The Novel" (1925). See *Study of Thomas Hardy and Other Essays,* 179–190.
6. See *D. H. Lawrence: A Personal Record*, by E. T. (Jessie Chambers), 1935, 103.

7. Those who do not have this Prologue in their editions can find it reprinted in *Phoenix II*, 92–108. As the essays in this present collection demonstrate, opinions differ as to whether or not it should be regarded as integral to the novel.

8. See *"The Will to Believe" and Other Essays in Popular Philosophy* (New York: Longmans, Green, and Co., 1899). Lawrence was interested in James and had read his *Pragmatism* (1907).

9. This phrase occurs in a letter to A. D. McCleod about Arnold Bennet's novel *Anna of the Five Towns*. See *Letters of D. H. Lawrence,* vol. 1, ed. James T. Boulton (Cambridge University Press, 1979), 459.

10. The report by Alfred Kuttner is reprinted in the Cambridge edition of *The Rainbow* (1989), ed. M. Kinkead-Weekes, 483–484.

11. *Sons and Lovers,* eds. Helen Baron and Carl Baron (Cambridge University Press, 1992), 224.

12. *Letters of D. H. Lawrence,* vol. 3, eds. James T. Boulton and Andrew Robertson (Cambridge University Press, 1984), 390.

13. *Letters of D. H. Lawrence,* vol. 1, 490.

14. Kate Millett, *Sexual Politics* (London: Rupert Hart-Davis, 1971), 260.

15. See Cornelia Nixon, *Lawrence's Leadership Politics and the Turn Against Women* (University of California Press, 1986).

16. *D. H. Lawrence: Novelist.* (London: Chatto and Windus, 1955), 27.

17. See example Mark Spilka, "Lawrence Up-tight or the Anal Phase Once Over," *Novel*, vol. 4, no. 5, Fall 1970, 252–267.

18. From "John Galsworthy" in *Study of Hardy and Other Essays,* 209.

Lawrence's *Götterdämmerung*

The Tragic Vision of Women in Love

JOYCE CAROL OATES

◆　◆　◆

And was he fated to pass away in this knowledge,
this one process of frost-knowledge, death by perfect cold? Was he a messenger, an omen of the universal dissolution into whiteness and snow?
　　　—Birkin thinking of Gerald, *Women in Love*

I N   A   L I T T L E - K N O W N   S T O R Y of Lawrence's called the "The
Christening" an elderly wreck of a man contemplates his illegiti-
mate grandchild and attempts to lead his embarrassed and impatient household in a prayer in "the special language of fatherhood."
No one listens, no one wishes to hear. He is rambling, incoherent,
bullying even in his confession and self-abnegation, yet his prayer is
an extraordinary one: he implores God to shield the newborn child
from the conceit of family life, from the burden of being a *son* with a
specific *father.* It was his own interference with his children, his im-
position of his personal will, that damaged them as human beings;
and he prays that his grandson will be spared this violation of the
spirit. Half-senile he insists upon his prayer though his grown-up
children are present and resentful:

> Lord, what father has a man but Thee? Lord, when a man says he
> is a father, he is wrong from the first word. For Thou art the Fa-
> ther, Lord. Lord, take away from us the conceit that our children
> are ours. . . . For I have stood between Thee and my children; I've
> had *my* way with them, Lord; I've stood between Thee and my
> children; I've cut 'em off from Thee because they were mine. And

they've grown twisted, because of me. . . . Lord, if it hadn't been for me, they might ha' been trees in the sunshine. Let me own it, Lord, I've done 'em mischief. It would ha' been better if they'd never known no father.

Between the individual and the cosmos there falls the deathly shadow of the ego: the disheveled old man utters a truth central to Lawrence's work. Where the human will is active there is always injury to the spirit, always a perversion, a "twisting"; that human beings are compelled not only to assert their greedy claims upon others but to manipulate their own lives in accord with an absolute that has little to do with their deeper yearnings constitutes our tragedy. Is it a tragedy of the modern era; is it inevitably bound up with the rise of industry and mechanization? Lawrence would say that it is, for the "material interests" of which Conrad spoke so ironically are all that remain of spiritual hopes; God being dead, God being unmasked as a fraud, nothing so suits man's ambition as a transvaluing of values, the reinterpretation of religious experience in gross, obscene terms. Here is Gerald Crich, one of Lawrence's most deeply realized and sympathetic characters, surely an alter ego of his—

> In his travels, and in his accompanying readings, he had come to the conclusion that the essential secret of life was harmony. . . . And he proceeded to put his philosophy into practice by forcing order into the established world, translating the mystic word harmony into the practical word organisation.[1]

Harmony becomes *organisation.* And Gerald dedicates himself to work, to feverish, totally absorbing work, inspired with an almost religious exaltation in his fight with matter. The world is split in two: on one side matter (the mines, the miners), on the other side his own isolated will. He wants to create on earth a perfect machine, "an activity of pure order, pure mechanical repetition"; a man of the twentieth century with no nostalgia for the superannuated ideals of Christianity or democracy, he wishes to found his eternity, his infinity, in the machine. So inchoate and mysterious is the imaginative world Lawrence creates for *Women in Love* that we find no difficulty in reading Gerald Crich as an allegorical figure in certain chapters and as a quite human, even fluid personality in others. As Gudrun's frenzied lover, as Birkin's elusive beloved, he seems a substantially different person from the Gerald Crich who is a ruthless god of the machine; yet as his cultural role demands extinction (for Lawrence had little doubt that civilization was breaking down rapidly, and Gerald is the very personification of a "civilized" man), so does his private emotional life, his confusion of the individual will with that of the cosmos, demand death—death by perfect cold. He is Lawrence's only tragic figure, a remarkable creation in a remarkable novel, and though it is a commonplace to say that Birkin represents Lawrence, it seems equally likely that Gerald Crich represents Lawrence—in his deepest, most aggrieved, most nihilistic soul.

Women in Love is an inadequate title. The novel concerns itself with far more than simply *women* in love; far more than simply women *in love*. Two violent love affairs are the plot's focus, but the drama of the novel has clearly to do with every sort of emotion, and with every sort of spiritual inanition. Gerald and Birkin and Ursula and Gudrun are immense figures, monstrous creations out of legend, out of mythology; they are unable to alter their fates, like tragic heroes and heroines of old. The mark of Cain has been on Gerald since early childhood, when he accidentally killed his brother; and Gudrun is named for a heroine out of Germanic legend who slew her first husband. The pace of the novel is often frenetic. Time is running out, history is coming to an end, the Apocalypse is at hand. *Dies Irae* and *The Latter Days* (as well as *The Sisters* and *The Wedding Ring*) were titles Lawrence considered for the novel, and though both are too explicit, too shrill, they are more suggestive of the chiliastic mood of the work (which even surprised Lawrence when he read it through after completion in November of 1916: it struck him as end-of-the-world" and as "purely destructive, not like *The Rainbow*, destructive-consummating").[2]

Women in Love is a strangely ceremonial, even ritualistic work. In very simple terms it celebrates love and marriage as the only possible salvation for twentieth-century man and dramatizes the fate of those who resist the abandonment of the ego demanded by love: a sacrificial rite, an ancient necessity. Yet those who "come through"—Birkin and Ursula—are hardly harmonious; the novel ends with their arguing about Birkin's thwarted desire for an "eternal union with a man," and one is given to feel that the shadow of the dead man will fall across their marriage. And though the structure of the novel is ceremonial, its texture is rich, lush, fanciful, and, since each chapter is organized around a dominant image, rather self-consciously symbolic or imagistic; action is subordinate to theme. The perversity of the novel is such that its great subject of mankind's tragically split nature is demonstrated in the artwork itself, which is sometimes a fairly conventional novel with a forward-moving plot, sometimes a gorgeous, even outrageous prose poem on the order of the work Aloysius Bertrand and Charles Baudelaire were doing in the previous century. Birkin is sometimes a prophetic figure, and sometimes merely garrulous and silly; Ursula is sometimes a mesmerizing archetypal female, at other times shrill and possessive and dismayingly obtuse. In one of Lawrence's most powerful love scenes Gerald Crich comes by night to Gudrun's bedroom after his father's death and is profoundly revitalized by her physical love, but Gudrun cannot help looking upon him with a devastating cynicism, noting his ridiculous trousers and braces and boots, and she is filled with nausea of him despite her fascination. Gudrun herself takes on in Gerald's obsessive imagination certain of the more destructive qualities of the Magna Mater or the devouring female, and she attains an almost mythic power over him; but when we last see her she has become shallow and cheaply ironic, merely a vulgar young woman. It is a measure of Lawrence's genius that every part of his immensely ambitious novel works (with the possible exception of the strained chapter "In The Pompadour") and that the proliferating images coalesce into fairly stable leitmotifs: water, moon, darkness, light, the organic, and the sterile.

Our own era is one in which prophetic eschatological art has as great a significance as it did in 1916; Lawrence's despairing conviction that civilization was in the latter days is one shared by a number of our most serious writers, even if there is little belief in the Apocalypse in its classical sense. The notion of antichrist is an archaic one, a sentiment that posits unqualified belief in Christ; and the ushering in of a violent new era, a millennium, necessitates faith in the transcendental properties of the world, or the universe, which contrast sharply with scientific speculations about the fate we are likely to share. Even in his most despairing moments Lawrence remained curiously "religious." It is a tragedy that Western civilization may be doomed, that a man like Gerald Crich must be destroyed, and yet—does it really matter? Lawrence, through Birkin, debates the paradox endlessly. He cannot come to any conclusion. Gerald is beloved, yet Gerald is deathly. Gerald is a brilliant young man, yet he is a murderer, he is suicidal, he is rotten at the core. It is a possibility that Birkin's passionate love for him is as foully motivated as Gudrun's and would do no good for either of them. *Can* human beings alter their fates? Though his pessimism would seem to undercut and even negate his art, Lawrence is explicit in this novel about his feelings for mankind; the vituperation expressed is perhaps unequalled in serious literature. Surely it is at the very heart of the work, in Birkin's strident ranting voice:

> "I detest what I am, outwardly. I loathe myself as a human being. Humanity is a huge aggregate lie, and a huge lie is less than a small truth. Humanity is less, far less than the individual, because the individual may sometimes be capable of truth, and humanity is a tree of lies. . . .
>
> ". . . I abhor humanity, I wish it was swept away. It could go, and there would be no *absolute* loss, if every human being perished to-morrow."

But Ursula also perceives in her lover a contradictory desire to "save" this doomed world, and characteristically judges this desire a weakness, an insidious form of prostitution. Birkin's perverse attachment to the world he hates is not admirable in Ursula's eyes, for Ursula is no ordinary woman but a fiercely intolerant creature who detests all forms of insincerity. She is Birkin's conscience, in a sense; his foil, his gadfly; a taunting form of himself. Yet later, immediately after Birkin declares that he loves her, she is rather disturbed by the starkly nihilistic vision he sets before her; and indeed it strikes us as more tragic than that of Shakespeare's:

"We always consider the silver river of life, rolling on and quickening all the world to a brightness, on and on to heaven, flowing into a bright eternal sea, a heaven of angels thronging. But the other is our real reality— . . . that dark river of dissolution. You see it rolls in us just as the other rolls—the black river of corruption. And our flowers are of this—our sea-born Aphrodite, all our white phosphorescent flowers of sensuous perfection, all our reality, nowadays."

Aphrodite herself is symptomatic of the death-process, born in what Lawrence calls the "first spasm of universal dissolution." The process cannot be halted. It is beyond the individual, beyond choice. It ends in a universal nothing, a new cycle in which humanity will play no role. The prospect is a chilling one and yet—does it really matter? Humanity in the aggregate is contemptible, and many people (like Diana Crich) are better off dead since their living has somehow gone wrong. No, Birkin thinks, it can't *really* matter. His mood shifts, he is no longer frustrated and despairing; he is stoical, almost mystical, like one who has given up all hope. For he has said earlier to Gerald, after their talk of the death of God and the possible necessity of the salvation through love, that reality lies outside the human sphere:

"Well, if mankind is destroyed, if our race is destroyed like Sodom, and there is this beautiful evening with the luminous land and trees, I am satisfied. That which informs it all is there, and can never be lost. After all, what is mankind but just one expression of the incomprehensible. And if mankind passes away, it will only mean that this particular expression is completed and done. . . . Humanity doesn't embody the utterance of the incomprehensible any more. Humanity is a dead letter. There will be a new embodiment, in a new way. Let humanity disappear as quick as possible."

Lawrence's shifts in mood and conviction are passionate, even unsettling. One feels that he writes to discover what he thinks, what is thinking in him, on an unconscious level. Love is an ecstatic experience. Or is it, perhaps, a delusion? Erotic love is a way of salvation—or is it a distraction, a burden? Is it something to be gone through in order that one's deepest self may be stirred to life? Or is it a very simple, utterly natural emotion? (In *Sons and Lovers* Paul Morel is impatient with Miriam's near-hysterical exaggeration of ordinary emotions; he resents her intensity, her penchant for mythologizing, and finds solace in Clara's far less complex attitude toward sexual love.) Lawrence does not really know, regardless of his dogmatic remarks about "mind-consciousness" and "blood-consciousness." He cannot *know*; he must continually strive to know, and accept continual frustration.[3]

Tragedy for Lawrence arises out of the fatal split between the demands of the ego and those of the larger, less personal consciousness: we are crippled by the shadow of the finite personality as it falls across our souls, as the children of the old man in "The Christening" are crippled by his *particular* fatherliness. If at one point in history—during the great civilization of the Etruscans, for instance—there was a unity of being, a mythic harmony between man and his community and nature, it is lost to us now; the blighted landscapes in Beldover through which Lawrence's people walk give evidence that humanity is no longer evolving but devolving, degenerating. ("It is like a country in an underworld," says Gudrun, repulsed but fascinated. "The people are all ghouls, and everything is ghostly. Everything is a ghoulish replica of the real world . . . all soiled, everything sordid. It's like being mad, Ursula.") One England blots out another England, as Lawrence observes in *Lady Chatterley's Lover* some years later.

In Lawrence's work one is struck repeatedly by the total absence of concern for community. In the novels after *Sons and Lovers* his most fully developed and self-contained characters express an indifference toward their neighbors that is almost aristocratic. Both Anna and Will Brangwen of *The Rainbow* are oblivious to the world outside their household: the nation does not exist to them; there is no war in South Africa; they are in a "private retreat" that has no nationality. Even as a child Ursula is proudly contemptuous of her classmates, knowing herself set apart from them and, as a Brangwen, superior. She is fated to reject her unimaginative lover Skrebensky who has subordinated his individuality to the nation and who would gladly give up his life to it. ("I belong to the nation," he says solemnly, "and must do my duty by the nation.") Some years later she and Gudrun express a loathing for their parents' home that is astonishing, and even the less passionate Alvina Houghton of *The Lost Girl* surrenders to outbursts of mad, hilarious jeering, so frustrated is she by the limitations of her father's household and of the mining town of Woodhouse in general. (She is a "lost" girl only in terms of England. Though her life in a primitive mountain village in Italy is not a very comfortable one, it is nevertheless superior to her former, virginal life back in provincial England.)

Lawrence might have dramatized the tragedy of his people's rootlessness, especially as it compels them to attempt desperate and often quixotic relationships as a surrogate for social and political involvement (as in *The Plumed Serpent* and *Kangaroo*); but of course he could not give life to convictions he did not feel. The human instinct for something larger than an intense, intimate bond, the instinct for community, is entirely absent in Lawrence, and this absence helps to account for the wildness of his characters' emotions. (Their passionate narrowness is especially evident when contrasted with the tolerance of a character like Leopold Bloom of *Ulysses*. Leopold thinks wistfully of his wife, but he thinks also of innumerable other people, men and women both, the living and the dead; he is a man of the city who is stirred by the myriad trivial excitements of Dublin—an adventurer writ small, but not contemptible in Joyce's eyes. His obsessions are comically perverse, his stratagems pathetic. Acceptance by Simon Dedalus and his friends would mean a great deal to poor Bloom, but of course this acceptance will be withheld; he yearns for community but is denied it.)

For the sake of argument, Gudrun challenges Ursula's conviction that one can achieve a new space to be in, apart from the old: "But don't you think you'll *want* the old connection with the world—father and the rest of us, and all that it means, England and the world of thought—don't you think you'll *need* that, really to make a world?" But Ursula speaks for Lawrence in denying all inevitable social and familial connections. "One has a sort of other self, that belongs to a new planet, not to this," she says. The disagreement marks the sisters' break with each other; after this heated discussion they are no longer friends. Gudrun mocks the lovers with her false enthusiasm and deeply insults Ursula. "Go and find your new world, dear. After all, the happiest voyage is the quest of Rupert's Blessed Isles."

Lawrence's utopian plans for Rananim aside, it seems obvious that he could not have been truly interested in establishing a community of any permanence, for such a community would have necessitated a connection between one generation and the next. It would have demanded that faith in a reality beyond the individual and the individual's impulses which is absent in Lawrence—not undeveloped so much as simply absent, undiscovered. For this reason alone he seems to us distinctly un-English in any traditional sense. Fielding and Thackeray and Trollope and Dickens and Eliot and Hardy and Bennett belong to another world, another consciousness entirely. (Lawrence's kinship with Pater and Wilde, his predilection for the intensity of the moment, may have stimulated him to a vigorous glorification of Nietzschean instinct and will to power as a means of resisting aestheticism: for there is a languid cynicism about Birkin not unlike that of Wilde's prematurely weary heroes.)

Halfway around the world, in Australia, Richard Somers discovers that he misses England, for it isn't freedom but mere *vacancy* he finds in this new, disturbingly beautiful world: the absence of civilization, of culture, of inner meaning; the absence of spirit.[4] But so long as Lawrence is in England he evokes the idea of his nation only to do battle with it, to refute it, to be nauseated by it. The upper classes are sterile and worthless, the working classes are stunted aborigines who stare after the Brangwen sisters in the street. Halliday and his London friends are self-consciously decadent—"the most pettifogging calculating Bohemia that ever reckoned its pennies." Only in the mythical structure of a fabulist work like *The Escaped Cock* can Lawrence imagine a harmonious relationship between male and female, yet even here in this Mediterranean setting the individual cannot tolerate other people, nor they him: "the little life of jealousy and property" resumes its sway and forces the man who died to flee. There is, however, no possibility of a tragic awareness in these terms; it is not tragic that the individual is compelled to break with his nation and his community because any unit larger than the individual is tainted and suspect, caught in the downward process of corruption.[5] The community, almost by definition, is degraded. About this everyone is in agreement—Clifford Chatterley as well as Mellors, Hermione as well as Ursula and Gudrun. Community in the old sense is based on property and possessions and must be rejected, and all human relationships not founded upon an immediate emotional rapport must be broken. "The old ideals are dead as nails—nothing there," Birkin says early in *Women in Love*. "It seems to me there remains only this perfect union with a woman—sort of ultimate marriage—and there isn't anything else." Gerald, however, finds it difficult to agree. Making one's life up out of a woman, one woman only, woman only seems to him impossible, just as the forging of an intense love-connection with another man—which in Lawrence's cosmology would have saved his life—is impossible.

"I only feel what I feel," Gerald says.

THE CORE OF OUR human tragedy has very little to do with society, then, and everything to do with the individual: with the curious self-destructive condition of the human spirit. Having rejected the theological dogma of original sin, Lawrence develops a rather similar psychological dogma to account for the diabolic split within the individual between the dictates of "mind-consciousness" and the impulses of "blood-consciousness." In his essay on Nathaniel Hawthorne in *Studies in Classic American Literature*, he interprets *The Scarlet Letter* as an allegory, a typically American allegory, of the consequences of the violent antagonism between the two ways of being. His explicitness is helpful in terms of *Women in Love*, where a rich verbal texture masks a tragically simple paradox. The cross itself is the symbol of mankind's self-division, as it is the symbol, the final haunting image, in Gerald Crich's life. (Fleeing into the snow, exhausted and broken after his ignoble attempt to strangle Gudrun, Gerald comes upon a half-buried crucifix at the top of a pole. He fears that someone is going to murder him. In terror he realizes "This was the moment when the death was uplifted, and there was no escape. Lord Jesus, was it then bound to be—Lord Jesus! He could feel the blow descending, he knew he was murdered.")

Christ's agony on the cross symbolizes our human agony at having acquired, or having been poisoned by, the "sin" of knowledge
and self-consciousness. In the Hawthorne essay Lawrence says:

> Nowadays men do hate the idea of dualism. It's no good, dual
> we are. The cross. If we accept the symbol, then, virtually we ac-
> cept the fact. We are divided against ourselves.
>
> For instance, the blood *hates* being KNOWN by the mind. It feels
> itself destroyed when it is KNOWN. Hence the profound instinct of
> privacy.
>
> And on the other hand, the mind and the spiritual conscious-
> ness of man simply *hates* the dark potency of blood-acts: hates the
> genuine dark sensual orgasms, which do, for the time being, ac-
> tually obliterate the mind and the spiritual consciousness, plunge
> them in a suffocating flood of darkness.
>
> You can't get away from this.
>
> Blood-consciousness overwhelms, obliterates, and annuls
> mind-consciousness.
>
> Mind-consciousness extinguishes blood-consciousness, and
> consumes the blood.
>
> We are all of us conscious in both ways. And the two ways are
> antagonistic in us.
>
> They will always remain so.
>
> That is our cross.

It is obvious that Lawrence identifies with the instinct toward formal allegory and subterfuge in American literature. He understands
Hawthorne, Melville, and Poe from the inside; it is himself he speaks
of when he says of Poe that he adventured into the vaults and cellars
and horrible underground passages of the human soul, desperate to
experience the "prismatic ecstasy" of heightened consciousness and
of love. And Poe knew himself to be doomed, necessarily—as
Lawrence so frequently thought himself (and his race). Indeed, Poe
is far closer to Lawrence than Hawthorne or Melville:

> He died wanting more love, and love killed him. A ghastly dis-
> ease, love. Poe telling us of his disease: trying even to make his

disease fair and attractive. Even succeeding. Which is the inevitable falseness, duplicity of art, American art in particular.

The inevitable duplicity of art: an eccentric statement from the man who
says, elsewhere (in an essay on Walt Whitman), that the essential
function of art is moral. "Not aesthetic, not decorative, not past-
time and recreation. But moral." Yet it is possible to see that the
artist too suffers from a tragic self-division, that he is forced to
dramatize the radically new shifting over of consciousness primarily in covert, even occult and deathly terms: wanting to write a
novel of consummate health and triumph whose controlling symbol is the rainbow, writing in fact a despairing, floridly tragic, and
rather mad work that resembles poetry and music (Wagnerian
music) far more than it resembles the clearly "moral" bright book
of life that is the novel, Lawrence finds himself surprised and disturbed by the apocalyptic nature of his greatest effort, as if he had
imagined he had written something quite different. The rhythm of
Lawrence's writing is that of the American works he analyzes so ir-
reverently and so brilliantly, a "disintegrating and sloughing of the
old consciousness" and "the forming of a new consciousness underneath." Such apocalyptic books must be written because old things
need to die, because the "old white psyche has to be gradually broken down before anything else can come to pass" (in the essay on
Poe). Such art must be violent, it must be outlandish and diabolic at
its core because it is revolutionary in the truest sense of the word.
It is subversive, even traitorous; but though it seeks to overturn
empires, its primary concerns are prophetic, even religious. As
Lawrence says in the poem "Nemesis" (from *Pansies*), "If we do not
rapidly open all the doors of consciousness / and freshen the putrid
little space in which we are cribbed / the sky-blue walls of our un-
ventilated heaven / will be bright red with blood." In any case the
true artist does not determine the direction of his art; he surrenders
his ego so that his deeper self may be heard. There is no freedom except in compliance with the spirit within, what Lawrence calls the
Holy Ghost.

The suppressed Prologue to *Women in Love* sets forth the terms of
Birkin's torment with dramatic economy.[6] "Mind-consciousness"

and "blood-consciousness" are not mere abstractions, pseudo-philosophical notions, but bitterly existential ways of perceiving and of being. When Birkin and Gerald Crich first meet they experience a subtle bond between each other, a "sudden connection" that is intensified during a mountain-climbing trip in the Tyrol. In the isolation of the rocks and snow they and their companion attain a rare sort of intimacy that is to be denied and consciously rejected when they descend again into their usual lives. (The parallel with Gerald's death in the snow is obvious; by suppressing the Prologue and beginning with the chapter we have, "Sisters," in which Ursula and Gudrun discuss marriage and the home and the mining town and venture out to watch the wedding, Lawrence sacrificed a great deal. "Sisters" is an entirely satisfactory opening, brilliant in its own lavish way; but the Prologue with its shrill, tender, almost crazed language is far more moving.)

Preliminary to the action of *Women in Love*, and unaccountable in terms of *The Rainbow*, which centers so exclusively upon Ursula, is the passionate and undeclared relationship between Birkin and Gerald, and the torturous split between Birkin's spiritual and "sisterly" love for Hermione and his "passion of desire" for Gerald. Birkin is sickened by his obsession with Gerald; he is repulsed by his overwrought, exclusively mental relationship with Hermione (which is, incidentally, very close to the relationship of sheer nerves Lawrence discusses in his essay on Poe: the obscene love that is the "intensest nervous vibration of unison" without any erotic consummation). That Birkin's dilemma is emblematic of society's confusion in general is made clear, and convincing, by his immersion in educational theory. What is education except the gradual and deliberate building up of consciousness, unit by unit? Each unit of consciousness is the "living unit of that great social, religious, philosophic idea towards which mankind, like an organism seeking its final form, is laboriously growing," but the tragic paradox is that there *is* no great unifying idea at the present time; there is simply aimless, futile activity. For we are in the autumn of civilization, and decay, as such, cannot be acknowledged. As Birkin suffers in his awareness of his own deceitful, frustrated life, he tries to forget himself in work; but he cannot escape a sense of the futility of all attempts at "social constructiveness." The tone of the Prologue is dark indeed, and one hears Lawrence's undisguised despair in every line:

> How to get away from this process of reduction, how to escape this phosphorescent passage into the tomb, which was universal though unacknowledged, this was the unconscious problem which tortured Birkin day and night. He came to Hermione, and found with her the pure, translucent regions of death in itself, of ecstasy. In the world the autumn itself was setting in. What should a man add himself on to?—to science, to social reform, to aestheticism, to sensationalism? The whole world's constructive activity was a fiction, a lie, to hide the great process of decomposition, which had set in. What then to adhere to?

He attempts a physical relationship with Hermione which is a cruel failure, humiliating to them both. He goes in desperation to prostitutes. Like Paul Morel he suffers a familiar split between the "spiritual" woman and the "physical" woman, but his deeper anxiety lies in his un-acknowledged passion for Gerald Crich. Surely homoerotic yearning has never been so vividly and so sympathetically presented as it is in Lawrence's Prologue, where Birkin's intelligent complexity, his half-serious desire to rid himself of his soul in order to escape his predicament, and his fear of madness and dissolution as a consequence of his lovelessness give him a tragic depth comparable to Hamlet's. He *wants* to love women, just as he wants to believe in the world's constructive activity; but how can a man create his own feelings? Birkin knows that he cannot: he can only suppress them by an act of sheer will. In danger of going mad or of dying—of possibly killing himself—Birkin continues his deathly relationship with Hermione, keeping his homoerotic feelings to himself and even, in a sense, secret from himself. With keen insight Lawrence analyzes Birkin's own analysis of the situation. "He knew what he felt, but he always kept the knowledge at bay. His a priori were: 'I *should* not feel like this,' and 'It is the ultimate mark of my own deficiency, that I feel like this.' Therefore, though he admitted everything, he never really faced the question. He never accepted the desire, and received it as part of himself. He always tried to keep it expelled from him." Not only does Birkin attempt to dissociate himself from an impulse that *is* himself, he attempts to deny the femaleness in his own nature by objectifying (and degrading) it in his treatment of Hermione and of the "slightly bestial" prostitutes. It maddens him that he should feel sexual attraction for the male physique while for the female he is capable of feeling only a kind of fondness, a sacred love, as if for a sister. "The women he seemed to be kin to, he looked for the soul in them." By the age of thirty he is sickly and dissolute, attached to Hermione in a loveless, sadistic relationship, terrified of breaking with her for fear of falling into the abyss. Yet the break is imminent, inevitable—so the action of *Women in Love* begins.

A tragedy, then, of an informal nature, experimental in its gropings toward a resolution of the central crisis: how to integrate the male and female principles, how to integrate the organic and the "civilized," the relentlessly progressive condition of the modern world. It is not enough to be a child of nature, to cling to one's ignorance as if it were a form of blessedness; one cannot deny the reality of the external world, its gradual transformation from the Old England into the New, into an enthusiastic acceptance of the individual as an instrument in the great machine of society. When Hermione goes into her rhapsody about spontaneity and the instincts, echoing Birkin in saying that the mind is death, he contradicts her brutally by claiming that the problem is not that people have too much mind, but too little. As for Hermione herself, she is merely making words because knowledge means everything to her: "Even your animalism, you want it in your head. You don't want to *be* an animal, you want to observe your own animal functions, to get a mental thrill out of them. . . . What is it but the worst and last form of intellectualism, this love of yours for passion and the animal instincts?" But it is really himself he is attacking: Hermione is a ghastly form of himself he would like to destroy, a parody of a woman, a sister of his soul.

Women in Love must have originally been imagined as Birkin's tragedy rather than Gerald's, for though Gerald feels an attraction for Birkin, he is not so obsessed with it as Birkin is; in the Prologue he is characterized as rather less intelligent, less shrewd, than he turns out to be in subsequent chapters. Ursula's role in saving Birkin from dissolution is, then, far greater than she can know. Not only must she arouse and satisfy his spiritual yearnings, she must answer to his physical desire as well: she must, in a sense, take on the active, masculine role in their relationship. (Significantly, it is Ursula who presses them into an erotic relationship after the death of Diana Crich and her young man. It is she who embraces Birkin tightly, wanting to show him that she is no shallow prude, and though he whimpers to himself, "Not this, not this," he nevertheless succumbs to desire for her and they become lovers. Had Ursula not sensed the need to force Birkin into a physical relationship, it is possible their love would have become as spiritualized, and consequently as poisoned, as Birkin's and Hermione's.) Ursula's role in saving Birkin from destruction is comparable to Sonia's fairly magical redemption of Raskolnikov in *Crime and Punishment*, just as Gerald's suicide is comparable to Svidrigailov's when both men are denied salvation through women by whom they are obsessed. Though the feminine principle is not sufficient to guarantee eternal happiness, it is nevertheless the way through which salvation is attained: sex is an initiation in Lawrence, a necessary and even ritualistic *event* in the process of psychic wholeness. Where in more traditional tragedy—Shakespeare's *King Lear* comes immediately to mind—it is the feminine, irrational, "dark and vicious" elements that must be resisted, since they disturb the status quo, the patriarchal cosmos, in Lawrence it is precisely the darkness, the passion, the mind-obliterating, terrible, and even vicious experience of erotic love that is necessary for salvation. The individual is split and wars futilely against himself, civilization is split and must fall into chaos if male and female principles are opposed. Lawrence's is the sounder psychology, but it does not follow that his world view is more optimistic, for to recognize a truth does not inevitably bring with it the moral strength to realize that truth in one's life.

Birkin's desire for an eternal union with another man is thwarted in *Women in Love*, and his failure leads indirectly to Gerald's death. At least this is Birkin's conviction. "He should have loved me," he says to Ursula and she, frightened, replies without sympathy, "What difference would it have made!" It is only in a symbolic dimension that the men are lovers; consciously, in the daylight world, they are never anything more than friends. In the chapter "Gladiatorial" the men wrestle together in order to stir Gerald from his boredom, and they seem to "drive their white flesh deeper and deeper against each other, as if they would break into a oneness." The effort is such that both men lose consciousness and Birkin falls over Gerald, involuntarily. When their minds are gone their opposition to each other is gone and they can become united—but only temporarily, only until Birkin regains his consciousness and moves away. At the novel's conclusion Birkin is "happily" married, yet incomplete. He will be a reasonably content and normal man, a husband to the passionate Ursula, yet unfulfilled; and one cannot quite believe that his frustrated love for Gerald will not surface in another form. His failure is not merely his own but civilization's as well: male and female are inexorably opposed, the integration of the two halves of the human soul is an impossibility in our time.[7]

HENCE THE CRUEL FROST-KNOWLEDGE of *Women in Love*, the death by perfect cold Lawrence has delineated. Long before Gerald's actual death in the mountains, Birkin speculates on him as a strange white wonderful demon from the north, fated like his civilization to pass away into universal dissolution, the day of "creative life" being finished. In *Apocalypse* Lawrence speaks of the long slow death of the human being in our time, the victory of repressive and mechanical forces over the organic, the pagan. The mystery religions of antiquity have been destroyed by the systematic, dissecting principle; the artist is driven as a consequence to think in deliberately mythical, archaic, chiliastic terms. How to express the inexpressible? Those poems in *Pansies* that address themselves to the problem—poems like "Wellsian Futures," "Dead People," "Ego-Bound," "Climb Down, O Lordly Mind," "Peace and War"—are rhetorical and strident and rather flat; it is in images that Lawrence *thinks* most clearly. He is too brilliant an artist not to breathe life even into those characters who are in opposition to his own principles. In a statement that resembles Yeats' (that the occult spirits of *A Vision* came to bring him images for his poetry) Lawrence indicates a surprising indifference to the very concept of the Apocalypse itself: "We do not care, vitally, about theories of the Apocalypse. . . . What we care about is the release of the imagination. . . . What does the Apocalypse matter, unless in so far as it gives us imaginative release into another vital world?"[8]

This jaunty attitude is qualified by the images that are called forth by the imagination, however: the wolfishness of Gerald and his mother; the ghoulishness of the Beldover miners; the African totems (one has a face that is void and terrible in its mindlessness; the other has a long, elegant body with a tiny head, a face crushed small like a beetle's); Hermione striking her lover with a paperweight of lapis lazuli and fairly swooning with ecstasy; Gerald digging his spurs into his mare's sides, into wounds that are already bleeding; the drowned Diana Crich with her arms still wrapped tightly about the neck of her young man; the demonic energy of Winifred's rabbit, and Gudrun's slashed, bleeding arm which seems to tear across Gerald's brain; the uncanny, terrifying soullessness of Innsbruck; the stunted figure of the artist Loerke; the final vision of Gerald as the frozen carcass of a dead male. These are fearful images, and what has Lawrence to set against them but the embrace of a man and a woman, a visionary transfiguration of the individual by love?—and even the experience of love, of passion and unity, is seen as ephemeral.

Birkin sees Gerald and Gudrun as flowers of dissolution, locked in the death-process; he cannot help but see Gerald as Cain, who killed his brother. Though in one way *Women in Love* is a naturalistic work populated with realistic characters and set in altogether probable environments, in another way it is inflexible and even rather austerely classical: Gerald is Cain from the very first and his fate is settled. Birkin considers his friend's accidental killing of his brother and wonders if it is proper to think in terms of *accident* at all. Has everything that happens a universal significance? Ultimately he does not believe that there is anything accidental in life: "it all hung together, in the deepest sense." (And it follows that no one is murdered accidentally: ". . . a man who is murderable is a man who in a profound if hidden lust desires to be murdered.") Gerald plainly chooses his murderer in Gudrun, and it is in the curious, misshapen form of Loerke that certain of Gerald's inclinations are given their ultimate realization. Gerald's glorification of the machine and of himself as a god of the machine is parodied by Loerke's inhuman willfulness: Gudrun sees him as the rock-bottom of all life. Unfeeling, stoic, he cares about nothing except his work, he makes not the slightest attempt to be at one with anything, he exists a "pure, unconnected will" in a stunted body. His very being excites Gerald to disgusted fury because he is finally all that Gerald has imagined for himself—the subordination of all spontaneity, the triumph of "harmony" in industrial organization.

Of the bizarre nightmare images stirred in Lawrence's imagination by the idea of the apocalypse, Loerke is perhaps the most powerful. He is at once very human, and quite inhuman. He is reasonable, even rather charming, and at the same time deathly—a "mud-child," a creature of the underworld. His name suggests that of Loki, the Norse god of discord and mischief, the very principle of dissolution. A repulsive and fascinating character, he is described by Lawrence as a gnome, a bat, rabbit, a troll, a chatterer, a magpie, a maker of disturbing jokes, with the blank look of inorganic misery behind his buffoonery. That he is an artist, and a homosexual as well, cannot be an accident. He is in Lawrence's imagination the diabolic alter ego who rises up to mock all that Lawrence takes to be sacred. Hence his uncanny power, his parodistic talent: he accepts the hypothesis that industry has replaced religion and he accepts his role as artist in terms of industry, without sentimental qualms. Art should interpret industry; the artist fulfills himself in acquiescence to the machine. Is there nothing apart from work, mechanical work?—Gudrun asks. And he says without hesitation, "Nothing but work!"

Loerke disgusts Birkin and Gerald precisely because he embodies certain of their own traits. He is marvelously self-sufficient; he wishes to ingratiate himself with no one; he is an artist who completely understands and controls his art; he excites the admiration of the beautiful Gudrun, and even Ursula is interested in him for a while. Most painful, perhaps, is his homosexuality. He is not divided against himself, not at all tortured by remorse or conscience. In the Prologue to the novel Birkin half-wishes he might rid himself of his soul, and Loerke is presented as a creature without a soul, one of the "little people" who finds his mate in a human being. It is interesting to note that the ratlike qualities in Loerke are those that have attracted Birkin in other men. Birkin has felt an extraordinary desire to come close to and to know and "as it were to eat" a certain type of Cornish man with dark, fine, stiff hair and dark eyes like holes in his head or like the eyes of a rat (see the Prologue); and he has felt the queer, subterranean, repulsive beauty of a young man with an indomitable manner "like a quick, vital rat" (see the chapter "A Chair"). The Nietzschean quality of Loerke's haughtiness and his loathing of other people, particularly women, remind us of the aristocratic contempt expressed by the middle-aged foreigner whom Tom Brangwen admires so much in the first chapter of *The Rainbow:* the man has a queer monkeyish face that is in its way almost beautiful, he is sardonic, dry-skinned, coldly intelligent, mockingly courteous to the women in his company (one of whom has made love with Tom previously), a creature who strangely rouses Tom's blood and who, in the form of Anna Lensky, will be his mate. There is no doubt but that Lawrence, a very different physical type, and temperamentally quite opposed to the cold, life-denying principle these men embody, was nevertheless powerfully attracted by them. There is an irresistible *life* to Loerke that makes us feel the strength of his nihilistic charm.

Surely not accidental is the fact that Loerke is an artist. He expresses a view of art that all artists share, to some extent, despite their protestations to the contrary. It is Flaubert speaking in Loerke, declaring art supreme and the artist's life of little consequence; when Loerke claims that his statuette of a girl on a horse is no more than an artistic composition, a certain form without relation to anything outside itself, he is echoing Flaubert's contention that there is no such thing as a subject, there is only style. ("What seems beautiful to me, what I should like to write," Flaubert said, in a remark now famous, "is a book about nothing, a book dependent on nothing external. . . .") Loerke angers Ursula by declaring that his art pictures nothing, "absolutely nothing;" there is no connection between his art and the everyday world, they are two different and distinct planes of existence, and she must not confuse them. In his disdainful proclamation of an art that refers only to itself, he speaks

for the aesthetes of the nineteenth century against whom Lawrence
had to define himself as a creator of vital, moral, life-enhancing art.
Though Lawrence shared certain of their beliefs—that bourgeois
civilization was bankrupt, that the mass of human beings were
hopelessly ignorant and contemptible—he did not want to align
himself with their extreme rejection of "ordinary" life and of nature
itself. (Too unbridled a revulsion against the world would lead one
to the sinister self-indulgent fantasies of certain of the decadent
poets and artists—the bizarre creations of Oscar Wilde and Huys-
mans and Baudelaire, and of Gustave Moreau and Odilon Redon
and Jan Toorop among others.) Loerke's almost supernatural presence drives Ursula and Birkin away, and brings to the surface the destructive elements in the love of Gudrun and Gerald. He is an artist
of decay: his effect upon Gudrun is like that of a subtle poison.

"Life doesn't *really* matter," Gudrun says. "It is one's art which is
central."[9]

Symbolically, then, Gerald witnesses the destruction of his love,
or of a part of his own soul, by those beliefs that had been a kind of
religion to him in his operating of the mines. Lawrence himself plays
with certain of his worst fears by giving them over to Loerke and
Gudrun, who toy with them, inventing for their amusement a
mocking dream of the destruction of the world: humanity invents a
perfect explosive that blows up the world, perhaps; or the climate
shifts and the world goes cold and snow falls everywhere and "only
white creatures, polar-bears, white foxes, and men like awful white
snow-birds, persisted in ice cruelty." It is Lawrence's nightmare, the
Apocalypse without resurrection, without meaning; a vision as
bleak and as tragically unsentimental as Shakespeare's.

ONLY IN PARABLE, in myth, can tragedy be transcended. In that
beautiful novella *The Escaped Cock*, written while Lawrence was dying,
the Christian and the pagan mate, the male and the female come together in a perfect union, and the process of dissolution is halted.
The man who had died awakes in his tomb, sickened and despairing,
knowing himself mortal, not the Son of God but no more than a
son of man—and in this realization is his hope, his true salvation.
He is resurrected to the flesh of his own body; through the warm,

healing flesh of the priestess of Isis he is healed of his fraudulent divinity. "Father!" he cries in his rapture, "Why did you hide this from me?"

Poetic, biblical in its rhythms, *The Escaped Cock* is an extraordinary work in that it dramatizes Lawrence's own sense of resurrection from near death (he had come close to dying several times) and that it repudiates his passion for changing the world. The man who had died realizes that his teaching is finished and that it had been a mistake to interfere in the souls of others; he knows now that his reach ends in his fingertips. His love for mankind had been no more than a form of egotism, a madness that would devour multitudes while leaving his own being untouched and virginal. What is crucified in him is his passion for "saving" others. Lawrence has explored the near dissolution of the personality in earlier works—in Ursula's illness near the end of *The Rainbow*, and in her reaction to Birkin's lovemaking in *Women in Love*; and in Connie Chatterley's deepening sense of nothingness before her meeting with Mellors—but never with such powerful economy as in *The Escaped Cock*. The man who had died wakes slowly and reluctantly to life, overcome with a sense of nausea, dreading consciousness but compelled to return to it and to his fulfillment as a human being. The passage back to life is a terrible one; his injured body is repulsive to him, as is the memory of his suffering. The analogy between the colorful cock and the gradually healing flesh of the man who had died is unabashedly direct and even rather witty. In this idyllic Mediterranean world a cock and a man are kin, all of nature is related, the dead Osiris is resurrected in the dead Christ, and the phenomenal world is revealed as the transcendental world, the world of eternity. Simply to live in a body, to live as a mortal human being—this is enough, and this is everything. Only a man who had come close to dying himself and who had despaired of his efforts to transform the human world could have written a passage like this, in awed celebration of the wonders of the existential world:

The man who had died looked nakedly onto life, and saw a vast resoluteness everywhere flinging itself up in stormy or subtle wave-crests, foam-tips emerging out of the blue invisible, a black-

and-orange cock, or the green flame tongues out of the extremes of the fig-tree. They came forth, these things and creatures of spring, glowing with desire and with assertion. . . . The man who had died looked on the great swing into existence of things that had not died, but he saw no longer their tremulous desire to exist and to be. He heard instead their ringing, ringing, defiant challenge to all other things existing. . . . And always, the man who had died saw not the bird alone, but the short, sharp wave of life of which the bird was the crest. He watched the queer, beaky motion of the creature. . . .

And the destiny of life seemed more fierce and compulsive to him even than the destiny of death.

The man who had died asks himself this final question: From what, and to what, could this infinite whirl be saved?

The mystic certitude of *The Escaped Cock*, like the serenity of "The Ship of Death" and "Bavarian Gentians," belongs to a consciousness that has transcended the dualism of tragedy. The split has not been healed, it has simply been transcended; nearing death, Lawrence turns instinctively to the allegorical mode, the most primitive and the most sophisticated of all visionary expressions. *Women in Love* is, by contrast, irresolute and contradictory; it offers only the finite, tentative "resurrection" of marriage between two very incomplete people. Like Connie Chatterley and her lover Mellors, the surviving couple of *Women in Love* must fashion their lives in a distinctly unmythic, unidyllic landscape, their fates to be bound up closely with that of their civilization. How are we to escape history?—defy the death-process of our culture? With difficulty. In sorrow. So long as we live, even strengthened as we are by the "mystic conjunction," the "ultimate unison" between men and women, our lives are tempered by the ungovernable contingencies of the world that is no metaphor, but our only home.

Notes

1. All quotations from *Women in Love* are taken from the Modern Library edition.

2. *Collected Letters*, ed. Harry T. Moore (New York, 1962), 482, 519.

3. As Lawrence says in an essay about the writer's relationship to his own work: "Morality in the novel is the trembling instability of the balance. When the novelist puts his thumb on the scale, to pull down the balance to his own predilection, that is immorality. . . . And of all the art forms, the novel most of all demands the trembling and oscillating of the balance," *Phoenix: The Posthumous Papers of D. H. Lawrence* (London, 1936), 529.

4. Richard Somers is fascinated and disturbed by Australia, into which he has projected the struggle of his own soul. The bush has frightened him with its emptiness and stillness; he cannot penetrate its secret. At one point it seems to him that a presence of some sort lurks in the wilderness, an actual spirit of the place that terrifies him. As for the social and political conditions of Australia—what is more hopelessly uninteresting than accomplished liberty? (See *Kangaroo*, Penguin edition, 33.)

5. That Lawrence might have dealt with the tragic implications of the individual's failure to find a home for himself in his own nation is indicated by remarks he makes elsewhere, for instance in the introductory essay, "The Spirit of Place," to *Studies in Classic American Literature:* "Men are free when they are in a living homeland, not when they are straying and breaking away. Men are free when they are obeying some deep, inward voice of religious belief. Obeying from within. Men are free when they belong to a living, organic, *bèlieving* community, active in fulfilling some unfulfilled, perhaps unrealized purpose." The *Studies* were written between 1917 and 1923.

6. The Prologue is available in *Phoenix II* (New York, 1968) and in a recently published anthology, *The Other Persuasion*, ed. Seymour Kleinberg (New York, 1977).

7. It is interesting to note Lawrence's intense dislike of the very idea of homosexuality in women. Miss Inger of *The Rainbow* is revealed as a poisonous, corrupt woman who makes an ideal mate for Ursula's cynical uncle Tom Brangwen. Ursula had loved them both but when she realizes that they are in the "service of the machine," she is repulsed by them. "Their marshy, bitter-sweet corruption came sick and unwholesome in her nostrils. . . . She would leave them both forever, leave forever their strange, soft, half-corrupt element" (*The Rainbow*, Penguin edition, p. 351). In *Lady Chatterley's Lover* Mellors begins to rant about women he has known who have disappointed him sexually, and the quality of his rage—which must be, in part, Lawrence's—is rather alarming. He goes through a brief catalogue of unacceptable women, then says, "It's astonishing how Lesbian women are consciously or unconsciously. Seems to me they're nearly all

Lesbian." In the presence of such a woman, Mellors tells Connie, he fairly howls in his soul, "wanting to kill her" (*Lady Chatterley's Lover*, Signet edition, p. 190).

8. *Phoenix*, 293–294.

9. Gudrun is an artist of considerable talent herself, one who works in miniatures, as if wishing to see the world "through the wrong end of the opera glasses." It is significant that she expresses a passionate wish to have been born a man, and that she feels an unaccountable lust for deep brutality against Gerald, whom in another sense she loves. Far more interesting a character than her sister Ursula, Gudrun is fatally locked into her own willful instinct for making herself the measure of all things: her vision is anthropomorphic and solipsistic, finally inhuman. We know from certain of Lawrence's poems, particularly "New Heaven and Earth," that the "maniacal horror" of such solipsism was his own. He seems to have been driven nearly to suicide, or to a nervous breakdown, by the terrifying conviction that nothing existed beyond his own consciousness. Unlike Lawrence, who sickened of being the measure of all things, Gudrun rejoices in her cruel talent for reducing everyone and everything—robins as well as people—to size. Her love affair with Gerald is really a contest of wills: in her soul she is a man, a rival. Like one of the seductive chimeras or vampires in decadent art—in the paintings of Munch and in the writings of Strindberg—Gudrun sees her lover as an "unutterable enemy," whom she wishes to kiss and stroke and embrace until she has him "all in her hands, till she [has] strained him into her knowledge. Ah, if she could have precious *knowledge* of him, she would be filled . . ." 379). At the novel's end she has become so dissociated from her own feelings and so nauseated by life that she seems to be on the brink of insanity. It strikes her that she has never really lived only worked, she is in fact a kind of clock, her face is like a clock's face, a twelve-hour clock dial—an image that fills her with terror, yet pleases her strangely.

The First *"Women in Love"*

JOHN WORTHEN

◆   ◆   ◆

I

On 1 October 1998, Cambridge University Press published a book which should have been published more than eighty years before, in the spring of 1917. It had been finished in November 1916, sent to the author's agent, and from there had gone to the publisher who had a contract to publish it.

But the author was D. H. Lawrence, the agent J. B. Pinker, the book the first version of *Women in Love*, and the publisher Algernon Methuen, who, just twelve months earlier, had been roundly criticized at Bow Street Magistrates Court for publishing the book's immediate predecessor, *The Rainbow*. The Magistrate, Sir John Dickinson, had then commented:

> how it ever could have passed through Messrs. Methuen's hands he failed to understand. It was greatly to be regretted that a firm of old standing and the highest repute, whose name on the title-

page of a book justified anyone in taking it into their home, should have allowed their reputation to be soiled, as it undoubtedly had been. . . . (*Daily Telegraph*, 15 November 1915, 12)

The Rainbow had, of course, been banned under the 1857 Obscene Publications Act. For the first time since 1910, Lawrence had then spent a period as long as seven months without working on a novel. There must have seemed little point in doing so, in spite of the fact that the other half of the old "Sisters" material remained to be developed. However, as he remarked in the spring of 1916, "a work of art is an act of faith . . . one goes on writing, to the unseen witnesses." He returned to novel-writing at the end of April 1916, to bring to a conclusion the fictional enterprise based on the lives of the Brangwen sisters which had occupied him since early in 1913.

Even by the standards of his own most intense periods of work, what he then accomplished, between late April and mid-November 1916, was extraordinary. He wrote the novel while living in isolation in Cornwall, unsure whether it would be published, quite uncertain how he would be able to earn his living, subject to constant uncertainty about the war and its progress, about the situation of Frieda's German family, and about his own status as unconscripted civilian. And he actually wrote this new novel twice within that seven-month period, producing in *The First "Women in Love"* what is arguably his most important piece of fiction of the second decade of the twentieth century—a novel which, until now, has been read by very few people, and whose very existence as an independent text has been largely ignored.[1]

II

Why was it not published in 1917? In November 1916, Pinker sent the typescript of the new book to Methuen. They kept it for a month, then returned it. They may have been consulting their lawyers about ending the contract (their June 1914 agreement with Lawrence had promised them his next three novels); and they may even have been wondering whether this new novel offered them any chance of recovering the advance they had paid Lawrence for *The Rainbow*, which they had demanded back in December 1915: "there has been a complete failure of the consideration for which we paid our money. Mr. Lawrence should now repay this sum" (*L* ii. 457 n. 2).[2] It is very unlikely that in the winter of 1916 they even considered publishing his new book; one which, in its own way, was as offensive about the war, and as potentially libelous about real people, as the previous one had been about marriage and sexuality. The month's delay was probably simply because Methuen saw no reason why they should hurry to make a decision about ending the contract of an author who had caused them so much trouble and embarrassment, and lost them money into the bargain. It was not until around 20 December 1916 that Lawrence heard that the contract had been canceled. He responded, with characteristic point and vigor, "I am glad not to be thrown any more under the snout of that particular swine" (*L* iii. 58).

Pinker could now offer *The First "Women in Love"* to other publishers. A copy of the typescript went to Duckworth, then to Constable and then to Secker, and there may well have been others who saw it too; Lawrence's friend Catherine Carswell believed that "it must have lain on the table at one time or another of every leading publisher in London" (80). But it was turned down everywhere; even Duckworth, who had all but one of Lawrence's books in print, and for whom Lawrence probably had the highest hopes, rejected it.[3] When sending Pinker a batch of manuscript for typing, on 25 October, Lawrence had remarked that it was "a terrible and horrible and wonderful novel. You will hate it and nobody will publish it. But there, these things are beyond us" (*L* ii. 669). When he sent in the final batch of manuscript a week later, he told a friend it was a novel "which everybody will hate completely" (*L* iii. 19); and he remarked to E. M. Forster that although it was "rather wonderful and terrible," "I don't suppose anybody will publish it" (*L* iii. 22). He was thus attempting to prepare himself for the worst, though he may well have been shocked by the absolute rejection the novel suffered in the winter of 1916–17. But after the *Rainbow* debacle, Lawrence was a marked man; what the new book said about the war, and the way in which it clearly used real people as fictional characters,[4] made it deeply unattractive to publishers who—with a growing wartime shortage of materials and labor—were cutting back on what they published and were increasingly unprepared to take risks. On one level, Lawrence remained confident that the novel would one day be published; a comment he made in February 1918—"I shall have some money when the war ends" (*L* iii. 216)—suggests the depth of that confidence. But it was not until December 1920 (in America) and June 1921 (in England) that the book was finally published (*WL* xxxix–1). I shall take as text of the 1921 novel the Cambridge edition of the novel, which incorporates the additions Lawrence made in proof for the English edition.

By 1921 it had become in many ways a different sort of book from the one which had circulated publishers in the winter of 1916–17. Pinker had had a clean typescript made of it in February 1917, and Lawrence had revised that typescript at various times during 1917 and then again in 1919. He rewrote about a tenth of the book completely, and made additions, cuts and changes throughout. What was published in 1921 demonstrated just how much work he had done during the intervening years.

The book which might have been published in 1917 is, of course, in one respect irrecoverable. Lawrence would certainly have revised it at the proof stage if a publisher had accepted it. He also mentioned twice during the week in November 1916 when he finished it that he planned "an epilogue—a small last chapter," but would not write it "until the whole is sent in to the printer" (*L* iii. 29): "that must wait for the wheel of time to turn" (*L* iii. 36). He had mentioned a similar idea back in July.[5] Such an "epilogue" might have taken the form of a surviving fragment of text (including the start of a letter from Gudrun describing the birth of Gerald's son), which Lawrence probably drafted and then abandoned sometime late in October 1916.[6] That seems a good deal more likely as material for an epilogue than the exchange between Ursula and Birkin which concludes the 1921 novel. On the other hand, no publisher in 1916 would have been prepared to accept a novel by Lawrence which was not yet complete, as Pinker may well have told him; and the typescripts which circulated publishers and friends in the winter 1916–17 had no indication of any ending apart from their conclusions on their (heavily revised) final pages. Perhaps significantly, Lawrence never mentioned the idea of an epilogue again.

III

The 1916 novel is a very different book from the 1921 novel, though large parts of it are almost identical.[7] This is a paradox which needs to be explored.

There are, to start with, some easily explained differences between the two texts. Lawrence wrote the 1916 novel before he had read James Pryse's *The Apocalypse Unsealed* or Madame Blavatsky's *The Secret Doctrine* (*L* iii. 151 and nn. 2 and 3): his 1917 reading left its mark (and more) on the revised version of the novel. When, towards the end of the "Excurse" chapter of the novel published in 1921, both Birkin and Ursula experience

> the most intolerable accession into being, the marvellous fulness of immediate gratification, overwhelming, outflooding from the Source of the deepest life-force, the darkest, deepest, strangest life-source of the human body, at the back and base of the loins. . . . (*WL*, 1987, 314).

then we may suspect that they too have been reading Pryse. The novel has acquired an idea of the Hindu chakras, probably from Pryse, which it is using for its own rather obscure purposes. But we are also aware that the novel is going up a *cul de sac.* This is not language which Lawrence would use again in fiction, and it is not a moment which any reader can grasp without prior knowledge of things esoteric. The same is true of other passages towards the end of this chapter: Ursula, stroking Birkin's back and buttocks, becomes aware of "The sense of the awfulness of riches that could never be impaired"; this sense "flooded her mind like a swoon, a death in most marvellous possession, mystic-sure" (*WL*, 1987, 316). All that the reader perhaps can do—like Halliday in the Cafe Pompadour, later in the novel—is to read out the passage in mockery of Ursula's mystic certainty; a certainty which two pages later becomes, quite bafflingly, "a full mystic knowledge of his suave loins of darkness" (*WL*, 1987, 318). Readers who have struggled with these passages, or been embarrassed for Lawrence's sake because of them, will be pleased to find that there had been nothing equivalent to them in the 1916 version of the novel.

However, that is not the only—or even the major—difference between the two versions at this point. The whole conclusion of what would become the "Excurse" chapter is different in the 1916 version. Some of the differences, of course, are fairly small; at times, the 1921 version simply clarified text which had been opaque or obscure in 1916.[8] When Ursula brings Birkin a flower at the end of the quarrel, for example, in *The First "Women in Love"* the short paragraph reads:

> "A pretty one," he said, vacantly, taking the flower. He sat looking at it unseeing. (*FWL*, 1998, 284)

In the 1921 *Women in Love*, the passage runs:

> "Pretty!" he said, looking up at her with a smile, taking the flower. Everything had become simple again, quite simple, the complexity gone into nowhere. But he badly wanted to cry: except that he was weary and bored by emotion. (*WL*, 1987, 310)

The text has developed, expanded, and made clear what had been a rather enigmatic moment.

In the 1916 text, Ursula and Birkin then drive to Southwell, where the minster clock is just striking six, and have their tea in the "Saracen's Head": all almost exactly as in the 1921 novel. After tea, they write their resignations, and plan to go away; again as in 1921. In the 1916 novel, however, they never leave the room; and they do not go to Sherwood Forest by car, do not spend the night there, do not make love. The love-declaration which Birkin makes to Ursula at this point of the novel takes on its own complexity, as he attempts to say both that he loves her, and that he has had enough of "voluptuousness, animal ecstasy" (*FWL*, 1998, 294). Ursula cannot really understand what he is talking about; and in spite of all her feelings for him, the episode ends with neither of them understanding the other, and Ursula in tears.

It is an extraordinarily moving episode, especially perhaps if one knows the esoteric excesses of the 1921 text. To start with, it is Ursula who is unsure of Birkin, and she expresses her uncertainty by saying:

> "I can't believe you love me even now."
>
> "What a Thomasine!—Do believe it then. I know you love me," he said.
>
> "Do you? Do I love you? Are you sure?" she asked, for she was mortally frightened. (*FWL* 286)

Her experience is that of feeling "delivered out of her own safe, enclosed keeping. And she could not, she could not allow it, she must draw back" (*FWL*, 1998, 287). This is quite different from anything in the 1921 novel, where—after a single moment of being "unassured" (*WL*, 1997, 312)—Ursula is happy in her new experience. In the 1916 novel, Birkin is a little bossy toward her, something of the know-all he is in other episodes ("Do believe it then"): ominously dominant. But, to start with, he is also a good deal more certain of what is happening:

> he seemed to have a new, star-like being, that was beyond suffering, so strange and steadfast and absolved.
>
> "Yes," he said, kissing her fresh cheeks. "I know you love me."
>
> "Do I?" she asked, looking up at him with a brow tortured by misgiving, a sort of hopelessness.
>
> "Yes," he said indifferently, hardly heeding her fears. . . . (*FWL*, 1998, 287)

In her "anguish of doubt" (*FWL*, 1998, 287), she eventually finds his confidence reassuring:

His finger-tips went delicately, finely over her face. They seemed to take away her fear, almost like removing a veil.

"And do you love me?" she asked, her heart bounding with joy. (*FWL*, 1998, 287)

He is unembarrassed by the question, and calls her "My love." But as she kisses him, and starts to feel liberated, it is his turn to start feeling uncertain:

"My love," he whispered, bending and kissing her, always kissing her, rather frightened and unsure in this new land.

She knew he was frightened. . . . (*FWL*, 1998, 287)

The kinds of confidence in self and other which the language of James Pryse introduced (and encouraged) in the 1921 novel are totally absent in the 1916 text. On the other hand, in 1916, what is going on between Birkin and Ursula is also clear. There is no esoteric language; instead, they inch their way painfully into a new kind of relationship.

He knew it was the first time in his life he had ever been happy, as flowers are happy, as the heedless things of the earth are happy. He had known ecstasy and delight before, but now, for the first time, he knew the grace of happiness, the strange, immortal serenity. (*FWL*, 1998, 287–288)

But as soon as we think that they might now be firmly and mutually happy, things shift again. Birkin wishes them to leave their jobs and go away together, but where in the 1921 novel "A new understanding dawned in her face" (*WL*, 1997, 315) when he suggests it (and her main difficulty is where they should go), the 1916 novel shows her rather more uncertain: "She was startled, and wondering" (*FWL*, 1998, 288). His certainty that he will just go away with her, and they will be happy, also worries her:

"Are you?" she said, slowly. "Are you going to make me be an an-
chorite and a hermitess, and you an ascetic? Don't—I don't want
to. Promise you won't be an ascetic. You are so terribly extreme."
(*FWL*, 1998, 288)

She quickly gets to her conclusion which, this time, is repeated word
for word in the 1921 version of the novel:

"You see, my love," she said, "I'm so afraid that while we are only
people, we've got to take the world that's given—because there
isn't any other." (*FWL*, 1998, 289; *WL*, 1997, 315)

But whereas, in 1921, Birkin in his way and Ursula in her own rather
different way agree not to part, the 1916 novel shows Birkin uncertain about any life which he might actually be able to lead with her.
He may say "One wants another, truer world," but his language be-
trays him even more than it does in the 1921 novel; he ends up, rue-
fully, "In the world, one must lie—one is a lie" (*FWL*, 1998, 289).

Ursula, too, is a good deal more rebellious (and less confident)
than she would be in 1921. Although she agrees to go away with
Birkin, into what he confidently assures her is his own world, her
reservations about spending all her time there take on the quality of
ironical criticisms of the idea: "I may go to London sometimes to the
music-hall, mayn't I? I love it so" (*FWL*, 1998, 290). Birkin can only
grumble at her : "It bores me. But you do as you like" (*FWL*, 1998,
290). When it comes to sending in their resignations, it is Ursula who
brings them to the point of doing so (in the 1921 novel the decision
is mutual); and it is she who objects to the idea of people suspecting
the simultaneity of their resigning. In 1921, she will say "I don't
care . . . it doesn't matter, does it?" (*WL*, 1997, 317). In 1916 she is
much more determined, compared with Birkin's casualness: "Isn't it
rather horrid, if everybody knows . . . I feel I don't want them to. It
isn't their affair" (*FWL*, 1998, 291).

Above all, they do not leave the room to go and make love cli-
mactically in Sherwood Forest, as in 1921. They have the same exchange—"Shall we go?" "As you like" (*FWL*, 1998, 291; *WL*, 1997,
317)—but what follows is one of Birkin's most revealingly honest

moments. He finds himself wanting Ursula sexually, whilst simultaneously desiring *not* to want her.

> It was not this, not this he wanted with her—not the poignant
> ecstasies of sex passion. Yet he did want them also, with an old
> craving of habit. And the desire seemed like death to him. For be-
> yond this was the small, yearning hope of a new sort of love, a
> new sort of intercourse, that was gentle and still and so happy, it
> was chastity and innocence of itself. This, this new, gentle posses-
> sion, should be the true consummation of their marriage (*FWL*,
> 1998, 291)

He is thus as theoretical—or hypothetical—about sex as he is elsewhere about relationship in general: it is he who has the *ideas* about
what their relationship could be like, what its "true consummation"
should be. He is looking for something which—whilst sexual—is
also not going to be as violent as "the old, fierce, destroying embrace" (*FWL*, 1998, 291); he fears that sex of the old kind (at least, of
the old kind which *he* has experienced) will destroy relationship. He
tells Ursula about his fears—and the last three pages of the chapter
concentrate on this subject almost exclusively.

Ursula is both fascinated and annoyed: "She had not been prepared for this. She felt as if he accused her, accused her of some har-
lotry" (*FWL*, 1998, 293). She, after all, shares none of his fears, nor
does she participate in his rebellion against the past. Rather sensibly,
she suggests that "one can't decide these things in this fashion . . .
One can't be so deliberate. It is indecent. We must take what comes"
(*FWL*, 1998, 293). Her slightly indignant insouciance is however met
by Birkin's customary stonewalling. He insists that "one chooses. At
length, one must choose. I know one must" (*FWL*, 1998, 293).

All the time, however, he is hoping against hope that she will ignore his theories and just give herself to him, so that he can indulge
in passion without blaming himself (presumably blaming her instead). But he ends up rather helplessly telling her that he has had
that kind of sex and is finished with it; or, to be exact, "whether I
have finished with it—heaven help us, I don't know—" (*FWL*, 1998,

294). This leaves her in the same state as it leaves him: " 'And I don't know,' she murmured, helplessly."

> At last he made a move to her.

> "At any rate," he said, looking down at her and touching her cheek with the tips of his fingers. "I know I love you—I love your face." The knowledge was a great comfort to him, a rock. "And if we go wrong—I shall know—ich habe es nicht gewollt. . . ." (*FWL*, 1998, 294)

Knowing that he loves her—at least, that he loves her face—is a very odd kind of "rock" on which to found a belief; the contrast between the softness of the face (and the touch), and the hardness of the rock, suggests how much Birkin is trying to convince himself. He also gives himself (in the Kaiser's "I did not want it") the excuse for possible failure with Ursula which—in the 1921 novel—is linked with his failure with Gerald Crich. Such things make Birkin's certainty about his love intensely ambiguous.

The novel is creating an ominous start to the relationship; but it is also showing something tender, paradoxical and realistic, and in particular true to Birkin's theoretical and spiritual nature (he comes to sound very much like the man who would shortly write *The Reality of Peace*). He ends up insisting, once again, that it is not passion which he wants:

> ". . . it isn't that.—This is peace, peace of soul—only peace. And the peace is the greatest reality, even if we make war—isn't it?" (*FWL*, 1998, 294).

Again, the 1917 reader would be getting a very clear signal: the larger stage of war and politics is here reduced to the purely personal stage—and peace is the greatest reality. The chapter thus ends, characteristically, with Birkin talking and talking, about certainty and commitment, and Ursula hardly saying anything. The last line of the chapter, however—the more striking precisely because Ursula has been so silent—reads: "But her eyes were full of sad tears, and she did not answer" (*FWL*, 1998, 294).

This is enough to suggest how different the episode is in the 1916 novel, even though it grows out of identical elements. The relationship deeply troubles Ursula; it is not (as at the end of the same chapter in the 1921 novel) a matter of her finding that "She had her desire fulfilled, he had his desire fulfilled," or that "she was to him what he was to her, the immemorial magnificence of mystic, palpable, real otherness" (*WL*, 1997, 320). That kind of esoteric language has no place in the 1916 novel, which is—appropriately for a novel which has the war so much in focus—continually about conflict and uncertainty.

It was not simply that Lawrence's reading during 1917 damaged the novel. It would be more truthful to say that in 1916 he would not have found Pryse and Blavatsky especially interesting, whereas by 1917–18 the agonies with which he responded to the world (specifically the world at war) meant that the alternative versions of experience which Pryse and Blavatsky offered him appealed to him deeply, and so almost inevitably infiltrated the text of his novel. The language he started to use—it got into the 1918–19 magazine versions of his *Studies in Classic American Literature* too—is esoteric, and he does not much care if it is shared by others, or whether "mystic, palpable, real otherness" makes much sense to anybody else; it is something which fascinates him. I would suggest that, here, the 1916 novel is much to be preferred to that of 1921.

IV

The 1916 text offers its reader an experience which constantly switches between what will already be known, from the 1921 text, and what will be quite new. At the start of the novel, for example, the first paragraph of the 1921 *Women in Love* is very close to what Lawrence had first typed in July 1916; nearly five years of revisions hardly affected it. The rest of the opening, however, changed massively between July 1916 and 1921; the opening dialogue itself had already changed completely during 1916.[9] Some of the changes appeared simply in individual words or descriptions: Gudrun, for example, wears "cherry-coloured stockings" (*FWL*, 1998, 4) in *The First "Women in Love"* rather than the "emerald green" ones (*WL*, 1997, 8) of *Women in Love*. However, as the episode goes on, it turns out that in *The First "Women in Love"* Gudrun—though wryly jesting about her experience—is a good deal more vulnerable when thinking of the man she might meet, now that she has come home, than she is in *Women in Love.* She says to Ursula that

> if there did happen to come along a highly attractive individual of considerable means, and we caught fire like anything, you know, with each other—I might immolate myself.—" She seemed wistful. "I'm getting bored," she went on, in pathetic complaint. "Things don't seem to materialise with me, I find. . . ." (*FWL*, 1998, 4).

The 1921 *Women in Love* offers a rather tougher-minded Gudrun, a different kind of "woman in love": poised and rhetorical:

> if there did happen to come along a highly attractive individual of sufficient means—well—" she tailed off ironically. Then she looked searchingly at Ursula, as if to probe her. "Don't you find, yourself getting bored?" she asked of her sister. "Don't you find, that things fail to materialise?. . . ." (*WL*, 1997, 8)

The sisters' dialogue about having children is also completely different in 1916 and 1921 (*WL*, 1997, 9) and, again, in *The First "Women in Love"* both are more vulnerable, less able to provide simple and ironic answers. These crucial changes happen without any change in the events or sequence of the episode; it is as if the characters had grown older, less vulnerable and more armoured, by 1921.

It is characteristic of the differences between the 1916 and 1921 novels that such passages of considerable difference are interspersed with sections which are not much changed, or only affected by small and detailed revisions. So, for example, when Gudrun is frightened of going through the crowd of ordinary collier folk at the wedding, in 1921 Ursula reassures her with the collusive and class-superior "they don't matter" (*WL*, 1997, 13). In 1916, however, it had been sisterly protectiveness and reassurance, not snobbery, which she had offered her sister: "they won't do anything" (*FWL*, 1997, 8). Such careful, local and precise working-over of the text is not, however, what is most remarkable about the revision evident in *Women in Love*. It may come as a surprise to a reader expecting continuous difference between *The First "Women in Love"* and *Women in Love* that lengthy passages regularly pass with hardly a change being made; chapter XV in its 1921 form, for example, is very nearly identical with its 1916 form. We should remember Lawrence reporting, in November 1916, when revising the part of the book originally written in May–June, that "there was a lot of the original draft that I couldn't have bettered" (*L* iii. 25); and he never did make substantial changes in some places.

When, however, he did start to revise, the new work could quickly take the form of a complete rewriting; and it could extend for pages or even chapters. For example, what became chapter XXV ("Marriage or Not")—apart from its first paragraph—is not just revised in 1921 but wholly rewritten; there is almost nothing similar in the 1916 text. The later part of Birkin's conversation with Gerald in the train on the way to London in chapter V ("In the Train") is much revised; while the conversation between Gerald and Birkin about the Pussum in chapter VIII ("Breadalby") is quite different, and so is a great deal of the conversation between Birkin and Ursula in chapter XI ("An Island"). Page after page between Gerald and Birkin in chapter XVI ("Man to Man"), as well as the conversation about marriage between Birkin and Gerald in chapter XXV, could come from a different novel completely; while I have already discussed the crucial changes made to the exchange between Birkin and Ursula in the *Saracen's Head* in chapter XXIII ("Excurse"). It is striking that a number of the particularly agonized quarrels are also heavily revised or completely rewritten: Birkin's rage with Hermione in chapter III ("Class-room") and his disagreement with Ursula in chapter XIII ("Mino") are both quite different, as are the arguments in chapter XIX ("Moony") and chapter XXVI ("A Chair"). A number of crucial monologues, too, are completely rewritten; for example, Birkin's version of "the black river of corruption" (*WL*, 1997, 172) in chapter XIV ("Water-Party"), and his musings in bed at the start of chapter XVI ("Man to Man"), as well as the extended meditation in chapter XIX ("Moony"), where again extra pages had to be added to the 1917 typescript to accommodate the changes; and Ursula's thinking aloud at the start of the same chapter is also heavily revised.

Lawrence's habits of revision thus ensured a general review of a good deal of the text of *The First* "Women in Love," the close revision of many passages, and the complete re-writing of a number of key episodes. Above all, it was the relationship between Birkin and Ursula which changed in the 1921 novel; the rewritten five pages which transformed the end of chapter XXVI ("A Chair") and the ending of the novel in chapter XXXII ("Exeunt") did more than most to change the relationship into a more dynamic, more robust one in 1921. In *The First* "Women in Love," the characters are often far less sure of themselves and of each other.

A particularly interesting aspect of the revision is that it regularly concentrates on the way sequences end; sometimes just by rewriting the last sentence of what (in the 1917–19 revision) were passages being turned into chapters, sometimes by revising almost up to the chapter ending itself, sometimes by completely rewriting the whole sequence culminating in that ending.[10] The number of chapters in the novel, eventually thirty-two, many of them created for the first time in the 1917–19 revisions, ensured that its structure would be very different from that of its predecessor *The Rainbow*, which although of similar length had had only sixteen chapters. The new, smaller units of *Women in Love* tended increasingly to become units where extensive change might be required by the development of a particular scene; but such changes might well not continue into, or very much affect, the next unit, so that (for example) the massive changes at the ends of chapter XIII ("Mino") and chapter XXVI ("A Chair") are succeeded by almost completely unchanged openings to chapter XIV ("Water-Party") and chapter XXVII ("Flitting"). The unusual character of the revised structure—thirty-two chapters which often have the quality of individual scenes or film stills—was still further developed in the final revision of 1921, when some (for example "Man to Man" and

"Woman to Woman," "Threshold" and "Excurse") were given titles suggesting parallel or balance, and as many as twenty were given single-word titles, stressing again their individual integrity as units. (The contrast with *The Rainbow* incidentally thus grew even more marked: chapter one of the earlier novel had been "How Tom Brangwen Married a Polish Lady": chapter one of the 1921 novel became "Sisters.")

V

I would like, finally, to consider the novel's ending and its crucial relationship with the First World War. The 1921 novel's penultimate chapter "Snowed Up" is very similar to the 1916 novel's penultimate chapter XII. There are additional sentences, extending, amplifying, but not essentially modifying the action. Only at moments—as when Gudrun feels "forlorn with insistence and triumph" (*WL*, 1997, 444), as opposed to "forlorn with insistence and terror" (*FWL*, 1998, 410)—is there a real change of meaning. Just occasionally the 1921 version appears a little too pointed; as when Gudrun—thinking about the following day, when she might go with Gerald to England, or to Dresden with Loerke, or to Munich to a girl-friend—draws her reflections to an end:

> And today was the white, snowy, iridescent threshold of all possibility. All possibility—that was the charm to her the lovely, iridescent, indefinite charm—pure illusion. (*FWL*, 1998, 432; *WL*, 1997, 468)

The openness is both attractive and ominous: it is, after all, "pure illusion." The 1921 novel however adds an additional sentence:

> All possibility—because death was inevitable, and nothing was possible but death. (*WL*, 1997, 468)

That cynical extra sentence is perhaps a little too deliberately focused upon what is going to happen next.

The strangest things are changed at times, however. After Gerald has attempted to strangle Gudrun—in a passage almost identical in 1916 and 1921—Loerke faintly protests: " 'That also,' he said in his thin, bitter voice: 'that's the sport.' He was acridly sarcastic" (*FWL*, 1998, 436). In 1921, his protest would become: " 'Monsieur!' he said, in his thin, roused voice: 'Quand vous aurez fini—' " (*WL*, 1997, 472). Why were such changes important? Loerke's first words to Gerald when the latter discovers them also changed, from " 's ist aus" (*FWL*, 1997, 435) to " 'All gone!' he said." (*WL*, 1997, 470). Some play with German and French and English appears to be going on; Loerke's characteristic slipperiness itself slides and slips.

Gerald's final walk to his death is nearly identical in the two texts. But the end of the novel, in the next chapter, shows one of the fundamental differences between 1916 and 1921. For one thing, Birkin's reaction to Gudrun is very different; he is "full of judgement," and she is conscious that he judges her (*FWL*, 1998, 440); his manner is "damning" (*FWL*, 1998, 441), altered to "abstracted" in 1921 (*WL*, 1997, 477). But this is linked with Birkin's utterly different series of responses to dead Gerald. Birkin's grief

> was chiefly misery. He could not bear that the beautiful, virile Gerald was a heap of inert matter, a transient heap, rubbish on the face of the earth, really. (*FWL*, 1998, 441)

His reflections on Gerald would, in the 1921 text, turn into a strange kind of consolation; he would develop his ideas of "the mystery of creation" as "fathomless, infallible, inexhaustible" (*WL*, 1997, 479), and he would find them a profound comfort. In 1916, just the opposite happens. Birkin is frozen too: dead like Gerald.

> And still Birkin's heart was frozen in his breast. This, then, was the end. He had loved Gerald, he loved him still. But the love was frozen in his breast, frozen by the death that possessed himself, as well as Gerald. (*FWL*, 1998: 442)

There are no consoling thoughts about creation or the creative mystery. Only when Birkin breaks down into tears do the 1916 and

1921 texts briefly come close again. But developments swiftly follow in 1921—Birkin's insistence to Ursula that he has loved Gerald, Ursula's complaint "You've got me" (*WL*, 1997 480), and the ending of the novel concentrating entirely on the relationship between Birkin and Ursula. It ends, of course, with them both back in England, talking about "two kinds of love," and (as always) disagreeing, down to the famous last line: " 'I don't believe that,' he answered" (*WL*, 1997, 481).

None of this had happened in 1916. Birkin's tears of grief over Gerald horrify Ursula and she slips wordlessly out of the room at the bottom of the novel's penultimate page—and thus out of the novel for good. It is not with the relationship of Birkin and Ursula that this text will end. There remains a single, strange, deeply moving final page of Birkin's mourning for Gerald, containing some of Lawrence's most emotional writing. It is not just grief for dead Gerald: "It was not the death he could not bear, but the nothingness of the life and the death put together. It killed the quick of one's life" (*FWL*, 1998, 443). And the novel ends like this:

He could not bear it. His heart seemed to be torn in his chest.

"But even then," he strove to say, "we needn't all be like that. All is not lost, because many are lost—I am not afraid or ashamed to die and be dead." (*FWL*, 1998, 443)

Against the grain, Birkin thus stresses what he barely believes: that all is not lost, in spite of the many who are lost. He is oddly like Milton's Satan, insisting against overwhelming odds that "All is not lost. . . ." (1971, i. 102). But what he feels is death.

In 1917, of course, this could only have been read as a direct reference to the war, and to its dreadful losses, with Birkin attempting to stand clear and see differently. But the novel was by now beyond all hope of being published, partly because of the final context in which the novel can be set: perhaps the most significant of all. The 1916 *First "Women in Love"* is a war novel to a much greater extent than the 1921 text; in part because one reads it differently, as the work of 1916, and in part because some passages which were subsequently cut, or changed, bore very heavily on the world of 1916–17 and would have struck 1917 readers with particular force.

VI

So, for example, the discussion of contemporary ideas in what was then the first chapter of the novel is significantly different from the discussion published in 1921, in which Hermione's discussion with the bridegroom about "nationality" (*WL*, 1997, 28) would be the starting point, and the discussion would go through ideas of patriotism, emulation, and capitalism. In 1916 the discussion had been "about the building of Dreadnoughts"[11]:

> "I cannot believe in these great armaments," she was saying. "The state forbids the individual to carry arms . . . Why should Britannia and John Bull go armed to the teeth, when you and I may hardly carry a pen-knife?" (*FWL*, 1998 23)

Theobald Lupton, the bridegroom, is of course a "naval officer, manly and up to his duty" (*FWL*, 1998, 18), and such a discussion is entirely appropriate. Gerald, of course, follows up the argument keenly: "Who is going to forbid nations to carry arms?" (*FWL*, 1998, 23). Birkin however offers the idea of an international police force which can "arrest" a nation behaving badly: it would be better, he says, to concentrate on nations which behave badly than on individuals. "It isn't the individual that wants watching, it is these great uncouth Bill Sykeses, the nations . . . your life isn't safe five minutes, in the hands of your nation" (*FWL*, 1998, 23–24). Reading all this in the spring of 1917 would have been an extraordinary and (for many people) a thoroughly offensive experience; it had only been in May 1916 that conscription had been introduced into the British army, but such writing offered a direct contradiction to ideas of conscription, as much as it did to patriotism. If Ursula had been offensive about the individual serving his country in *The Rainbow* (in ways that may have contributed to the decision to prosecute the book[12]), this was a good deal worse.

And the book keeps up a kind of running battle with the fact of the war. In the classroom with Hermione and Ursula, Birkin's monologue just before they all leave is, in 1916, twice as long, and directly applicable to the war-situation:

> We are the last products of the decadent movement, the analytic, lyrical, emotional, scientific movement which has had full sway since the Renaissance, and which we've been so proud of . . . it is knowledge, knowledge all the while, this passion, this emotionalism, this soldiering, it is a form of immediate anthropology, we study the origins of man in our own immediate experience, we push right back to the first, and last, sensations of procreation and of death. (*FWL*, 1998, 36–37)

Birkin's ideas, caught thus on the wing, are barely comprehensible; but it is clear that, to him, "soldiering" is one of the revealing catastrophes of our civilization. Birkin continues by stressing how

> in reality, the whole of the people in the world are going one way now, in a helpless herd, down the last slopes of sensational knowledge into the gap of darkness we came out of. It is the road to death. But if we want death, then nothing but death will do for us—like the leaves in autumn. (*FWL*, 1998, 37)

Again, the apocalyptic idea would, in 1917, inevitably have translated itself into a commentary on the contemporary situation. England and Germany are both helpless herds, going down the last slopes into death. Talking to Ursula on the island, Birkin asks if "we are not going all merely to perish in the final glistening experience of death and killing" (*FWL*, 1998, 119); talking to her in his Nottingham rooms, he explains why he thinks contemporary men are so futile: "they take to fighting and killing each other, and raking up old phrases" (*FWL*, 1998, 139). So much for contemporary appeals to patriotism and nationhood. The allusion to the rising waters at the start of the chapter which became "Moony" was, in 1916, not simply to "the tide of nothingness" (*WL*, 1997, 244) but to "the tide of destruction": "The world was in flood again, and there was no Noah, and no Noah's ark this time" (*FWL*, 1998, 225).[13] Even when Ursula sings so that Gudrun can do eurhythmic movements, in the 1916 novel she incongruously comes up with "It's a long long way to Tipperary," that most famous of wartime marching songs: it would have been hard to locate the novel more precisely in wartime (the song had only been published in 1912). None of these examples survived into the 1921 novel.

Alongside these continual allusions to war and death, too, other references and allusions take on a new meaning. When Birkin looks out of the train window on the way to London, and thinks "Well, if mankind is destroyed, if our race is destroyed like Sodom. . . ." (*FWL*, 1998, 49), in 1917 it would have been clear that he was continuing his attack on the barbarity of contemporary England at war. When he comments about Gerald, in the Café Pompadour, "He was in the last war" (*FWL*, 1998, 54; *WL*, 1997, 64), the 1917 context would immediately have suggested, to a contemporary, "i.e. the war before this one"; when he says to Ursula, in the episode on the island, that people "maintain a lie, and run amok at last" (*FWL*, 1998, 113; 1997, *WL* 127), it would have been clear what form he thought that running amok had recently taken.

These examples could be multiplied many times, of course. There is still one final way, however, in which we can think of the book as a 1917 novel; by considering its potential appearance in print in the spring of 1917.

VII

In 1917, publication of *The First "Women in Love"* would have coincided closely with *Prufrock and Other Observations*, T. S. Eliot's first book of poems, which came out in an edition of 500 copies in June 1917; with the first three cantos by Ezra Pound, which appeared in *Poetry* in June, July, and August 1917; the novel would have appeared a few months before Edward Thomas' first book of poems (*Poems* by Edward Eastaway), published on 10 October (Thomas had been killed on 9 April; and it would closely have followed works such as Isaac Rosenberg's "Break of Day in the Trenches" (published in *Poetry* in December 1916) and (strikingly) the first English publication of James Joyce's *A Portrait of the Artist as a Young Man*, which appeared in an edition of 750 copies on 12 February 1917.

We tend today to think of *Women in Love* as a novel which—appearing as it did in England in June 1921—finds its natural place among postwar works such as Joyce's *Ulysses*, published early in 1922, and Eliot's *The Waste Land*, written late in 1921 and appearing the following year. But *Women in Love* began as a novel of the middle of the war, and might well have been published alongside the writing of Joyce and Eliot which was coming out in 1917. Its publication in 1917 would have made it not just possible but necessary to read it as a novel which, while deliberately not involving itself with the period of war, placed its version of society's mechanical obsession and violent break-up right in the middle of the war. Lawrence once remarked that "The book frightens me: it is so end-of-the-world" (*L* iii. 25): an appropriate book for a Europe poised between the horrors of the battle of the Somme in the summer of 1916, and the longer nightmare of Passchendaele, which would begin with the rains of August 1917. But he also hoped that "it is, it must be, the beginning of a new world too" (*L* iii. 26); not a new world fitfully and uncertainly re-building itself in the weariness of the post-war period, but one which challenged the whole ethos of what one publisher's reader (who advised the rejection of the novel in January 1917) called "the forms of English civilisation." The report by that reader (for the publisher Constable) ran, in part:

> . . . we feel that the present would be a most unfavourable time for the publication of the book in its present form. In the first place, there are the writer's expressions of antipathy to England and the forms of English civilisation. At the present time, when people are sacrificing all that is dearest to them for their country, such expressions are we think bound to rouse the resentment both of the reviewers and the public. In the second place, the destructive philosophy as it is expressed in this book would we think be particularly unwelcome at the present time, and the same might perhaps be said of the author's 'detached' attitudes toward the events of the present day. (*WL*, 1997, xxxiv)

The accusation that Lawrence expressed "'detached' attitudes toward the events of the present day" shows how much the war was setting the report's agenda; and it is true that the "new world" which Lawrence thought his book might initiate turned out to be one which neither he nor anyone else would be allowed to inhabit. That, however, should not prevent us from seeing *The First "Women in Love"* as a piece of fiction generated in—and in many ways poignantly addressed to—the England, and the Europe, of the First World War: not to a post-war world disillusioned with society, and resigned to its fate, but one actually fighting a war. In the book's analysis, the "forms of English civilisation" were symptomatic of the very civilization which, as a final irony, prevented the book itself from appearing.

In the 1916 novel, too, Gudrun and Loerke fantasize about the end of the world in terms of the limitations of democracy: they imagine how "the world became so perfect that by unanimous consent it committed suicide, because it had come to pass that any step taken by any man was an infringement of the rights of some other man" (*FWL*, 1998, 418). But, in an eerie prediction of the future, they also enjoy "some mocking dream of the destruction of the world by the ridiculous catastrophe of man's invention: a man invented such a perfect explosive that it blew the earth in bits among the stars . . ." (*FWL*, 1998, 418). The summer of 1917 would be marked by massive explosions of mines at Messines Ridge, in the greatest series of man-made explosions the world had ever seen. One eye-witness commented: "None of us had seen anything like it ever. It was just one mass of flames. The whole world seemed to go up in the air" (Macdonald, 1978, 42). The 1916 novel was abreast of its time in ways for which it has not yet been given credit. In the 1921 novel, Gudrun and Loerke develop the explosive fantasy a little further, but this time in irony: a perfect explosive is again invented, which

> blew the earth in two, and the two halves set off in different directions through space, to the dismay of the inhabitants. . . . (*WL*, 1997, 453)

Not, thus, with the point and attack of the 1916 novel; but there is evidence that Lawrence was revising at least some of the Loerke/Gudrun passages in September 1917, when he would have known about the events of Messines Ridge,[14] and might very well have wanted to offer a mocking prediction about the future, rather than a dreadful confirmation of the present.

In that way, the novel itself moved on in its response to the war. As Lawrence would write in 1919,

> it is a novel which took its final shape in the midst of the period of war, though it does not concern the war itself. I should wish the time to remain unfixed, so that the bitterness of the war may be taken for granted in the characters. (*WL*, 1997, 485)

That bitterness can now, I think, at last be seen for what it is, in the 1916 novel. What is, finally, dreadful to Birkin—and perhaps to the reader—is experience in which the individual manages "never to struggle clear—never to struggle clear" (*FWL*, 1998, 443). Although Lawrence in 1916 did his best to stress the novel's positive qualities—"it is, it must be, the beginning of a new world"—he also showed how deliberately he had reached that conclusion ("it is, it must be"). And the first part of that sentence remarks "The book frightens me: it is so end-of-the-world."[15] That, I think, properly suggests the quality of *The First "Women in Love."* Birkin is haunted by the tragedy of Gerald because "It was not the death he could not bear, but the nothingness of the life and death put together" (*FWL*, 1998, 443). The wartime novel found not just the deaths in war unbearable, but "the nothingness of the life and death put together": its summing-up of the civilization which led to such a war. *The First "Women in Love"* may come to be regarded as a minor offshoot of a major work, or it may—and I believe it should—come to be seen as a great novel in its own right. I suspect, too, that it may come to haunt its readers as that rare thing, an authentically tragic twentieth-century novel.

Notes

1. The history of the publication of early versions of Lawrence's texts offers no real parallel to *The First "Women in Love."* The first surviving long

draft of *Sons and Lovers* will shortly be published as *Paul Morel* in the *Cambridge Edition of the Works of D. H. Lawrence*. It was, however, never finished, let alone submitted to a publisher. The first draft of *The Plumed Serpent* has been published as *Quetzalcoatl*, ed. Louis L. Martz (Redding 1995), but this was a state of the text which Lawrence himself had no intention of publishing, as he always knew that he was going to rewrite the book. The two surviving early drafts *of Lady Chatterley's Lover*, of 1926 and 1927, have been published, as *The First Lady Chatterley* (New York, 1944) and *John Thomas and Lady Jane* (1972). In July 1929, Lawrence did consider publishing the first, but only as a solution to his English and American publishers' desire for a *Lady Chatterley* novel which they could publish: he himself was very dubious about bringing it out. He could "easily make it passable. But shall I? shall I print a crude first version?" (*L* vii. 383–384, 391). Up to July 1929 he showed no desire to publish it; and he never made any attempt to publish the second version.

2. DHL did not do so, and Methuen apparently made no attempt to enforce the repayment. Methuen had also declared that no copyright could exist in *The Rainbo* (*L* ii. 457 n. 2), thus presumably attempting to rule it out as one of the three novels for which they had a contract.

3. *The Trespasser, Love Poems, Sons and Lovers, The Widowing of Mrs. Holroyd*, and *The Prussian Officer* were all still available from Duckworth in 1916; by 1915 they had also acquired the rights to DHL's first novel *The White Peacock* and had published a new edition.

4. In the spring of 1917, Ottoline Morrell threatened action if the book were published; in 1921, Philip Heseltine managed to extract £50 from Secker (and have changes made) on the grounds of the book's libels on him. At least twelve people might, however, have found recognizable versions of themselves or their family members in the book: Heseltine, Minnie Lucy Channing, Ottoline and Philip Morrell, Louie Burrows and the Burrows family, Thomas Philip Barber and members of the Barber family, John Middleton Murry, Maxim Litvinov, Bertrand Russell, William Henry Hocking, Anne Estelle Rice, Gordon Campbell, and Eleonora Duse. See *FWL* Introduction xl, pp. xlviii.

5. "I have finished my novel—except for a bit that can be done any time" (*L* ii. 621); "There is a last chapter to write, some time, when one's heart is not so contracted" (*L* ii. 627).

6. See *FWL* xxxi and *WL* xxxi. The fragment runs:

> A year afterwards, Ursula in Italy received a letter from Gudrun in Frank furt am Main. Since the death of Gerald in the Tyrol, when Gudrun had gone away, ostensibly to England, Ursula had had no news of her sister.

"I met a German artist who knew you," Gudrun said "and he gave me your address. I was silent for so long because there was nothing I could say.

I have got a son—he is six months old now. His hair is like the sun shining on the sea, and he has his father's limbs and body. I am still Frau Crich—what actually happened is so much better, to account for one's position, than a lie would be. The boy is called Ferdinand Gerald Crich.

As for the past—I lived for some months with Loerke, as a friend. Now I am staying (*WL*, 1997, xxxi).

7.   "His revision [of the TS which became *Women in Love*] affected over 90 per cent of the pages of TSII; he also rewrote 10 per cent of it. He inserted nine pages in his own handwriting; he typed and inserted a further eight replacement or additional pages; he inserted interlinear revision on thirty-five pages so extensive that at most only a few words of the original typescript remained, and often not even those; on a further 24 pages his revision was so heavy that only a few pages of the original typescript survived. In this way, seventy-six pages out of 766 were effectively rewritten" (*WL*, 1997, lvi).

8.   For full discussion of the 1917 changes see *Triumph to Exile*, pp. 391–98.

9.   The original July 1916 dialogue appears in *FWL*, explanatory note on 2:25.

10.   From *WL*, chapters II, IV, IX, XII, XIII, XVII, XVIII, XIX, XXI, XXIII, XXIV, XXV, XXVI, XXXI, and XXXII end significantly differently in the 1921 novel from their equivalent appearance in the 1916 novel.

11.   Dreadnought was the name of the first of a new class of heavy British battleships launched on 18 February 1906, which provoked Germany and other maritime powers into building similar ships; the name quickly became applied to any large battleship with its armaments all of one calibre.

12.   See *Triumph to Exile*, p. 278.

13.   The allusion may have provoked his suggestion of a title in November 1917, when it is possible that this section was revised and the reference removed: "I think I'll call it 'Noah's Ark' " (*L* iii. 183).

14.   See *WL*, explanatory note on 427:2.

15.   The Introduction to the Cambridge edition of *Women in Love* used those 1916 comments as its final comment on the novel (*WL* 1xi), but the remarks apply, of course, to *The First "Women in Love"* rather than to the later book.

Works Cited

Carswell, Catherine. *The Savage Pilgrimage*. London: Chatto and Windus, 1932.

Kinkead-Weekes, Mark. *D. H. Lawrence: Triumph to Exile 1912–1922*. Cambridge: Cambridge University Press, 1996.

Lawrence, D. H. *The First Lady Chatterley*. New York: Dial, 1944.

———. *The First "Women in Love."* Ed. John Worthen and Lindeth Vasey. Cambridge: Cambridge University Press, 1998.

———. *John Thomas and Lady Jane*. New York: Viking, 1972.

———. *The Letters of D. H. Lawrence: Volume II: June 1913–October 1916*. Ed. George J. Zytaruk and James T. Boulton. Cambridge: Cambridge University Press, 1981.

———. *The Letters of D. H. Lawrence: Volume III: October 1916–June 1921*. Ed. James T. Boulton and Andrew Robertson. Cambridge: Cambridge University Press, 1984.

———. *The Letters of D. H. Lawrence: Volume VII: November 1928–February 1930*. Ed. Keith Sagar and James T. Boulton. Cambridge: Cambridge University Press, 1993.

———. *Quetzalcoatl*. Ed. Louis L. Martz. Redding Ridge, Calif.: Black Swan, 1995.

———. *Women in Love*. Ed. David Farmer, Lindeth Vasey, and John Worthen. Cambridge: Cambridge University Press, 1987.

Macdonald, Lyn. *They Called It Passchendaele*. London: Joseph, 1978.

Milton, John. *Paradise Lost*. Ed. Alastair Fowler. London: Longman, 1971.

Into the Ideological Unknown

Women in Love

DAVID PARKER

◆　◆　◆

I

Recent poststructuralist theory has rejected the notion of a literary canon, largely on the now-familiar grounds that the canonical works univocally speak the ideology of a hegemonic class, thus marginalizing such groups as blacks, women, and the working class.

Of particular concern to the poststructuralists is the pretension of these texts to ethical authority. As Frederic Jameson has said: "it is ethics itself which is the ideological vehicle and legitimation of concrete structures of power and domination" (*The Political Unconscious: Narrative as a Socially Symbolic Act*, London, 1981, 114). He goes on to outline his (sub-Nietzschean) idea of ethics as a system of binary oppositions, of good versus evil, where "evil" inevitably denotes imagined characteristics of those who are Other to the hegemonic class. For this reason ethical criticism, which—hoodwinked by these texts' strategies of containment—confines itself to "surface" exposition of them, is worse than useless because it perpetuates the work of legitimation, giving it added institutional authority. Nor does the newer psychological criticism fare much better in Jameson's book, for this is merely a sub-genre of the ethical, replacing "myths of the re-unification of the psyche" for the "older themes of moral sensibility and ethical awareness" (60).

The canonical texts are said to repress their ideological function, consigning it to their unconscious where it can only be retrieved by political analysis. To this extent they are mad texts, dangerously so, because, unless we are capable of analysing them politically, they can only offer, as Lennard J. Davis says, to reinforce in us "those collective and personal defences" which are our "neurotic" constructs of the world (*Resisting Novels: Ideology and Fiction*, London, 1987, 15). Using Freud's famous essay, "Remembering, Repeating and Working Through," Davis argues that in reading novels we merely "repeat" repressed narratives which in the long run impair our capacity to know "what really is" 24).

Just why it should be supposed that political analysis alone can confront us with non-ideological reality is rarely made clear in the criticism I've been citing. The question that is so often asked remains unanswered: what privileges Marxist history? Or why should it be true to say, as Jameson does, that "everything is 'in the last analysis' political" and not equally true that, according to a different sort of analysis, everything is ethical? Or psychological? What these questions reveal in such theory is a not very thinly disguised will-to-*über*narrative that mirrors closely its own account of the hegemonic narrative it wants to supplant. If, for a moment, we entertain the neurotic fantasy that everything is in some sense psycho-ethical, we might say that this usurpation of the old authority looks—as Dirk den Hartog suggested in *The Critical Review* in 1988—like an Oedipal reaction. The point of making this observation is that almost everywhere this new discourse finds its identity, not by coming to terms inclusively and dialectically with humanist criticism and the texts it helped to canonize, but by attempting to marginalize all of them. This comes out plainly in the apparent disinclination or inability of many theorists to look with care and disinterest at the works they are adducing; instead they offer straw-man accounts of them that often grossly underestimate their complexity and intelligence.

In fact a significant sign of the intelligence of many canonical works—e.g. *Middlemarch, Anna Karenina,* and *Women in Love*—is their understanding of the narcissistic or neurotic impulses often involved in insurgent theorizing: Casaubon's wish, for instance, to possess a Key to All Mythologies; or Koznyshev's need to picture threatening otherness simplistically and distortedly in order to contain it; or the merely reactive will in Gerald Crich's mechanistic rationalism, which remains unconsciously bound to his father's troubled Christian philanthropy, the very principle it struggles to efface.

The danger, and perhaps the wished-for neurotic pay-off, for theorists such as Jameson is that this sort of ethico-psychological insight will become the unconscious of *their* discourse. And once again, that's something that wouldn't have been lost on the canonical authors themselves. As Ursula Brangwen says to the artist Loerke: "As for your world of art and your world of reality . . . you have to separate the two, because you can't bear to know what you are." The capacity of art to reveal what artists in that sense *are* in their works is irreducible, and the impulse to theorize the revelation away, together with the sort of criticism that would highlight it, is itself always going to be psychologically revealing. What this suggests is yet another *raison d'etre* of the canonical works and of humanist criticism—as subversive Other to the suppressive will of hegemonic Theory.

Not all such recent theory wants to suppress the canon though. According to Jonathan Culler, de Manian deconstruction provides at least one justification for canonical texts—that they are often "the most powerful demystifiers of the ideologies they have been said to promote" (*Framing the Sign: Criticism and its Institutions,* Oxford, 1988, 52). This at least gestures in the direction of noting the true complexity of such works, though here again the point would hardly have been news to the authors themselves. Lawrence makes the point almost identically in his *Study of Thomas Hardy* (ed. E. McDonald, New York, 1936, 476, 479):

> Yet every work of art adheres to some system of morality. But if it
> be really a work of art, it must contain the essential criticism on

the morality to which it adheres. And hence the antinomy, hence the conflict necessary to every tragic conception.

The degree to which the system of morality, or the metaphysic, of any work of art is submitted to criticism within the work of art makes the lasting value and satisfaction of that work.

A few pages later, Lawrence expands on the same point:

It is the novelists and dramatists who have the hardest task in reconciling their metaphysic, their theory of being and knowing, with their living sense of being. Because a novel is a microcosm, and because man in viewing the universe must view it in the light of a theory, therefore every novel must have the background or structural skeleton of some theory of being, some metaphysic. But the metaphysic must always subserve the artistic purpose beyond the artist's conscious aim. Otherwise the novel becomes a treatise.

All too often, ideological analysis produces straw-man readings precisely by taking works of art as univocal treatises, seeing only "the conscious aim" and not the "artistic purpose"—its sources in part unconscious—that transcends the intentional "system of morality" or "theory of being" of the author. What this involves is reading not simply for static hermeneutic structures or systems of signification but also for *process*, for art as discovery, exploration. When he points to the lack of a properly "*dynamic* intentional structure" in Jameson's reading of Conrad's *Lord Jim*, Jacques Berthoud (in *Narrative: From Malory to Motion Pictures*, ed. Jeremy Hawthorn, London, 1985, 112, his italics) is making a similar point. Whatever static binary oppositions the author may start out with, one test of the true classic is the degree to which the work either clings to them or entertains doubts, uncertainties, dialogic "criticisms," which allow these terms to interact, become unstable, fluid, even altogether to change places. *Women in Love* is interesting and important as a work of art not because it expresses a Romantic ideology of "innocence" versus "social being," or opposes preconceived "good" human possibilities to "evil" ones, but because it explores these things in their dynamic interrelatedness.

What follows from this is that a work such as *Women in Love*, far from simply confirming a conscious structure of repressive ethical fixities, contributes to what Alcorn and Bracher call "blurring or dissolving various artificial boundaries on the reader's cognitive map" ("Literature, Psychoanalysis, and the Re-Formation of the Self: A New Direction for Reader-Response Theory," *P.M.L.A.*, 1984, 344). Moreover, *Women in Love* especially foregrounds in the lives it represents the ways in which fixed ideas, modes of what it calls "knowing"—that is, consciously constructing—the world, are actually a defence against repressed feelings and realizations. The novel's searching, in fact, is a good deal directed towards understanding the conditions under which such defences can be dropped and one can move into what it terms "the unknown." It is a novel very much *about* transformation, selves in process, about both reinforcing psychic resistances and "working through" them. At the same time, in a process analogous to and reflecting the represented ones, the novel's ultimate "artistic purpose" can be seen as a "working through" of that over-insistent will-to-vision which keeps threatening Lawrence's art from *The Rainbow* on.

II

Most accounts of *Women in Love*, such as the one in Dan Jacobson's recent book ("*Women in Love* and the Death of the Will" in *Adult Pleasures*, London, 1988), stress the polarization between two sets of characters, one struggling through to freedom and life, the other going down the slope, with the rest of the race, to various forms of death. This view of the novel has, of course, a lot to be said for it. The opening dialogue, for instance, immediately presents a distinction between two ways of thinking about something—which turn out to be, more importantly, two ways of being.

On the one hand, there is Ursula, "calm and considerate", deciding that she doesn't know whether she *really wants* to get married; for her, it will depend on what sort of man turns up, which can't be known in advance. Her calm already hints at a fundamental trust, or underlying ease, in face of this unknown future. The prose is soon to suggest the shaping underlife from which these thoughts and words come. Though she feels curiously "suspended," we're told, Ursula accedes to what she senses darkly at centre: a new potential life like an infant in the womb, held in by "integuments" but pressing for birth. Leaving aside for the moment the ideological question of the sort of transformation-narrative this image might seem to imply, it's clear after a few pages that Ursula's capacity to be at ease with uncertainty is connected with a strong potentiality for growth. In this first page, her "I don't know" and "I'm not sure" are the first hints of that, and it's important to note that they indicate an openness, not least of *mind.*

Gudrun, by contrast, wants to be "quite definite"; for her it seems possible that "in the abstract" one might need the *experience* of having been married. The dramatic imagining also suggests that, despite this drive for definiteness, Gudrun isn't, as Ursula is, really "considering" possible consequences of marrying for the experience. When Ursula points to the most likely consequence, that it will be the end of experience, Gudrun "attends" to the question as if for the first time. Two things then happen; the conversation comes temporarily "to a close," and Gudrun, almost angrily, rubs out part of her drawing in a way that indicates suppressed emotion. These little closures keep occurring, and always they're brought about by Gudrun. A bit later, Ursula questions her about her magnificently stated motive for coming back home—"*reculer pour mieux sauter*":

> "But where can one jump *to*?"
> "Oh, it doesn't matter," said Gudrun, somewhat superbly. "If one jumps over the edge, one is bound to land somewhere."
> "But isn't it very risky?" asked Ursula.
> A slow, mocking smile dawned on Gudrun's face.
> "Ah!" she said, laughing. "What is it all but words!"
> And so again she closed the conversation. But Ursula was still brooding.
> "And how do you find home, now you have come back to it?" she asked.
> Gudrun paused for some moments, coldly, before answering. Then, in a cold, truthful voice, she said:

"I find myself completely out of it."

"And father?"

Gudrun looked at Ursula, almost with resentment, as if brought to bay.

"I haven't thought about him: I've refrained," she said coldly.

"Yes," wavered Ursula; and the conversation was really at an end. The sisters found themselves confronted by a void, a terrifying chasm, as if they had looked over the edge.

They worked on in silence for some time. Gudrun's cheek was flushed with repressed emotion. She resented its having been called into being. (Ed. D. Farmer, L. Vasey and J. Worthen, Cambridge, 1987, 10. All references to this edition.)

Gudrun's conversational closures show a way of talking and thinking—or rather, *not*-thinking—that's at least as interested in the impression it's making on others as it is in getting at the truth of something. As the fashionable cynicism of "What is it all but words!" reminds us, this is the sociolect of glittering Chelsea bohemia. It is what poststructuralism would call a "discourse": the cynical "words" to some extent speak Gudrun. It's a discourse, above all, of power, which is exercised precisely in clipping off whatever subject might reveal one, give one away, show a chink in the armour. The chilly formality of "I've refrained" does this to Ursula, who until then wants to go on thinking about the matter of father, to think it through, not least for her own sake. Like everything else, the words add to Gudrun's impressiveness, but they also instantly resist any possibility either of closer contact with Ursula or, more significantly, of getting at the blocked feelings that are obviously calling out for expression within herself. For Lawrence's imagining insists that the expressed "words" of any individual or group, their sociolect or discourse, can't really be understood as such without reference to the whole state of being they involve. Gudrun in a sense *is* in a prison house of language ("what is it *all* but words"), but that's only intelligible in terms of the underlying "repressed emotion" her particular language both manifests and helps to contain. It's a language of repression, of resistance, in other words, designed, like her stockings, to cover up magnificently. And already, the novel is suggesting the price to be paid for this magnificence—thwarted energy, the feeling of everything withering in the bud.

In Hermione Roddice we see a similar thing in a more extreme case. As she walks into the church she shows the continuities between the drive for definiteness, the need to "know," and the need to cover up vulnerabilities. The repeated "knew" in she "knew herself to be well-dressed . . . knew herself the social equal . . . knew she was accepted" dramatize an inner texture of thoughts which cloak sublinguistic states that the novel quickly puts before us. Hers is assuredly, if you like, a neurotic text in that the story it has to keep repeating about her and about the world is always going to be containment, rationalization, compensation, projection, and so on, of what lies beneath. And it's worth pointing out that the novel puts clearly before the reader in her the ways in which "aesthetic knowledge, and culture, and world-visions, and disinterestedness" (17)—in short, the impulses to theorize, to ideologize—can all be "defences", ways precisely of blocking and resisting insight. *Women in Love* is a good deal about theories and "world visions" as false consciousness, symptoms of resistances that need to be worked through.

At the same time, the novel's own impulse isn't to "know" with this sort of drive for finalizing definiteness. The central figures certainly aren't, as most of the wedding guests are for Gudrun, "sealed and stamped and finished with" (14). What the usual thematizing readings fail to see is the whole process of signification by which the novel questions its leading intuitions as it registers them. No sooner do we think we have a settled sense of the contrasts being drawn between Ursula and Gudrun than the novel turns about and re-*minds* us of what has also been implied in the imagining of them: that they are, as the chapter-heading says, sisters. Another characteristic of these little scene-closures is the way they serve to defeat ideological closure in our reading of them—construing the issues simply as "innocence" versus "social being"—by pointing to what the women have in common: "The sisters found themselves confronted by a void, a terrifying chasm, as if they had looked over the edge". A little earlier: "They both laughed, looking at each other. In their hearts they were frightened. . . . The sisters were women. . . . But both had the remote, virgin look of modern girls . . ." (8).

What these sentences illustrate in miniature is that dialectical in-
terplay between difference and similarity which is another aspect of
the "frictional to-and-fro" characteristic at every level of Lawrence's
thinking at its best. It's above all a *movement* of dramatic exploration
and signification that never lets differences harden into structures of
static opposition but keeps turning back on them, threatening to
dislodge them. One moment we find Gudrun wanting to be quite
definite, the next we find her *not* wanting to be (9)—and *Ursula* afraid
of the depth of feeling within her (11) or saying to herself, in a way
that faintly echoes Hermione's intensely apprehensive projections
about Birkin in the church: "The wedding must not be a fiasco, it
must not" (18). This conventionality in Ursula, which Birkin will
spend a lot of energy trying to dislodge, is in part the self-protective
"integument" preventing her at moments from peering over the
edge into that "void" or "terrifying chasm" of the unknown faced
by "both" sisters. It too manifests itself as self-concealing discourse—Ursula's being of the less sophisticated "things are just
dandy" kind—especially when the vertiginous chasm gets too close.
"I know!" she cries in response to Gudrun's *reculer pour mieux sauter*—
"looking slightly dazzled and falsified, and as if she did *not* know".
This tendency of Ursula's to lie to herself comes out as *looking* false
because of that vigorous life coming into being within her, which
simply *won't* be falsified. Gudrun is in better control of herself than
that, except at those moments when she darkens and the held-in
life appears on her cheek as a resented "flush". At such moments she
and Ursula show themselves to be sisters in a full sense.

It's important to reflect on what this sisterhood means. Nearly all
accounts of the novel, including Leavis's pioneering one, either
overlook or understate the degree to which, at least in all four
major figures, the novel keeps sight of that core of "innocent" life in
them which remains as a *permanent possibility*. This is why it is seriously
reductive to say, as Dan Jacobson does, that the "others"—that is,
other than Birkin and Ursula, whom he calls the "good" characters—"can barely say or do anything—make love, give to charity,
paint, teach, talk—without revealing or being said to reveal how ad-
vanced, how gangrenous, their condition really is" (op. cit. 96).
What this ignores is that these figures can barely do these things or

reveal their "dissolution" without, at the same time, also revealing the thwarted or twisted *life* in them which continues to express itself in their deathward disintegration, in a sense as its very motive-force. Lawrence describes the process in a contemporary essay, "The Crown" (1915):

> Still the false I, the ego, held down the real, unborn I, which is a blossom with all a blossom's fragility.
>
> Yet constantly the rising flower pushed and thrust at the belly and heart of us, thrashed and beat relentlessly. If it could not beat its way through into being, it must thrash us hollow. (*Phoenix II: Uncollected, Unpublished and Other Prose Works by D. H. Lawrence*, ed. W. Roberts and H. T. Moore, London, 1968, 388)

What this underlines is the profound interrelatedness established at the beginning of *Women in Love* between Ursula's "unborn I" and that bud—"Everything withers in the bud"—which is the image of the same undeveloped possibility in Gudrun, a blossom very much "held down," suppressed, by her Chelsea-nurtured "ego." What beats its way through into being in Ursula and Birkin is the same life-source that thrashes Gudrun and Gerald hollow.

In part this inter-relatedness makes itself felt metaphorically: there's a far-reaching suggestive continuity between the flowers, say, that Ursula gives Birkin—in place of those rings—in "Excurse," and the "open flower" of Gerald's love in "Snowed Up." In each case, the implication is precisely the same: to be given over to the other is to be open both to the possibilities of transformation and of annihilation. Which way the process goes is seen to depend on a complex interactive enablement or disablement between the lovers, where each of these courses continues to be imagined in terms of the opposite possibility. The destruction of Gerald is so final precisely because, to the extent of his capacity for it, he *is* so open to Gudrun; his love-wound and his death-wound are one and the same thing: "This wound, this strange, infinitely-sensitive opening of his soul, where he was exposed, like an open flower, to all the universe, and in which he was given to his complement, the other, the unknown, this wound, this disclosure, this unfolding of his own covering, leaving him incomplete, limited unfinished, like an open flower under the sky, this was his cruelest joy" (446). For Gudrun, being the object of Gerald's "cruelest joy" feels like being torn open, a feeling that underlines the incapacities of both; yet with her too the imagery also hints at what might otherwise have been realized: "She felt, with horror, as if he tore at the bud of her heart, tore it open, like an irreverent, persistent being. Like a boy who pulls off a fly's wings, or tears open a bud to see what is in flower, he tore at her privacy, at her very life, he would destroy her as an immature bud, torn open, is destroyed" (446).

This sort of writing, far from dismissing Gerald and Gudrun as "gangrenous," presents their inter-destruction as a tragic inevitability involving all that they are, including their most valuable possibilities. Gerald dies because he can't be, as Loerke is and Gudrun becomes, merely "indifferent"; his nature is, as we're told, "too serious" (445). At the same time, Gudrun seems to bury with Loerke a longing for belief in something more than her modish ironies will ordinarily allow. At unguarded moments, such as when—significantly—Gerald is asleep in bed beside her, she works through to a realization of what, at centre, she longs for:

Her heart was breaking with pity and grief for him. And at the same moment, a grimace came over her mouth, of mocking irony at her own unspoken tirade. Ah, what a farce it was! She thought of Parnell and Katherine O'Shea. Parnell! After all, who can take the nationalisation of Ireland seriously? After all, who can take political Ireland really seriously, whatever it does? And who can take political England seriously? Who can? Who can care a straw, really, how the old, patched-up Constitution is tinkered at any more? Who cares a button for our national ideals, any more than for our national bowler hat? Aha, it is all old hat, it is all old bowler hat?

That's all it is, Gerald, my young hero. At any rate we'll spare ourselves the nausea of stirring the old broth any more. You be beautiful, my Gerald, and reckless. There *are* perfect moments, oh convince me, I need it.

He opened his eyes, and looked at her. She greeted him with a mocking, enigmatic smile in which was a poignant gaiety. Over his face went the reflection of the smile, he smiled too, purely unconsciously.

That filled her with extraordinary delight, to see the smile cross his face, reflected from her face. She remembered, that was how a baby smiled. It filled her with extraordinary radiant delight.

"You've done it," she said.

"What?" he asked, dazed.

"Convinced me."

And she bent down, kissing him passionately, passionately, so that he was bewildered. He did not ask of what he had convinced her, though he meant to. He was glad she was kissing him. She seemed to be feeling for his heart, to touch the quick of him. And he wanted her to touch the quick of his being, he wanted that most of all. (419)

Here Gudrun is as given over to Gerald as she will ever be, and while the scene dramatizes what *is* alive between them—it almost is a perfect moment—the imagining never loses touch with what must thwart that life. On the one hand, there's Gerald's regressive "wanting"—the baby-smile hinting at the way in which, for him, the world is an udder to feed his supreme self. Before long, he will be exultant; she will feel used. At the same time, Gudrun's characteristic defences have only been able to fall because she is alone. In fact her thinking here has an exploratory freedom that it never seems to have in conversation; others, even her sister and her lover—perhaps especially these—always inhibit the open expression and so the true discovery of the fundamental needs, we see displayed here. Afraid above all of giving herself away, she can only fully be herself by herself. And the clear price to be paid for being like that, for remaining enclosed in a defensive sheath of cynicism, is to remain an immature bud.

And yet—as Lawrence would put it, using his most significant connective—the imagining here is so inward as to present a problem with even that formulation. The problem is that Gudrun's defensive cynicism here is so close to the novel's own attitude to these political and social questions. Or, to put the point in a more pointed way, we wouldn't be surprised to hear *Birkin* saying all that about political England and Ireland. At moments he says things that are even more extremely disillusioned. At the beginning of "Excurse," for instance, he thinks thoughts that show his kinship with the nihilism of Loerke:

> His life now seemed so reduced, that he hardly cared any more. At moments it seemed to him he did not care a straw whether Ursula or Hermione or anybody else existed or did not exist. Why bother! Why strive for a coherent, satisfied life? Why not drift on in a series of accidents—like a picaresque novel? Why not? Why bother about human relationships? Why take them seriously—male or female? Why form any serious connections at all? Why not be casual, drifting along, taking all for what it was worth? (302)

This couldn't be Loerke, of course, partly because for him these wouldn't have been questions but settled convictions. Yet there is something in what Leo Bersani says about the novel when he talks of Lawrence playing "dangerously with similarities; we are always being asked to make crucial but almost imperceptible distinctions" (*A Future for Astyanax: Character and Desire in Literature*, London, 1978, 176). This is over-stated, as the present case illustrates: neither Loerke nor Gudrun would have gone on to reflect, as Birkin does, that they were "damned and doomed to the old effort at serious living." And yet there can be no doubt that Lawrence does endow many of the characters, including those who are usually thought of as objects of his critique, with his own characteristic thoughts. Bersani goes on to make a similar point when he says that "Lawrence nonchalantly exposes what the realistic novelist seems anxious to disguise: the derivation of his work from a single creative imagination" (178). There's nothing "nonchalant" or merely modernist in this, however. What it shows, in fact, is the strenuous innerness of Lawrence's dramatic thinking about the various life-possibilities his work is exploring: very little is merely external or notational in this novel, or left as unrealized "metaphysic."

Which is to say, above all, that there's very little in the novel that remains merely Other to the novel's thinking and feeling. One good reason for thinking of this as a canonical text is that, like *Middlemarch* and—supremely—*Anna Karenina, Women in Love* is for the most part both supple-minded and imaginatively generous enough *not* to fall into the repressive ethical oppositions which, according to Jameson, are supposed to characterize such books. In these books the over-defended "social beings" ever retain a core of innocence, a mostly unrealized capacity, and unconscious longing, for change and growth; while the "innocents" must always struggle against defensive integuments in themselves if they are to *beat their way through* into being. The necessity for permanent struggle in these figures precludes the simple idealization of them that George Eliot falls into with Dorothea towards the end of *Middlemarch*, for instance, or our thinking of them as "good" characters. This is why it's a notable strength in *Women in Love* that Birkin, even as late as "Excurse," is still tempted to chuck in the whole thing with Ursula and retire back into his shell, for the moment a Loerke look-alike.

Right from the beginning, Birkin has been saying other characters' lines in a way that reveals the repressed "social being" in him. One extremely telling moment is at the wedding at Shortlands when Mrs Crich hints that she'd like him to be Gerald's friend:

> Birkin looked down into her eyes, which were blue, and watching heavily. He could not understand them. "Am I my brother's keeper?" he said to himself, almost flippantly.
>
> Then he remembered with a slight shock, that that was Cain's cry. And Gerald was Cain, if anybody. Not that he was Cain, either, although he had slain his brother. There was such a thing as pure accident. . . . Or is this not true, is there no such thing as pure accident? Has *everything* that happens a universal significance? Has it? Birkin pondering as he stood there, had forgotten Mrs Crich, as she had forgotten him.
>
> He did not believe that there was any such thing as accident. It all hung together, in the deepest sense. (26)

Assuming that Birkin is right and there's no such thing as pure accident, then what are we to make of Birkin "accidentally" uttering

Cain's cry, and then when he remembers whose cry it is instantly associating it with Gerald? What it all suggests is something that Freud, who didn't believe in accidents either, would have seen as a significant slip, a revelation "in the deepest sense" of an aspect of Birkin that he didn't want to know about—namely the Cain in himself. One way in which Birkin is Cain isn't hard to see; after all, he is a mass brother-murderer in his often-expressed wish that the rest of mankind would simply disappear. He has just said so to Mrs Crich:

> "Not many people amount to anything at all," he answered, forced to go much deeper than he wanted to. "They jingle and giggle. It would be much better if they were just wiped out. Essentially, they don't exist, they aren't there."

Saying this kind of thing is obviously much more disturbing to Birkin than he can allow himself to know, which is one reason for resisting Dan Jacobson's assertion that Birkin is allowed by the novel to get away with this sort of sentiment "without being accused by the narrative voice or the other characters of manifesting a murderously diseased will" (op. cit., 96). What this overlooks is a much more subtle form of placing: Birkin's annihilating wishes and Gerald's brother-killing as a ruthless mineowner—thus annihilating his father's sort of troubled brotherhood—are being unmistakably linked.

In this and in other ways Birkin and Gerald are seen to be brothers in spirit if not in blood long before explicit *Blutbruderschaft* comes into question. As with the sisterhood of Ursula and Gudrun, this is so even when the imagining of them draws strong attention to difference. The dialogue that concludes "Shortlands" for instance has Birkin analysing Gerald's conventionality and opposing it to true spontaneity, when suddenly the focus shifts to what connects them:

> There was a pause of strange enmity between the two men, that was very near to love. It was always the same between them; always their talk brought them into a deadly nearness of contact, a strange, perilous intimacy which was either hate or love, or both. They parted with apparent inconcern, as if their going apart

were a trivial occurrence. And they really kept it to the level of trivial occurrence. Yet the heart of each burned from the other. They burned with each other, inwardly. This they would never admit. They intended to keep their relationship a casual free-and-easy friendship, they were not going to be so unmanly and unnatural as to allow any heart-burning between them. They had not the faintest belief in deep relationship between man and man, and their disbelief prevented any development of their powerful but suppressed friendliness (33–34).

Here it is *Birkin*, as much as Gerald, who's showing that, as Birkin himself has just said, "It's the hardest thing in the world to act spontaneously on one's impulses . . ." (32). This is only remarkable because in context it was a dictum directed at *Gerald's* supposedly Cain-like suppressed desire/fear of having his gizzard slit. What Birkin's whole argument suppresses in fact is his own suppressed feeling for Gerald, which has a good deal to do with why it *is* such a provocatively cutting sort of argument. In yet another Cain-like way then, Birkin is denying that in himself which is common to both men; and he has the analytical knife out for Gerald precisely because, at some level, that brotherhood itself is deeply "perilous" to him.

Brotherhood, commonality, movements of responsibility or pity for others, notably Hermione, are ever the threatening Other in Birkin's psyche. His conscious ethic is that of Nietzschean singleness and self-responsibility. The sentence on spontaneity continues: ". . . and it's the only really gentlemanly thing to do—*provided you're fit to do it*" (my italics). The problem is that most of mankind are evidently not fit. As he said to Mrs Crich, they "just jingle and giggle. It would be much better if they were just wiped out." But fortunately it doesn't have to come to that because, as he says, "Essentially they don't exist, they aren't there." Which isn't simply saying all over again that they don't really *live*, spontaneously and with *übermensch* singleness. It's saying, rather, that one doesn't have to take them into account. They don't matter; one can forget them. And Birkin does that, very largely, for he seems to know, in advance, that any larger political responsibility or social consciousness is a form of false consciousness—a strategy for avoiding the responsibility of looking closely into oneself.

Granting Birkin's point, that social consciousness can be a form of false consciousness, or unconsciousness, his own refusal to know about the jinglers and gigglers surely involves another form of false consciousness, what Trigant Burrow in the book that Lawrence himself praised called "the social unconscious." This is the "fallacy of implied subjective differentiation," which is for Burrow "the whole meaning of unconsciousness and the basis of all delusion" (*The Social Basis of Consciousness: A Study in Organic Psychology Based upon a Synthetic and Societal Concept of the Neuroses*, London, 1927, 125). It's the thank-God-I-am-not-as-other-men attitude that George Eliot has in her sights in the figures of Bulstrode and Lydgate, when the whole burden of her imagining is to underline the realities of mutual inter-dependence and Burrovian "subjective continuity"— whereby we only begin to know others by looking into the depths of ourselves. Where Eliot's emphasis runs the risk of sentimentality, Birkin's "disquality," in emphasizing discontinuity—the other side of the truth about others—is always in danger of the sort of delusive belief in his own superiority and uniqueness that George Eliot called "egoism" and Burrow the "social unconscious".

It's here that *Women in Love* itself is most open to criticism because there are strong grounds for thinking that Lawrence largely backs Birkin in his thoughts about "disquality." Indeed, one might say that his text fulfils Birkin's murderous wishes by hardly allowing these jinglers and gigglers to exist in it. Only a superior class of people *does* exist in *Women in Love*. Most of them, of course, belong to the artistic and intellectual *avant-garde*, but at centre-stage are those potentially able to beat their way through to new life. The novel leaves us in no doubt that is a very tiny elite indeed, surrounded by a great mass— typified by Palmer the electrician, the middle-aged Will Brangwen, and the couple who take the Birkins' chair—about whom there is nothing interesting, and certainly nothing hopeful, to be said. The rest presumably belong to meaningless mediocrity or to the great industrial machine. It's usual to say at this point that Lawrence himself, surrounded by the originals of most of these characters, had lost any touch he once had with the world in which such ordinary people lived. This doesn't quite go far enough, because after all he was the author of one of the most compelling novels about English working-class and provincial life ever written—and (what partly accounts for this triumph) one written *from within*. That the Midlands colliers of *Women in Love* are caricatured as sexually potent underworld automata, imagined in the mass rather than as individual Walter Morels, needs another explanation: Lawrence was denying his social roots, suppressing many things he knew—in the service of an ethic of individual self-transcendence.

Marxists have already had their say about this, and I don't think there's any point in denying the force of the case here. *Women in Love* does have a political unconscious; to this extent it is ideology-bound, symptom of a particular historical process. But this can only be the final word about the novel if one is prepared to grant, as I am certainly not, some sort of trans-historical privilege to Marxism that guarantees it against counter-deconstruction. In the absence of this, one can only say that there are various different stories about what is real and important—and about transformation. All, as Lawrence freely admitted, have in them the bones of an ideology. What matters for art is the extent to which that is criticized from within, subjected to a dialectical pressure that will bring to light its characteristic suppressions—in this way "working through" them into what I can only provisionally call an "ideological unknown".

III

Women in Love takes up the bold experimentalism of *The Rainbow* and perfects it by grafting it back onto the formal stem of the "old" novel. Clearly Lawrence found the most uncompromisingly "modernist" and stylized sections of *The Rainbow*, which are shaped almost entirely around alternations of inward response, difficult either to sustain or to resolve, and he more or less abandoned the mode long before he finished the book. These sections raised a more profound difficulty too. For all their undoubted interest and power, the rhythmic withdrawals and returns of Will and Anna come to seem claustrophobically over-focused on their own significance and, lacking the imaginative resistances of a realistic surface, ultimately programmatic. The paradox is that the most formally exploratory mode in the novel is at the same time the most insistent on its own *terms* of exploration: unlike the "old" novel of Eliot and Tolstoy, it offers us no other terms.

The heart of the problem with *The Rainbow* can be seen in Lawrence's famous letter about the novel to Edward Garnett of 5 June 1914 where he outlines his limited affinity with Marinetti and the Futurists:

> I don't care so much about what the woman *feels*—in the ordinary usage of the word. That presumes an *ego* to feel with. I only care about what the woman *is*—what she *is*—inhumanly, physiologically, materially—according to the use of the word: but for me, what she *is* as a phenomenon (or as representing some greater inhuman will), instead of what she feels according to the human conception. (*The Letters of D. H. Lawrence*, vol. 2, ed. George J. Zytaruk and James T. Boulton, Cambridge, 1981, 83)

Lawrence of course also carefully distinguishes himself from the Futurists in this letter, but what is not usually noticed is that his own tone is continuous to some extent with theirs: "I only care about what the woman *is* . . . inhumanly, physiologically, materially . . ." is almost pure 1914-manifestoese, the sort of formulation that might have come out of the pages of *BLAST*. The point is worth making because a determination to make it new is at the centre of *The Rainbow*. "I *only* care . . ." corresponds to its modernist *foreshortening or stylization* of experience that is achieved by jettisoning much of the "human conception" of the "old" novel. At the same time, it's important not to overlook the prominent "me" in this sentence ("but for me . . ."), which reminds us that this is his *own* distinctive vision of newness, that is, as distinct from Marinetti's or Pound's or Gaudier-Brzeska's or any of the other Cubists or Vorticists competing for the limelight in those heady brink-of-war days.

The formulation also raises substantive questions. If it is asked how one tells "what the woman *is*" as distinct from what she herself "*feels*," the answer is given time and again in *The Rainbow*: one "knows." Lydia may not consciously feel the "vacancy" at the heart of her existence, but Tom Brangwen, seeing her walk by, instinctively "knows" of it. This sort of "knowing", or "blood"-knowing, is of course one of those vital capacities handed on from generation to generation: it is possessed as much by Ursula peering into her microscope ("she only knew that it was not limited mechanical energy . . .") as it was by the ancestral Brangwens who "knew the wave which cannot halt." At the same time, the novelist's own way of apprehending experience in *The Rainbow* is clearly continuous with theirs. Tom's intuition of a connection between Lydia and himself largely expresses the novel's own:

> It was coming, he knew, his fate. The world was submitting to its transformation. He made no move: it would come, what would come. (ch. 1)

Tom is of course more or less right about this, and in context the rightness of his "knowledge" seems imaginatively compelling. But this is only because the novel gives no space here to other possibilities, such as (as is the case so often in *Middlemarch*) that the lover may be confusing projected need or wish with actuality—and that Lydia may in fact feel that his intuition is wrong. Such possibilities presumably belong to the old "human conception" that Lawrence no longer "cares about" here: they're irrelevant to the foreshortened vision of things that largely controls the novel. Which is to say that the importance given to blood-knowing in some ways imposes an element of ideological closure in *The Rainbow*; or, to revert to Lawrence's own terms, the presented world of the novel in some respects lacks that implied internal "criticism" of its "metaphysic" which "makes for the lasting value and satisfaction of that work."

It is significant that, as we have seen, "knowing" in *Women in Love* mostly means something very different: it's usually a form of *false* consciousness clung to in order to suppress subconscious realizations. At the same time, without rejecting the essential intuitions or formal discoveries of *The Rainbow*, the later novel goes back to a realistic surface of things that includes, crucially, an interest in what the person "feels," as distinct from what she or he is "known" to "be." Indeed one of the primary nodes of interest in *Women in Love* is often the gap between what is intuitively—that is, projectively—

"known" about one character by another and what is in other ways revealed.

We see this in a particularly telling way in Gudrun's attempts to come to terms with Gerald. By the chapter "Death and Love" it begins to become clear that her intense desire to "know" him—led on by all that seemed desirably unknown about him—is actually a subtle form of resistance to his otherness. Right from the beginning, her response to him has been passionately visionary, alive with an imaginative energy that, for her, seems to be indistinguishable from sexual desire. She's momentarily taken out of her self-consciousness by what she sees as his arctic dangerousness, his wolf-like singleness, a conception which both genuinely lights him up for us and yet makes him curiously difficult to square with, for instance, the man Birkin loves. In short, there's an element of abstraction in Gudrun's Gerald, of assimilative vision, that's related to her own modernist carvings and beyond them to Loerke's futuristic friezes. In *Women in Love*, the stylizations of modernism are now themselves problematic—and deeply implicated in the mechanical reductions of the modem world.

As we see when Gudrun and Gerald kiss under the railway bridge—and she yields passionately to an *idea* of Gerald as the powerful "master" of all the colliers—Gudrun's sexuality is bound up with imaginative appropriation, this being an ultimate sort of light-in-the-darkness, a form of control that can never lapse finally in surrender to *him*. She in fact seems partly to recognize this:

> She reached up, like Eve reaching to the apples on the tree of knowledge, and she kissed him, though her passion was a transcendent fear of the thing he was, touching his face with infinitely delicate, encroaching, wondering fingers. Her fingers went over the mould of his face, over his features. How perfect and foreign he was—ah how dangerous! her soul thrilled with complete knowledge! (331–332)

The thrill of Gudrun's exploratory way to trying to "know" Gerald's face—we never forget that she is a sculptor—is itself rendered exploratorily, in prose that focuses the limits of her knowledge. To put it simply, Lawrence's imagining of her experience, unlike her sense of Gerald, is sympathetically inward.

In fact Gudrun's fear of knowing Gerald in *that* way, of understanding "the thing he was" (as the flow of Lawrence's sympathetic consciousness has given him to us), is linked with those conversational closures of hers in the conversation with Ursula at the very beginning of the novel. There we see that, for all her apparently dazzling originality, Gudrun is very much bound by the language of the society that she affects to despise. Unlike Birkin and Ursula, Gerald and Gudrun mostly talk in conventionalities, even at their most intense moments, which is associated with their inability either to push through or to lapse into new understanding:

"Why don't I love you?" he asked, as if admitting the truth of her accusation, yet hating her for it.

"I don't know why you don't—I've been good to you. You were in a *fearful* state, when you came to me."

Her heart was beating to suffocate her, yet she was stony and unrelenting.

"When was I in a fearful state?" he asked.

"When you first came to me. I *had* to take pity on you—but it was never love."

It was the statement 'It was never love,' which sounded in his ears with madness.

"Why must you repeat it so often, that there is no love?" he said in a voice strangled with rage.

"Well you don't *think* you love me, do you?" she asked.

He was silent with cold passion of anger.

"You don't think you *can* love me, do you?" she repeated, almost with a sneer.

"No," he said. (442)

The novel suggests that the conventional terms in which Gudrun and Gerald mostly talk to each other are partly a sign of the blockage from which they can provide no release: whatever the lovers may think they want from each other, they can only "repeat" the same limited set of sentiments over and over again. The present is hostage to the past. In Freudian terms, Gudrun and Gerald seem merely able to "repeat" the past to each other symbolically rather than "work through" their mutual resistances to an understanding of the other's separate being.

In the case of Gerald, the Freudian terms are especially relevant because part of our sense of "the thing he was" is provided by the story of childhood trauma that hovers over all accounts of him like a suggestive pathogenesis. It's merely suggestive because the novel reaches for no definite explanation about its importance in Gerald's life, but rather questions the various versions that enter the characters' heads. In Birkin's meditation on Gerald's shooting of his brother, two possible ways of regarding this episode are raised. At first, Birkin thinks of the shooting as an "accident" that has "drawn a curse across the life that had caused the accident." But he quickly moves away from this more ordinary "surface" explanation to ponder another one—that there is "no such thing as pure accident," that "*everything* that happens [has] a universal significance," such that "it all [hangs] together in the deepest sense." These are obscure reflections, of course, and we can only make sense of them cumulatively as the novel goes on pondering them. From the hints that emerge, we see that this "deepest sense" of all human actions is that they are obscurely *willed*, as in the extreme case Birkin envisages, of murderer and murderee in which even the victim desires his execution. This is of course about as close *ad absurdum* as any *reductio* can be allowed to go, and it keeps us wondering about the state of the man putting it forward.

The novel by no means simply backs the idea that everything that happens is in some ultimate sense willed, though it by no means rejects it either: time and again events are shaped so as to disclose the "deepest" will in them. And yet, as is already evident, the drive for single coherent vision, the drive to see things *simply* "in the deepest sense" as opposed to a more ordinary, commonsense, "surface" way of seeing them, is something about which the novel is properly sceptical. In fact, it is constantly opening a space to see some things as accidental, including Gerald's childhood trauma, which is much more generous to him than Gudrun or Birkin sometimes are.

More specifically, Birkin's drive for coherence at the "deepest" level of vision is seen as partly a variant of Gudrun's will to "know" things, a will that obscurely resists entertaining their otherness. Especially at the beginning of Birkin and Ursula's various love-scenes, we see his sort of drive to "know" partly as an elaborate *defence* against her, a way of fending her off. They are unable to connect; she slips into an embarrassed conventionality, he into a brutal intellectualizing directness:

> "How nice the fuchsias are!" she said, to break the silence.
> "Aren't they!—Did you think I had forgotten what I said?"
> A swoon went over Ursula's mind.
> "I don't want you to remember it—if you don't want to," she struggled to say, through the dark mist that covered her.
> There was silence for some moments.
> "No," he said. "It isn't that. Only—if we are going to know each other, we must pledge ourselves for ever. If we are going to make a relationship, even of friendship, there must be something final and infallible about it."
> There was a clang of mistrust and almost anger in his voice. She did not answer. Her heart was much too contracted. She could not have spoken.
> Seeing she was not going to reply, he continued almost bitterly, giving himself away:
> "I can't say it is love I have to offer—and it isn't love I want. It is something much more impersonal and harder,—and rarer."
> There was a silence, out of which she said:
> "You mean you don't love me."
> She suffered furiously saying that.
> "Yes, if you like to put it like that . . ." (145)

This is characteristic of Birkin: even as he talks of final pledges and being "without reserves and defences, stripped entirely into the unknown" (147), he is bristling with them, untrustingly throwing the theory in her face precisely as a way of holding off those things in her. This "abstract earnestness" is exactly what wouldn't enable Ursula to be stripped entirely, as Birkin, beside himself with deep fears, obscurely knows.

At the same time, Birkin's drive to theorize about this "something more impersonal" has an importance that can't simply be psychologized away. As he realized himself: "There was always confusion in speech. Yet it must be spoken. Whichever way one moved, if one were to move forwards, one must break a way through the walls of the prison, as the infant in labour strives through the walls of the womb" (186). This reminds us why clinging to the conventional language of love—as Gudrun and Gerald do, and Ursula wants to—doesn't get anywhere. As we've seen, it is indeed a "prison"; it's a repressed and ultimately repressive language that obscures the often ambiguous underlife of sexuality. For Birkin, to move forward to new life is partly to *force* one's way through into expression, to break through the current limits of thought and language to new vision, however crude or violent or confused or abstract the first attempts might be. *This* sort of breaking through—as opposed to the flow of *sympathetic* consciousness—applies in one way to the novel as a whole, of course, but it applies in a particular way to Birkin, who clearly dramatizes a similar impulse in Lawrence himself. He embodies Lawrence's own insurgent will-to-vision, the discursive or ideologizing drive of the essays and pamphlets that gets all too much free rein in the later novels.

It's revealing that Lawrence in the famous letter to Garnett sounds rather like Birkin when he's trying to explain something to Ursula and ends up sounding, as she would say, too "cocksure." Indeed, in "Mino" his terms are strikingly similar to those in the letter:

> "I want to find you, where you don't know your own existence, the you that your common self denies utterly. But I don't want your good looks, and I don't want your womanly feelings, and I don't want your thoughts nor opinions nor your ideas—they are all bagatelles to me."
>
> "You are very conceited, Monsieur," she mocked. "How do you know what my womanly feelings are, or my thoughts or my ideas? You don't even know what I think of you now."
>
> "Nor do I care in the slightest." (147)

The crucial difference, of course, between the letter and the novel is that in *Women in Love* the woman is there to talk back and to insist on the importance of those womanly feelings that Birkin says he doesn't care about. In doing so, she also insists on the importance of a more ordinary sense of "knowing"—not blood-knowing, but mere acquaintance with facts, such as what she actually *does* think, as opposed to what he "knows" her to be thinking, or not thinking.

The importance of Ursula to the imaginative process and power of *Women in Love* can hardly be overestimated. It's usual to say that the strength of Birkin as a creation—as opposed, say, to Mellors—is that he's constantly being revealed and illuminated, his views being tested, refined and contradicted, by the drama of which he's part. And Ursula provides much of the internal "criticism that makes the lasting value and satisfaction of [the] work of art." Yet her part in the novel is very much more important than this. Not only is she Birkin's complement, his other, the one in whom he finds what he is after; she is the one in whose realized resistant spirit Lawrence's own will to "utterance" finds its complement and other too.

We can see this at the end of "Mino," where Birkin and Ursula are in contact in a new way:

> "Proud and subservient, proud and subservient, I know you," he retorted dryly, "proud and subserved, then subservient to the proud—I know you and your love. It is a tick-tack, tick-tack, a dance of opposites."
>
> "Are you so sure?" she mocked wickedly, "what my love is?"
>
> "Yes I am," he retorted.
>
> "So cocksure!" she said. "How can anybody ever be right, who is so cocksure? It shows you are wrong."
>
> He was silent in chagrin.
>
> They had talked and struggled till they were both wearied out.
>
> "Tell me about yourself and your people," he said.
>
> And she told him about the Brangwens, and about her mother, and about Skrebensky, her first love, and about her later experiences. He sat very still, watching her as she talked. And he seemed to listen with reverence. Her face was beautiful and full of baffled light as she told him all the things that had hurt her or

perplexed her so deeply. He seemed to warm and comfort his
soul at the beautiful light of her nature.

"If she *really* could pledge herself," he thought to himself, with
passionate insistence but hardly any hope. Yet a curious little irresponsible laughter appeared at his heart. (153)

The "curious little irresponsible laughter" that comes to Birkin here
is a hint that something like the star-equilibrium he's been talking
about is beginning to take place between himself and Ursula. It's important to note that, although it might signal the beginning of what
he's after, it doesn't come simply *because* he's been after it. In that important sense it comes from beyond his conscious aim, from the
"unknown" to which at last he seems to be open.

Birkin is slowly transformed in these love-scenes. Ursula's un-
fearful loving mockery sets in train something like a Freudian
"working through" of his defences, his tendency to neurotic repetition, such that he comes slowly to understand that she is not like
the Hermione he "knows" and fears she is. The key sign of this is
that his ideas fall away and are reborn as experience—experience all
the more remarkable for being, at the same time, so ordinary. When
Birkin can be quiet enough to allow it to happen, their relations take
on a simplicity and an ordinariness that is itself extraordinary in the
world of this novel: Ursula tells him about her past; they have tea;
they joke with each other, tease each other.

It's important to see that this remarkable ordinariness—which is
so valuable because it lies, so to speak, on the other side of the prison
walls from which all of the characters long to be released—reveals a
good deal about the art that embodies it. The transformation of
Birkin in these love-scenes recursively mirrors the novel's own creative transformation of the psycho-ethical thinking from which it
partly springs into an art that goes "beyond the artist's conscious
aim." Ursula's loving subversion of the preacher in him reflects the
novel's "working through" of the sort of prophetic will that came to
express itself more and more in the latter half of *The Rainbow* as over-
certain knowledge of what the world is like.

The world of *Women in Love* is much more mind-resistant than the
one that keeps disclosing its meanings to the student Ursula in the

earlier novel. Which is partly to say that the later novel's "theory of being," like Birkin's is constantly being met dialectically by a "living sense of being" that refuses simply to be badgered into passive agreement with it. The cats in "Mino," for instance, altogether shrug off not only the sort of anthropomorphizing signification that both Birkin *and* Ursula try (half-seriously) to force upon them—and which readers commonly try to read into them—but they lie altogether beyond human ken. Their apparent handiness to the characters', and what is often taken to be Lawrence's, argument, dissolves when the focus comes back to the "uncanny fires" of the cats' eyes that are constantly looking beyond or through the human beings into a landscape that is utterly "unknown."

The cats' final un-knowableness means that, so far as the human drama is concerned, they aren't part of that remorseless coherence "in the deepest sense" which is often supposed to characterize *Women in Love*. Their most important role in fact is that they *tempt* the characters (and us) to read them as symbolic, and then run off, fundamentally unread and unsymbolized. To that extent they remain *accidental* to the thrust of the drama, part of what might be called, not a realistic surface, but a realistic depth, of things that keeps impinging on events in ways that are utterly unexpected. Just at the point at which the quarrel between Birkin and Ursula is about to flare up again, Mrs. Daykin comes in with a tray:

> "*You prevaricator!*" she cried, in real indignation.
> "Tea is ready, sir," said the landlady from the doorway.
> They both looked at her, very much as the cats had looked at them, a little while before.
> "Thank you, Mrs. Daykin."
> An interrupted silence fell over the two of them, a moment of breach.
> "Come and have tea," he said.
> "Yes, I should love it," she replied, gathering herself together.
> (151)

The essential action here is what it always is for Lawrence, the ebb and flow of vital feeling within and between the two lovers. By this point in their quarrel, we sense that Ursula's "real indignation" is on the point of playing itself out and metamorphosing into something quieter and more responsive to Birkin. Yet Mrs. Daykin really does impinge on this process, enforcing on both of them (and us) a vital sense of relativity: compared to someone really on the outside of their little world, they are, for all their momentary antagonisms, in profound connection with each other. And that implied realization helps to precipitate the shift of feeling that is already coming into being between them.

It's one sign of what's so deeply convincing about *Women in Love* that its "living sense of being" includes realistic rhythms of episode and accident as subtly reshaping cross-currents to the master-rhythms of love and withdrawal between the lovers. Here mutual defences fall away partly because the lovers are distracted by tea or because they get simply "wearied out"—too fatigued to argue any longer. The transformed, "worked through" quality of these moments is extremely important: Lawrence is defining an ordinariness that is significantly different from the mere conventionality of Gerald and Gudrun. At a given moment, tea with beautiful china can revive closeness for Ursula and Birkin as easily as the great living continuum of the fields can for Anna Brangwen. In *Women in Love*, realistic episode and detail aren't simply subsumed and effaced as they are in the most modernist sections of *The Rainbow*, with its rather fixed pattern of variation within endless repetition. The imagining in the later novel is able to embrace much more of a world that, like Mrs. Daykin and the cats, quite cuts across the rhythms of the lovers' connection.

The importance that small accidents and unexpected events have in *Women in Love* draws attention to the importance of the "unknown" in the imaginative process that produced them. Lawrence is constantly working on an edge where precise ends aren't pre-known—in such a way that decisive moments can spring into being (in the novel's own phrase) "accidentally on purpose," out of the suggestive interstices of surface happenings. In fact, Birkin downing his champagne accidentally on purpose before giving the wedding-speech nicely illustrates the combination of willed ends yet unwilled means that characterizes the artistic process of this novel. The "ordinary" moments between Ursula and Birkin are, from their point of view, so poised and free and, in a certain sense, blessed, precisely because they seem to happen so spontaneously: one minute Ursula is attacking Birkin as a prevaricator, the next she is drinking tea and telling him about her people. At the same time, the art that embodies this moment is only "right" because it too comes into being in an utterly unsignalled way that simultaneously takes up and clinches the deeper purposes that have been latent in the imagining of the whole scene and indeed the whole novel. The story Ursula tells of her mother and of Skrebensky shows the necessary connection here between the represented life and the art itself: in remembering them she is dramatizing the return to conscious expression of latent purposes that go right back into the prehistory of *Women in Love*—to a time when this novel and *The Rainbow* were one story.

Looked at from this larger perspective, the will for the lovers to connect in some such way has of course been there all along (in both their minds and their creator's), and has been expressing itself even in their quarrelling. Indeed it is expressed *especially* in their quarrelling: though they aren't conscious of it, their arguing, unlike that of Gerald and Gudrun, is itself part of the process of "working through" their resistances to each other. And just as it's impossible for them to plan consciously the overcoming of these defences, so it's impossible for Lawrence to plan consciously the precise realization of these unplanned moments that are at the same time a consummation of all that he's been "in the deepest sense" striving to realize. In a real sense, such moments come out of an "unknown" that keeps transcending, even as it completes, the artist's will-to-meaning.

The notion that art can in a certain sense transcend its so-called ideological underpinnings isn't one that would be necessarily persuasive or even intelligible to someone committed to seeing *any* representation of personal transformation as "neo-Freudian nostalgia for some ultimate moment of *cure*" (Jameson, op. cit., 283) Nor would pointing out that, in this novel, there is no "ultimate moment", only continuing process. There is in short no answer here to those who insist ideologically that there can be nothing in a work of art but enfleshed ideology. Yet clearly *Women in Love* demonstrates that, to conceive, as some do, of embodied morality in a novel as a static system of binary oppositions is to miss the *dynamic* nature of intentionality as a restless process of undermining, interrogating and repositioning the work's key terms. And to insist, as others do, that novels can only reinforce our resistances to non-ideological reality, is to miss the fact that some significant ones actually represent such resistances and are centrally concerned with the possibility of "working through" them. Not only this, but as *Women in Love* also demonstrates, the dynamic intentionality of some novels is an embodiment of the "working through" process itself, whereby ideological purpose issues in represented meanings that were unplanned and, in a relevant sense, "unknown."

Lawrence in Another Light
Women in Love *and Existentialism*

JOHN B. HUMMA

ESPECIALLY WHEN VIEWED AS THE RESPONSE or reaction to or development away from the seemingly dead end of naturalism, existentialism, though currently out of fashion, is nonetheless among the more important literary-philosophical developments of the twentieth century. And yet, though the whole tenor of Lawrence's thought is anti-deterministic and though he almost certainly is one of the three or four most important English-language novelists of the century, D. H. Lawrence only infrequently is considered in the context of existentialism. To be sure, for Norman Mailer, Lawrence's greatest interest lies precisely in his existentialism. Mailer represents Lawrence's thinking in this way: "People can win at love only when they are ready to lose everything they bring to it of ego, position, or identity—love is more stern than war—and men and women survive only if they reach the depths of their own sex down within themselves. They have to deliver themselves over to the unknown." Mailer believes that "No more existential statement of love exists."[1] Eliseo Vivas also has recognized an important existentialist element in Lawrence. Writing before *Sein und Zeit* and *L'etre et le neant* and therefore "lacking the terminology that existentialism has put at our disposal," Lawrence, Vivas says, "had to put his quarrel in terms of mind against the blood, reason against instinct,"[2] dichotomies that are fundamentally existential. More recently, T. H. Adamowski has examined *Lady Chatterley's Lover* within an existentialist frame, though chiefly with respect to the sexual components of that novel.[3] Otherwise, the slate, mainly, is blank.[4] One, of course, would not expect to find Joyce's fiction construed as existentialist since it is, though hardly naturalistic, nonetheless strongly deterministic. On the other hand, critics often find existentialism to be an appropriate frame of reference for Conrad's fiction. This does not surprise since his situations, and the ways leading into and out of them, are similar to those of the later French writers whom we indeed call *existentialists*. I would like to make the case here for considering Lawrence, in essentials, to be a profoundly existentialist writer. After all, writers whom we often discuss in relation to Lawrence, as influences or as writers offering significant analogues or parallels—I am thinking chiefly of Dostoevsky and Nietzsche—frequently are themselves cited as existentialists or as precursors of existentialism. Why, then, not Lawrence if the label fits and if it helps to illuminate his writing?

Death, dread, nausea, the absurd, nothingness, contingency, possibility, mystery, passion, "existence precedes essence," choice, freedom, commitment, authenticity (and inauthenticity)—these are informing bywords and themes of existentialism. These are terms that, when scooped into the appropriate configurations, characteristically embrace what existentialism is. Many of the words appear frequently and importantly in Lawrence's writings, and they are especially prominent in *Women in Love*, which, as Lawrence's richest and probably best novel—certainly one of the two or three masterpieces—is the work I want to use here to illustrate Lawrence's existentialism.[5] All of the above terms, whether or not Lawrence uses the same phrases, are a part of the dynamics of his fiction and his thought. My aim is to show how our seeing Lawrence's writings in the light of existentialism helps us to see another important dimension to his thought and writings and to recognize further the extent of the artistic *cum* "philosophical" accomplishment. It is a further way, I think, toward seeing Lawrence whole.

Walter Kaufmann, until his death a few years ago perhaps the leading contemporary proponent in America of existentialism, writes, "In the end, Rilke, Kafka, and Camus pose a question, seconded by Dostoevsky and Sartre's plays and fiction: could it be that at least some part of what the existentialists attempt to do is best done in art and not philosophy?"[6] Thinking along the lines of Jaspers and Heidegger, for whom "reason" and analytic thinking are reductive, Kaufmann seems to believe it is. To be sure, there is a certain programatic quality in the fiction and plays of self-conscious "existentialists" (who frequently resisted the label itself) like Camus and Sartre. That is, they are trying, at least in some measure, to illustrate existentialist concepts in their imaginative works. But it does seem appropriate, as Kaufmann suggests, to see existentialism as much as a literary phenomenon as a philosophical one. This, of course, does not state the matter quite accurately since literature, at its best, *is* philosophical. If I am correct, though, in my assertions about Lawrence as an existentialist, then Kaufmann may as well have included an excerpt from *Women in Love* (or *St. Mawr*, say) as Kafka's "Three Parables" in his anthology of existentialist writings, *Existentialism from Dostoevsky to Sartre*. And not because, in isolation, the selection merely has an existentialist component or two but because it represents the book in its entirety as a comprehensive, coherent, and persuasive document of the ethic one knows as existentialism and because, also, it represents its author who, though writing before Jaspers and Heidegger had published their most important works, was writing within an "existentialist" frame or context. It is interesting that Jaspers (1883), Ortega (1883), and Heidegger (1889) were all born within four years of Lawrence. It should not be surprising, then, considering the intellectual currents of the time, that Lawrence, building on Dostoevsky and Nietzsche, should anticipate these writers. What is surprising is the degree of completeness with which he anticipates them together with the fact that the relationship has gone essentially unobserved. It is important to establish here that Lawrence did not read any of the twentieth-century existentialists and that they, apparently, did not (except for Sartre) read him. (This is not an influence study.) Significantly, however, he shares with them a fairly deep acquaintance with Dostoevsky and

Nietzsche. In Dostoevsky he finds the treatment of one of his own
important themes, "reduction through sensation,"[7] one of the central bogeys in *Women in Love*.

   Women in Love begins where existentialism begins: with the positing
of the fact that God does not exist. ("Christian" existentialism is another matter, of course.) Early in *Women in Love* Birkin tells Gerald
"that one needs some one *really* pure activity,"[8] love perhaps, though
he does not love anyone at the moment. "It seems to me there remains only this perfect union with a woman—sort of ultimate
marriage—and there isn't anything else" (58). Gerald says, "And
you mean if there isn't the woman, there's nothing?" Birkin: "Pretty
well that—seeing there's no God" (58).[9] The substance of this conversation and its implications are basic Lawrence and basic existentialism both. Each starts with the proposition that "God" does not
exist and that, consequently, the individual must generate his own
values and meanings. That is, the individual must make choices,
then act for what he chooses. The courses that the two men's lives
take establish and become themselves definitions of "authentic" and
"inauthentic" existence. What Lawrence makes clear is that Birkin
chooses life and that Gerald *chooses* his death. These are not chosen for
them. We are not, for all of Lawrence's sense of mystical identity
with Hardy, in a Hardyan universe. No "Immanent Will" consigns
Gerald's life to "dissolution" or "disintegration" and his death by
snow. Lawrence makes it clear that he could have chosen life
through, in part, a relationship with Birkin. But Gerald lets go the
grasp of the saving hand. It may seem, as has seemed for some, that
Gerald is not in control of his fate (I use the word aware of the contradiction contained in it). But the fact that he is blond and Nordic
and has "the mark of Cain" on him for having killed his brother
does not excuse him from self-responsibility, as Lawrence makes
clear. It is significant that Ursula holds Gerald responsible for the
brother's death; that Gudrun does not: "It seems to me the purest
form of accident," she says. Ursula says, "No. I couldn't pull the trig-
ger of the emptiest gun in the world, not if someone were looking
down the barrel. One instinctively doesn't do it—one can't" (49).
Birkin's reflections earlier seem to convey the heart of the matter:

Gerald as a boy had accidently killed his brother. What then? Why seek to draw a brand and a curse across the life that had caused the accident? A man can live by accident, and die by accident. Or can he not? Is every man's life subject to pure accident, is it only the race, the genus, the species, that has a universal reference? Or is this not true, is there no such thing as pure accident. Has *everything* that happens a universal significance? Has it?

He did not believe that there was any such thing as accident. It all hung together, in the deepest sense. (26)

The word *accident* itself becomes an important metaphor in the novel. There are those lives led by "accident," and there are those that proceed through choice and commitment. The way of the former embraces the "drift toward death," toward nothingness.

Connected with the belief that God does not exist, or is dead, is the sense of the tremendous presence, or looming, of "nothingness." Kierkegaard, in *The Concept of Dread*, gave the later existentialists one of their chief notions. "Nothing . . . begets dread," Kierkegaard wrote, and out of dread comes "freedom's reality as possibility for possibility."[10] ("Freedom," of course, is going to be important in this discussion of Lawrence's existentialism.) Kierkegaard speaks of man as a synthesis of "soul" and "body" with a third factor that he calls, somewhat confusingly, "spirit." Spirit is a friendly power which has precisely the function of constituting the relationship between the first two components. "How is spirit related to itself and to its situation? It is related as dread. The spirit cannot do away with itself, nor can it grasp itself so long as it is outside of itself. Neither can man sink down into the vegetative life, for he is determined as spirit" (*CD*, 1969, 40). Without pursuing this very far, one finds the passage interesting in its gloss of an incident from Lawrence's novel. After Hermione strikes Birkin with the lapis lazuli, he goes off in a state of what we can accurately call "dread" in the broad existentialist sense—a profound despair and nausea at the revealed nothingness of things (this is one of Birkin's darkest moments in the novel)—and immerses himself in the at first soft and then bristly and coarse grass and firs: "Nothing else would do, nothing else would satisfy, except this coolness and subtlety of vegetation travelling into one's blood. How fortunate he was, that there was this lovely, subtle, responsive vegetation" (107). Birkin can find relief in the vegetation, but he cannot be sustained by it. Afterwards, he sinks into an overwhelming body-and-soul sickness. But the way out is through what Lawrence in later writings called "thought adventure," Kierkegaard's "spirit." Kierkegaard's next sentence, which shows his love for paradox, also illuminates Lawrence: "He [the individual] cannot flee from dread, for he loves it; really he does not love it, for he flees from it" (*CD*, 1969, 40). One loves it as one loves-hates the ordeal both terribly difficult and essential that he must undertake. It empowers the individual to act, to seek a way through: Birkin, in other words. He does not love it and flees from it because he refuses to accept, at this time, self-responsibility. The dread and nausea overwhelm him and he goes the way of dissolution, death: the way of Gerald. Kierkegaard goes on to say that God's judgment on Adam and Eve ("Thou surely must die") induces a "notion of the terrible," which becomes "dread": "the infinite possibility of being able, (awakened by the prohibition) draws closer for the fact that this possibility indicates a possibility as its consequence" (*CD*, 1969, 41). That is, "Possibility means I can" (*CD*, 1969, 44). In *Women in Love*, it would seem that we have two pairs of the archetypal Adam and Eve. The "I can" in the face of "possibility"—we will see Lawrence's significant use of this word also—takes on extremely interesting configurations for each of the couples. Kierkegaard writes, "Thus dread is the dizziness of freedom which occurs when the spirit would posit the synthesis, and freedom then gazes down into its own possibility, grasping at finiteness to sustain itself. In this dizziness freedom succumbs" (*CD*, 1969, 55). Because it has to. And then begins again. As Birkin tells Ursula at one point, before he succumbs: love is a "direction that excludes all other directions" (152). One has to lose, or give up, the particular freedom to begin others.

Nothingness looms immense throughout *Women in Love*. I have pointed out a couple of instances of it already. A particularly striking one occurs in the "Moony" chapter when Ursula feels herself "a tiny little rock with the tide of nothingness rising higher and higher" (244). We find another in "Continental": as on the boat they leave behind the "nowhere . . . called England," Ursula seems to feel them, she and Birkin, "fall[ing] away into the profound darkness," and "they seemed to fall like one closed seed of life falling through dark, fathomless space" (388). Existentialists have given us a number of concrete images of the human condition, but I do not believe that any are so graphically apposite, or characteristic, as this one. Nothingness, too, is not just out there: we make it, also, ourselves. Ursula, with Birkin, visiting the symbolically empty house of her parents for the last time, comments: "So *nothing*—their two lives—there's no *meaning* [Lawrence's italics both times, in fact] in it." If Will and Anna had not met, and married, "it wouldn't have mattered, would it?" (373). Ursula's criticism here, of course, is that her parents had failed to make, or create, their lives, had failed in their choices.

Heidegger and Sartre elaborate on what Kierkegaard said about dread and nothingness in ways particularly instructive of matters in *Women in Love* and of Lawrence in general. By the same token, I think that *Women in Love* helps to elucidate some of the statements we encounter in Heidegger and Sartre. For Heidegger, as for Kierkegaard, "dread reveals Nothing."[11] Confronted with this nothingness, the rational faculty by itself is baffled and put off: "Science wishes to know nothing of Nothing" (WM, 1949, 329). But we reach the "what-is" when face to face with nothing. "What-is," or "Da-sein," or "being there," results from our "being projected into Nothing" (WM, 1949, 339). The terms describe the situation of a person with existential awareness, of one who exists within a context. It is only in this state, it is only by being projected into nothing, that what Heidegger (and Sartre) call "transcendence" is reached: "Without the original manifest character of Nothing there is no self-hood and no freedom" (WM, 1948, 339–340).

One can see how this leads to, or reflects, Lawrence. Heidegger writes, "Nothing is the source of negation, not the other way. If this breaks the sovereignty of reason in the field of enquiry into Nothing and Being, then the fate of the rule of 'logic' in philosophy is also decided." And the *coup de grace*: "The very idea of 'logic' disintegrates in the vortex of a more original questioning" (WM, 1949, 342). The "more original questioning" is the sort that a novelist like Lawrence does. I shall discuss later how novel writing—a certain kind of novel writing—is itself a form of existentialist activity, and how the notion of art, including novel writing, is central to the meaning of *Women in Love*. Heidegger's breaking inquiry down into two categories is similar to Lawrence's dichotomies of mind and blood knowledge, though I suspect that Lewis's "third eye" in *St. Mawr*, rather than "blood-consciousness" *per se*, comes closer to what Heidegger means by a "more original questioning." The point is, though, that science, or reason, or intellect, is not enough. Something other, something interior, must be reckoned. If Lawrence had written philosophy as such, this is how he might have sounded (the words are Heidegger's): "Readiness for dread is to say 'Yes!' to *the inwardness of things* [my italics here]" (WM, 1949, 355). And like this: "But Being is not a product of thinking. It is more likely that essential thinking is a product of Being" (WM, 1949, 356). And this: "The animus against 'logic' . . . derives from the knowledge that thinking . . . has its source not in the observation of the objectivity of what-is, but in the experience of the truth of Being." And logic, or "calculative thought," has "no notion that in calculation everything calculable is already a whole before it starts working out its sums and products, a whole whose unity naturally belongs to the incalculable which, with its mystery, ever eludes the clutches of calculation" (WM, 1949, 356–357). The reader of Lawrence feels on familiar ground here. Heidegger had not, as I have indicated, read Lawrence. "What Is Metaphysics" was written in 1929, with a "Postscript," from which the latter quotations were taken, added in 1943, but the vocabulary—"inwardness," "mystery," and, in another passage, "soundless voice of hidden springs" (WM, 1949, 360)—especially with the attack upon logic, sounds very much like Lawrence (by way of Nietzsche perhaps).

The nothingness that one faces is the result of the "thrownness," as Heidegger calls it,[12] a person's sense of abandonment. Sartre writes, "And when we speak of 'abandonment'—a favorite word of Heidegger—we only mean to say that God does not exist, and that it is necessary to draw the consequences of his absence right to the end."[13] It makes the possibility of our deaths all the more terrifying and bewildering and absurd because we mean *nothing* to the universe: "For there is no God and no prevenient design, which can adapt the world and all its possibilities to my will. When Descartes said, 'Conquer yourself rather than the world,' what he meant was, at bottom the same—that we should act without hope" (*EH*, 1948, 39). But Sartre does not see existentialism as being pessimistic. Rather, he says, when people reproach existentialists it is for "the sternness of our optimism" (*EH*, 1948, 42). In the "Water-Party" chapter, toward the end of the discussion between Birkin and Ursula about the processes of dissolution and creation, Birkin says:

> "Dissolution rolls on, just as production does . . . It is a progressive process—and it ends in universal nothing—the end of the world, if you like.
> —But why isn't the end of the world as good as the beginning?"
> "I suppose it isn't," said Ursula, rather angry.
> "Oh yes, ultimately," he said. "It means a new cycle of creation after—but not for us. If it is the end, then we are of the end—fleurs du mal, if you like. If we are fleurs du mal, we are not roses of happiness, and there you are."
> "But I think I am," said Ursula. "I think I am a rose of happiness."
> "Ready-made?" he asked ironically.
> "No—real," she said, hurt.
> "If we are the end, we are not the beginning," he said.
> "Yes we are," she said. "The beginning comes out of the end."
> "After it, not out of it. After us, not out of us."
> "You are a devil, you know, really," she said. "You want to destroy our hope. You *want* us to be deathly."
> "No," he said, "I only want us to *know* what we are."
> "Ha!" she cried in anger. "You only want us to know death."
> "You're quite right," said the soft voice of Gerald, out of the dusk behind. (173)

In the way that it connects up with what Heidegger and Sartre have said, this passage is extremely interesting. Birkin squashes Ursula's too easy and essentially phony statement "I think I am the rose of happiness." His position is essentially that of Nietzsche's *Amor Fati,* which is much what Sartre meant by existentialism's "stern optimism": Birkin accepts the inevitable. Ursula, who is still to be persuaded to embrace at least a portion of Birkin's ethic, then remarks that he wants to destroy "hope"—which, of course, in the Sartrean sense, he does wish to do. The starting point for authenticity is truthfulness: "I only want us to *know* what we are," he tells her. Gerald's reply of "You're quite right" to Ursula's rejoinder that he wants her to know only death has meaning on two levels: it comes "out of the dusk" of Gerald's own inclination toward death. And it means what it literally says. We have to face death—or nothingness—if we are to experience freedom—allow it to be—and achieve the stern optimism possessed by those who live authentically.

Sartre's famous definition of existentialism, adumbrated by Heidegger but not stated in quite the same terms, is that existence comes before essence:

> Atheistic existentialism, of which I am a representative, declares with greater consistency that if God does not exist there is at least one being whose existence comes before its essence, a being which exists before it can be defined by any conception of it. That being is man or, as Heidegger has it, the human reality. What do we mean by saying that existence precedes essence? We mean that man first of all exists, encounters himself, surges up in the world—and defines himself afterwards. If man as the existentialist sees him is not definable, it is because to begin with he is nothing. He will not be anything until later, and then he will be what he makes of himself. Thus, there is no human nature, because there is no God to have a conception of it. Man simply is. Not that he is simply what he conceives himself to be, but he is what he wills, and as he conceives himself after already existing—as he wills to be after that leap towards existence. Man is nothing else but that which he makes of himself. That is the first principle of existentialism. (*EH*, 1948, 27–28)

"Man is nothing but what he makes of himself": this seems to me to be the subtext of the entire novel. It is subtextual because Lawrence never puts it into so many words; nonetheless, it underlies the development of the four principal characters and of Hermione, and in important though inconspicuous ways of the Brangwen and Crich parents (Birkin seems to have no parentage). It also underlies the development of the relationships involving the principal characters.

Consequent upon the proposition that existence precedes essence is the proposition that in making ourselves we are helping to make mankind: "I am thus responsible for myself and for all men, and I am creating a certain image of man as I would have him to be. In fashioning myself I fashion man" (*EH*; 1948, 30). This self-responsibility—and the failure to realize it—is at the center of *Women in Love*. Gerald especially represents the failure since his own fashioning of himself affects the greatest number: "Whilst his father lived Gerald was not responsible for the world. But now his father was passing away, Gerald found himself left exposed and unready before the storm of living, like the mutinous first mate of a ship that has lost his captain, and who sees only a terrible chaos in front of him" (221). Gerald never does fashion a coherent self. The "self" he does fashion is instrumentalist (like Gudrun's), that sees relationships in terms of power. This poses no problems for him with a Minette. But in a relationship with a Gudrun, who is the stronger, he cannot survive. Gudrun understands implicitly "they were of the same kind, he and she, a sort of diabolic free masonry subsisted between them. Henceforward, she knew, she had her power over him" (122). This is in the early "Sketchbook" chapter. In the preceding chapter, "Coal-Dust," she had seemed outraged at his forcing of the free nature of the horse at the railroad crossing. Probably, though, the powerful effect the incident has on her is the result as much of his *having* his power over the horse as it is any injury to the horse. (In "Rabbit" she and Gerald are one in the cruel enmity they have toward Bismarck's free nature, toward "the mystery that is in him"). Afterward her mind is drugged "by the sense of indomitable soft weight of the man, bearing down into the living body of the horse." The scene looks forward to the battle between them for sexual power that is played out against the frozen mountain landscape in the last chapters. For here she cannot rid herself of the image of the "strong, indomitable thighs of the blond man clenching the palpitating body of the mare into pure control" (113). Gerald's reduction, then, of the process of mining to "pure instrumentality" is of a piece with his own essence as he has created it: "they were all subordinate to him," his "instruments" (222–223). He fashions "a new world, a new order," which the men submit to with "exaltation," since it provides them "a sort of freedom" that was "beyond feeling or reason, something really godlike" (231). Gerald's way leads him directly into the existentialist error of making men into things for his use. Sartre said of existentialism that it "alone is compatible with the dignity of man, it is the only [theory] which does not make man into an object" (*EH*, 44–45).

Usually when critics treat this passage the focus is on the disintegration of the "organic" principle and its replacement by that of "mechanical organization." And this is important, to be sure. But if we focus on the phrasing, on Lawrence's choice of words in the passages above, we get a further sense of the powerful existentialist implications of the novel. The sort of "freedom" the men get is, of course, no freedom at all. But they desire it because they do not have to choose any longer (although they have indeed chosen their submission). "Feeling and reason" are the two modes of our understanding: they are now "beyond" both of these, beyond freedom and dignity at it were. Finally, they have a "god" now, with Gerald, the "high priest" who relieves them of their responsibility. But their high priest, like their new deity, is hollow. Gerald has always been governed by a sense of fatality, which Sartre calls "self-deception": "Since we have defined the situation of man as one of free choice, without excuse and without any help, any man who takes refuge behind the excuse of his passions, or by inventing some deterministic doctrine, is a self-deceiver" (*EH*, 1948, 51). Birkin contemns the "strange sense of fatality in Gerald, as if he were limited to one form of existence, one knowledge, one activity, a sort of fatal halfness, which seemed to him wholeness" (207). Similarly, the murderer-murderee concept reaches its full development when Gerald, at the end, feels he is going to be "murdered," that "he was bound to be murdered" (473). Not so at all: he makes, or "fashions," his own death. He might have fashioned otherwise. To believe differently is to negate the meaning of the final chapter when Birkin, beside Gerald's corpse, reflects how it could have been different. In establishing Gudrun's inauthenticity at the end, *her* failure to choose, Lawrence uses other terms that are remarkable for their existentialist flavor and import. Gudrun prefers not-acting, leaving her future indecisive: "Her tomorrow was perfectly vague before her. This was what gave her pleasure" (467–468). Unlike Birkin and Ursula, who know that one must give up some courses if one is to take others, Gudrun desires "all possibility." It is this that has "charm" for her: "All possibility—because death was inevitable, and *nothing* was possible but death" (468). Thus "she did not want things to materialize, to take any definite shape" but always "to be wafted into an utterly new course" (468). Sartre quotes Dostoevsky's "If God did not exist, everything would be permitted" as "the starting point" for existentialism. "That is what I mean when I say that man is condemned to be free and from the moment he is thrown into the world he is responsible for everything that he does" (*EH*, 1948, 34). Gudrun, though, does not want to fashion a reality. Sartre says, "We define man only in relation to his commitments" (*EH*, 1948, 50). Gudrun refuses commitments. She therefore never really "rises above the dreariness of actuality, the monotony of contingencies" (p. 460), as Lawrence effectively puts it. Consequently, though she will manifest all this in her Gudrun-way, she will become like her father, "not a coherent human being" but "a roomful of old echoes" (257). Such, then, though never "fated," are the fatal consequences of "self-deception" and the avoidance of choice, or commitment.

Sartre's statement that our actions, right or wrong, become examples for all mankind, that in fashioning ourselves we fashion men, applies directly to Birkin's belief that the world needs someone who will "give new values to things," a "new attitude to life" (54). If Gerald and Gudrun represent the main negative pole of the novel, fashioning men and women negatively, then Birkin and Ursula represent, correspondingly, the positive pole, the existentially authentic ones. In Birkin resides the necessary urge toward freedom. In a conversation early on at Shortlands about knowledge, Hermione gushes that the "greatest thing in life" is "*to know*," which allows one "to be *free*" (86). Sir Joshua Malleson agrees with her, and it is left to Birkin to refine the theory, to put it into a significant, because precise, context. "You can only have knowledge, strictly," he says, "in the past" (86). What this means, when looked at closely, is that the present and future are open. Existence precedes, and makes, essence.

Essence is not *to be* there, necessarily—that is, any given essence. The past stops with the past. Ursula, much later, after she and Birkin are married, feels that she has "just come into life": and asks, "What had she to do with parents and antecedents?" She realizes, existentially, that she "had no father, no mother" (409) in the sense that, in making herself, she had to parent herself. As Birkin at one point says, "One must throw everything away, everything—let everything go, to get the one last thing one wants" (132). Many of the terms of the novel, then, establish themselves in what in retrospect we would call a definite "existentialist" context. Here is Ursula, late in the novel, thinking about the *distance* between her past and now: "My God, how far was she projected from her childhood" at Cossethay, "and how far she was still to go!" As she travels "into the unknown with Birkin, an utter stranger," she seems to have "no identity," it seems "that the child she had been, playing in Cossethay churchyard, was a little creature of history, not really herself" (390). Though it is true that we are the sum of our actions, the consequence of our history, it is also true that our history is not us in that we are free to make, to remake, ourselves at any moment. Our history is not our essence. Obviously, if it were, our free will would be purely nominal. When at the end of this chapter ("Continental") the two couples are talking about the deathliness of England and the nature of "Englishness," Gerald, trying to phrase Birkin's ideas, says: "I think Rupert means . . . that *nationally* all Englishmen must die, so that they can exist individually" (397). The purport of this is perfectly existentialist: if individuals are to be, they must be free of any national essence.

What defeats Hermione, and what almost defeats Ursula, is that Birkin resists the essence they would confer upon him. At Shortlands, watching him dance, the Contessa sees him "as a changer," and Hermione, shuddering at this observation, "hates" him because of "his power to escape, to exist, other than she did, because he was not consistent" (92). Lawrence has built in a fine contrapuntal scene late in the novel when Birkin, with Ursula at the hostelry, dances with her "licentiously," "frightening" her. But now she has accepted Birkin's ethic, and can accept the dangers his existentially free being pose. Later, in their room, she asks him why he is "like this." But he only looks at her, first with "satiric contempt," then with "remorseless suggestivity." She sees then that "he might do as he would. His licentiousness was repulsively attractive. But he was self-responsible, she would see what it was" (412–413). They are, of course, *both* self-responsible, and can explore for themselves the "degrading": "Who cared? Degrading things were real, with a different reality." She asks herself, much as Connie Chatterley will, "Why not be bestial, and go the whole round of experience? . . . Why not?—She was free" (413). The vital difference between *her* freedom and the freedom that Gudrun only imagines is hers, is that Ursula's respects the dignity and freedom of others; Gudrun's is founded on the instrumentality, the object-ness, of others.

It is not difficult to see how the novel's central and unifying thematic image—that of "star-equilibrium"—embraces this most integral existentialist notion. At the end of "Excurse," which is the pivotal chapter in Ursula's development, Ursula comes to feel that "she was to him what he was to her, the immemorial magnificence of mystic, palpable, real otherness" (320). Until now she had resisted the "mutual unison in separateness" (264). Birkin, in "Moony," remembering the West African figure with its beetle sensibilities gone "far beyond phallic knowledge," the sun-destructive counterpart to the Northern, frost-destructive process of dissolution embodied in Gerald (and Gudrun as well), thinks of "the other way, the remaining way" that he must follow, "the way of freedom": for

> "There was the paradisal entry into pure, single being, the individual soul taking precedence over love and desire for union . . . a lovely state of free proud singleness, which accepts the obligation of the permanent connection with others." (254)

Here is the novel's crucial opposition: the first way lacks freedom and dignity, the second sponsors and enables these. The qualifier that Lawrence adds, the acceptance of the "obligation of the permanent connection with others," is also crucial. Gerald and Gudrun's way is selfish in its instrumentality. If existentialism is a humanism, as Sartre says, then the ethic of Gerald and Gudrun is an inhumanism.

It seems to me that of the great existentialist thinkers, Jaspers is the one that Lawrence is closest to. Like Heidegger, as we have seen, Jaspers was a contemporary of Lawrence, experienced most of the same intellectual and cultural phenomena, was strongly influenced by Nietzsche. And although his ideas really do not differ essentially from those of Heidegger or, later, Sartre, his expression of them (perhaps because of the influence of Nietzsche), seems at times "Lawrencian." What Lawrence called "thought adventure," for instance, in *Kangaroo* and elsewhere, sounds like Jaspers, who is speaking here: "The history of philosophy is not, like the history of the sciences, to be studied with the intellect alone. That which is receptive in us and that which impinges upon us from history is the reality of man's being, unfolding itself in thought."[14] "Thought," then, is not just "intellect," but the whole of man's responses to the world outside him. In "Books," published posthumously, Lawrence puts it this way: "Man is a thought-adventurer. But by thought we mean, of course, discovery. We don't mean this telling himself stale facts and drawing false deductions, which usually passes as thought. Thought is an adventure, not a trick."[15] It is "an adventure of the whole man, not merely of his wits." This "whole man" includes the blood which "also thinks . . . It thinks in desires and revulsions, and it makes strange conclusions," "strange" because they are not necessarily in accord with "head" and "spirit," which have "led [man] wrong."[16] Again, what Jaspers calls "Transcendence" (along with Heidegger and Sartre) and the "Encompassing" resonates with Lawrence's "thought adventure":

Does not the sum of all objects form the totality of Being? No. As the horizon encompasses all things in a landscape, so all objects are encompassed by that in which they are. As we move towards the horizon in the world of space without ever reaching it, because the horizon moves with us and reestablishes itself ever anew as the Encompassing at each moment, so objective research moves towards totalities at each moment which never become total and real Being, but must be passed through towards new vistas. Only if all horizons met in one closed whole, so that they formed a finite multiplicity, could we attain, by moving through all the horizons, the one closed Being. Being, however, is not closed for us and the horizons are not finite. On all sides we are impelled towards the infinite. (OMP, 1975, 176)

Birkin's wanting what is "beyond the influence of love" (145), the desire to stay "unfinished" like a Rodin sculpture, "so that you are never contained, never confined, never dominated from the outside" (356–57), is part of his effort to keep free of what Jaspers calls "determinate Being" (OMP, 1975, 176). How like Lawrence's "star-equilibrium" this notion in the central passage from Jaspers sounds: "The thesis of my philosophizing is: The individual cannot become human by himself. Self-being is only real in communication with another self-being. Alone, I sink into gloomy isolation—only in community with others can I be revealed in the act of mutual discovery. *My own freedom can only exist if the other is also free* [my italics]. Isolated or self-isolated Being remains mere potentiality or disappears into nothingness" (OMP 1975, 174). Birkin and Ursula in the first part of this quotation; Gerald and Gudrun in last sentence.

The opposition between Jaspers' "Reason"[17] and "Existenz" looks much like the vital oppositions (mind vs. blood knowledge, lion vs. unicorn) in Lawrence:

> Reason without Existenz even in the richest possible field finally passes into an indifferent thinking, a merely intellectual movement of consciousness as such, or into a dialectic of the spirit. And as it slips away into intellectual universality without the binding root of its historicity, it ceases to be reason.
>
> Irrational Existenz which rests upon feeling, experiencing, unquestioned impulse, instinct, or whim, ends up as blind violence, and therewith falls under the empirical laws which govern these actual forces. Without historicity, lost in the mere particularities of contingent empirical existence in a self-assertion unrelated to Transcendence, it ceases to be Existenz.
>
> Each without the other loses the genuine continuity of Being and, therefore, the reliability which, although it can not be calculated, is nevertheless appropriate to genuine reason and Existenz. They separate themselves from one another only to become violent powers lacking any communication. In isolation they no longer mean what they should; only formulas without either basis or purpose remain, in a narrowing sphere or empirical existence.[18]

The one needs the other as the blood needs the intellect to complete the whole man and as the lion needs the unicorn and vice-
versa: The unicorn might think of the lion, "If he ceased to exist, I
should be supreme and unique and perfect. Therefore I will destroy
him." The lion, however, must not and "will not be destroyed. If he
were, if he were swallowed into the belly of the unicorn, the unicorn would fly asunder into chaos."[19] As Jaspers put it, "Each without the other loses the genuine continuity of Being." The recognition is a fundamentally existentialist one.

Finally, this again about Transcendence, to move us back to
Women in Love: Jaspers writes, "Understanding the meaning of the
Encompassing has the significance of creating a possibility. The
philosopher therein says to himself: preserve the open space of the
Encompassing! Do not lose yourself in what is merely known! Do
not let yourself become separated from Transcendence!"[20] Thus
Birkin and Ursula going round to the bow of the ship as they depart
for the Continent: " 'Let us go forward, shall we?' said Birkin. He
wanted to be at the tip of their projection. So they left off looking at
the faint sparks that glimmered out of nowhere, in the far distance,
called England, and turned their faces to the unfathomed night in
front" (387). In great novels, the most ordinary sentences and images, it seems, exert an irresistible tendency to take on symbolic
overtones. In one sense, this passage contains so much of the shared
existence of Ursula and Birkin; and it is the seed of "The Nightmare"
chapter in *Kangaroo*, even before the event that was to be written *was*
written. I am speaking of the coherence of both the novel and the
novels, as *Women in Love* as a chapter in the greater novel: Lawrence's
works in their entirety. This leads to a consideration of one last coherence, this one involving *Women in Love* as a novel about the writing
of novels, the creation of "art."

For all existentialists, and for Jaspers in particular, "philosophy is
practice" (OMP, 1979, 161). That is, it is life lived. The creations of the
existentialist writer are the practicing of his or her life as an artist and
existentialist and will have authenticity or not according to how well
or indifferently, honestly or dishonestly, the task is practiced. Early in
Women in Love Birkin thinks of his life as being without "organic mean-

ing" (53). In the course of the novel the lives of Birkin and Ursula come to achieve organic meaning; the lives of the others do not.[21] Driving with Ursula in "Excurse," just before he gives her the rings, Birkin experiences one of his lowest mental and emotional moments in the entire novel. He thinks, "Why bother? Why strive for a coherent, satisfied life? Why not drift on in a series of accidents—like a picaresque novel? Why not? Why bother about human relationships? . . . Why form any serious connections at all? Why not be casual, drifting along, taking all for it was worth?" The outlook is similar to the one that Gudrun comes to rest in. "And yet, still, he was damned and doomed to the old effort at serious living" (302). He is speaking of what existentialists call commitment or involvement—connection with others, human relationships (though Lawrence himself would resist becoming "*engagé*" in a social "cause").

The remark about life as a picaresque novel is significant beyond its service as simile for a way of living, for living by drift and accident, rather than by purpose and decision. It is no accident that artists together with the practice of their art are important throughout *Women in Love*. Early in the novel Gerald asks Birkin if Gudrun one day will be a "well-known artist." Birkin doubts it: "She drops her art if anything else catches her. Her contrariness prevents her taking it seriously—she must never be too serious, she feels she gives herself away. And she won't give herself away— she's always on the defensive. That's what I can't stand about her type" (94–95). One notices the presence of the word "seriously." In these passages certain key words tend to recur, like touchstones: "drift," "accident," "coherence," "serious." Lawrence has not been afraid to give himself away in the novel, as Birkin is not in his letter writing ("Gudrun in the Pompadour" chapter). In the Foreword, Lawrence tells his readers that the book is "a record of the writer's own desire, aspirations, struggles: in a word, a record of the profoundest experiences of the self. Nothing that comes from the deep, passional soul is bad, or can be bad" (485). The picaresque novel, of course, lacking linear development, lacks a certain kind of coherence. It tends to be neither serious nor profound. It is "a series of accidents" that, in the end, have led nowhere. In these respects it is the mirror of the lives that Gudrun and Gerald—and another artist, the German "industrial" artist, Loerke—have written for themselves.

Gudrun believes Loerke to be "a fellow craftsman, a fellow being" (458) to her. He tells Gudrun that "art should *interpret* industry, as art once interpreted religion" (424). But industry, of course, as presented in the novel, has no coherence; religion, in its larger, deeper sense, is about coherence. In effect, Lawrence is saying, art has gone wrong, which is one of the reasons this is a time of "crisis," as he puts it in the Foreword. Loerke is unconnected to everything: "he cared about nothing, he was troubled about nothing, he made not the slightest attempt to be at one with anything. He existed a pure, unconnected will" (427). He is the purest instance and culmination of that process of "disintegration" that Lawrence has been at pains earlier to describe so thoroughly. Gudrun, naturally enough, feels a "certain violent sympathy" for this "mud-child" of "the underworld of life," who swims, as Birkin says "like a rat in the river of corruption" (427–28). His is the most extravagant and grotesque form that the circumstance of not living in organic relation to anything takes in the novel. In response to Ursula's criticism of the horse in the photo of his nymphet-Godiva sculpture, Loerke tells her "derisively" that it is "a work of art" and as such "has nothing to do with anything but itself, it has no relation with the everyday world of this and the other, there is no connection between them, absolutely none." And then he tells her with great emphasis: "Do you see, you *must not* confuse the relative world of action, with the absolute world of art. That you *must not do*" (430–431). In existentialist terms, in separating life and humanity from art, in making himself, as Jaspers said, "the immediate object of his efforts," he finds himself "on his last and perilous path"; for "he will lose the Being of the other and then no longer find anything in himself" (OMP, 1979, 168). Except that he has already, in fact, well-nigh completed himself, this could hardly be bettered as a description of Loerke.

In reading the novel in existentialist terms, I find that the characters of Birkin and Ursula, especially Birkin, take on measurably greater dimensions than those significant ones they already have. As each of them struggles, frequently blundering, toward a coherent, organic meaning, toward authentic being, they both assume, partly in being so alone in the novel in their determination and persistence, an even more distinctly heroic quality. Gerald at the end, in a finely integrative and epitomizing passage, after nearly killing Gudrun, "drifted, as on a wind, veered, and went drifting away . . . drifted up the slope" away from "any further contact" (472). But Birkin and Ursula resist "drift," they resist living as though life were a picaresque novel. Life is an art, and must be lived organically, which is to say coherently, just as art organically must come from life and be about life. And the practice of it can be "terrible" since one is free to write his life or to live his art (if he or she is an artist), as though in fact it *were* a picaresque novel. Ortega writes, "At every moment of my life there open before me diverse possibilities: I can do this or that. If I do this, I shall be A the moment after; if I do that, I shall be B." Then, in a statement that encapsulates an important meaning in *Women in Love*, Ortega says that "It is too often forgotten that man is impossible without imagination, without the capacity to invent for himself a conception of life, to 'ideate' the character he is going to be. Whether he be original or a plagiarist, man is the novelist of himself."[22] Like Birkin, that is, man must create "organic meaning" for himself, avoid drift and the accidental life, must fashion his life.

At the very beginning of the novel, Ursula feels that although "her active living was suspended . . . underneath, in the darkness, something was coming to pass." She must "break through the last integuments. She seemed to try to put her hands out, like an infant in the womb, and she could not, not yet. Still she had a strange prescience, an intimation of something yet to come" (9): that something is "That Individual," to borrow the famous chapter title from Kierkegaard's *Concluding Unscientific Postscript*. The novel is about those, then, who do, or do not, in the language of Jaspers, Heidegger, and Sartre, achieve "transcendence" or "self-surpassing." In Lawrence's fiction, only a few make, out of their "dread," authentic lives for themselves: choose freedom. Of "people," Birkin says, "Essentially, they don't exist" (25). *Women in Love*, essentially, is an existentialist novel.

Notes

1. Norman Mailer, *The Prisoner of Sex* (Boston: Little Brown, 1971), 147–48.

2. Eliseo Vivas, *D. H. Lawrence: The Failure and the Triumph of Art* (Bloomington: University of Indiana Press, 1960), 109.

3. T. H. Adamowski, "The Natural Flowering of Life: The Ego, Sex, and Existentialism," in *D. H. Lawrence's "Lady,"* ed. Michael Squires and Dennis Jackson (Athens: University of Georgia Press, 1985), 36–57.

4. The only general study that I know of is S. D. Sharma's "D. H. Lawrence's Existential Vision," in *Essays on D. H. Lawrence*, ed. T. R. Sharma (Meerut: Shalabh Book House, 1987), 153–161. Fewer than eight pages of text, it devotes no more than a sentence or two to Lawrence novels other than *Lady Chatterley's Lover*, to which it gives about a page and a half, Daniel J. Schneider, in *D. H. Lawrence: The Artist as Psychologist* (Lawrence: University of Kansas Press, 1987), speaks briefly of Lawrence's theories of psychology in existentialist terms. The slate, it seems, mostly is blank.

5. One might well select several other works as primary instances of Lawrence's existentialism. Earlier, "The Prussian Officer" comes to mind and, later, *St. Mawr* and *The Escaped Cock*. But in its intellectual density and complexity and general richness of theme, *Women in Love*, of all Lawrence's works, should be the one by which one is able, or not, to make the claim I am making here.

6. Walter Kaufmann, *Existentialism from Dostoevsky to Sartre* (New York: New American Library, 1975), 49.

7. D. H. Lawrence, "The Crown," in *Death of a Porcupine and Other Essays*, ed. Michael Herbert (Cambridge: Cambridge University Press, 1988), 195–200.

8. D. H. Lawrence, *Women in Love*, ed. David Farmer, Lindeth Vasey, John Worthen, Cambridge: Cambridge University Press, 1988), 57. Subsequent page references will be to this edition.

9. In later works, Lawrence would speak of the "dark gods," of the "Holy Ghost," etc. I do not believe, however, that there is any contradiction (though to be sure there is development). Nietzsche, himself, in the poem "To an Unknown God," addressed a similar "Being." Both were technically atheists, though one resists the use of the term with Lawrence.

10. Soren Kierkegaard, *The Concept of Dread*, trans. Walter Lowrie (Princeton: Princeton University Press, 1968), 38. Cited hereafter as *CD*. The syntax here seems strange, to be sure. Lowrie writes, in a note, "From the context, what one expects is 'possibility for freedom,' and the Danish editors do not hesitate to say that this is what is meant" (*CD* 1968, 149).

11. Martin Heidegger, "What Is Metaphysics?" trans. R.F.C. Hull and Alan Crick, in *Existence and Being* (Chicago: Henry Regnery Co., 1949), 336; hereafter cited at WM.

12. Martin Heidegger, *Being and Time*, trans, John Macquarrie and Edward Robinson (New York and Evanston: Harper and Row, 1962). See especially pp. 174–79, where the term is introduced. It is everywhere thereafter.

13. Jean-Paul Sartre, *Existentialism and Humanism*, trans. Philip Mairet (London: Methuen & Co., 1948), 32–33; hereafter cited as *EH*.

14. Karl Jaspers. "On My Philosophy," trans. Felix Kaufmann, in *Existentialism from Dostoevsky to Sartre*, ed. Walter Kaufmann (New York: New American Library, 1975), 161; hereafter cited as OMP.

15. D. H. Lawrence, "Books," in *Death of a Porcupine and Other Essays*, 198.

16. D. H. Lawrence, "Books," 198.

17. One should note that "Reason" is not synonymous with Lawrence's "mind knowledge." Reason's function actually is to "seek a relation with everything, denying communication with nothing" and is "to be distinguished radically from *intellect*" (177). Nonetheless, in its paired relationship with *Existenz*, I think I am safe in making the comparison.

18. Karl Jaspers, *Reason and Existenz*, trans. Wiliam Earle (New York: Noonday Press, 1955), 68.

19. Lawrence, "The Crown," 255.

20. Jaspers, *Reason and Existenz*, 61–62.

21. The life of Gerald's father achieves a sort of organic meaning in relation to the mine operations. Mr. Crich seems to have been committed to the welfare of the workers and to an ideal of responsible and caring mine ownership. Lawrence writes of the transition from Mr. Crich to Gerald: "The whole unifying idea of mankind seemed to be dying with his father, the centralising force that held the whole together seemed to collapse with his father, the parts were ready to go asunder in terrible disintegration" (221). The process, then, is one from integration to disintegration, from coherence to incoherence, from humane purpose to either mechanistic organization or "drift." To be sure, Mr. Crich's marriage lacked organic meaning.

22. Jose Ortega y Gasset, *History as a System and Other Essays Toward a Philosophy of History*, trans. Helene Weyl (New York: W. W. Norton, 1961), 201–203.

Ars Erotica or Scientia Sexualis?

Narrative Vicissitudes in D. H. Lawrence's Women in Love

GERALD DOHERTY

◆　　◆　　◆

IN *THE HISTORY OF SEXUALITY* (VOLUME ONE),
Michel Foucault remarks that, historically, there have been two
great procedures for producing the truth about sex. Some societies,
mainly Eastern ones—Indian, Japanese, Chinese (Rome being Foucault's sole Western candidate)[1]—have generated an *Ars Erotica*
where truth is drawn from pleasure itself, i.e., from its subtleties, in-
tensities, progressive duration, liberating effects, and its access to
other planes of existence. Essentially esoteric, its knowledge is held
in the greatest reserve, passed on by a master who, through initia-
tory rituals, guides the acolyte along the erotic path to enlightenment. For the latter, the result is transfiguration—in Foucault's elo-
quent phrases—"an absolute mastery of the body, a singular bliss,
oblivious of time and limits, the exile of death and its threats" (*History*, 1981, 57–58).[2]

What Foucault does not remark on, however, is that the *Ars Erotica* theory of pleasure (in contradistinction to Western theories of
desire) is profoundly resistant to articulation in narrative form. In
positing states of consciousness induced by intense pleasure but be-

yond the linguistic articulations that engender desire, *Ars Erotica* practice elides the basic structures of narratability.[3] (Traditionally it has found its natural embodiment in the treatise—largely expository works that offer specific instructions, explain occult symbolism, and provide philosophical explanations of the transcendent modalities it holds out to the acolyte.[4]) If, as Paul Ricoeur maintains, narrative "attains its full meaning when it becomes a condition of temporal existence" (1984, 52), then in its destruction of temporal limits and its eradication of desire *Ars Erotica* locates itself beyond the scope of emplotment, of incorporation into narrative succession and sequence, whose modalities feed off those very desires that *Ars Erotica* seeks to abolish. As such, it confirms D. A. Miller's general observation that "narrative appropriately ceases where mysticism begins, for there is nothing more for a narrative to produce . . . except the same 'rapturous consciousness' " (1989, 131).

Because it seems so inhospitable to novelistic appropriation, the English novel, not surprisingly, has left *Ars Erotica* severely alone, steering away from its concept of pleasure, and from its mystical resolutions, achieved through the art of initiation, to erotic conflicts. Only one major work in the English tradition—*Women in Love*—takes a contrasting course, co-opting *Ars Erotica* as the vehicle for its states of "rapturous consciousness," and as the source of its ultimate values from which perspective other values are critiqued and opposed. Part II of the present essay explores the problems for narrative that such an unlikely and, narratologically speaking, perverse adoption of an alien and unassimilable modality entails.

By contrast, Foucault's second "great procedure"—*Scientia Sexualis* (or sexology, as I shall call it, for convenience[5])—is profoundly complicit with storytelling, embracing a theory of desire based on an insatiable hunger and striving that binds it indissolubly to narrative forms.[6] Associated historically by Foucault with the vast nineteenth-century proliferation of discourses about sex—psychological, psychiatric, pedagogic—sexology turns on the art of making sex speak, of transforming its affects into stories, and thus constituting the subject through those sexual discourses that go to make up his or her identity. As such, sexology feeds into the novelistic, supplying it with plots (in the form of case-histories), configurations, and themes, as well as with a pathology of sexual aberrations—symptoms and perversions—against which sexual norms are established. In the broadest sense, both sexology and novelistic narration are interpretative disciplines that submit human desire to the rigours of hermeneutic interrogation.

Among novelists in the English tradition, Lawrence is especially attuned to sexological pressures. Located at the historical moment when the novelistic and the sexological converge, he was, as Stephen Heath puts it, supremely aware of "current thinking in sexology and sexual psychology and psychoanalysis" (1982, 102). Indeed, such prose treatises as *The Crown* (1915), *Fantasia of the Unconscious* (1922) and *Psychoanalysis and the Unconscious* (1921) wage an open polemic against sexological thinking, in its drive to scientize eros, and to reduce the unconscious to a discursive phenomenon.

What Lawrence aggressively disputes at the ideological level, however, he urgently commits himself to at the narratological one. Put differently, he co-opts some of sexology's major conceptions and strategies precisely because they provide the motor force of good plots and the very motive of narrative. Two such strategies are of special significance for *Women in Love*, and are the pivots of the present essay's concerns. First, the pathologization of the sexual psyche in terms of symptoms, perversions, dysfunctions, generating complex plots to explain and interpret them; second, the cultivation of the confessional mode (*the* sexological strategy, as defined by Foucault) to uncover the disquieting truths underlying these pathological states.

To take the latter point first: Foucault identifies confession as the Western strategy for eliciting the truth about sex, exposing not only what the subject wishes to hide, but also what is hidden from him or her. Indeed, Occidental literature is essentially a confessional genre, "ordered according to the infinite task of extracting from the depths of oneself . . . a truth which the very form of confession holds out like a shimmering mirage" (*History* 59).[7] It institutes analytical introspection as *the* form of constructed experience, and interrogation as its basic strategy for establishing sex as the hidden clue to identity. In so doing, it casts the novelistic narrator in the role of silent interlocutor who *hears* his characters' life-histories as confessions made to themselves or to one another or to him. Such strategies allow for a wide spectrum of narratorial postures toward the extraction of intimate secrets, ranging from the tactful/benign (George Eliot), through the tentative/empathic (Forster and Woolf) and the self-consciously detached (Joyce) on to the (frequently) ruthless, aggressive and alienating narrator of *Women in Love*. There Lawrence exploits sexological techniques of investigation to expose states of desire he deplores.

Through its recodification of confession as therapeutic, sexology brings sexuality under the rule of the normal and pathological (Foucault, *History*, 1981, 67). In so doing, it generates a nosography of desire and its satisfactions, establishing norms against which aberrations may be classified and defined.[8] Such recognitions in turn produce complex narrative structures—interpretative systems or codes—to decipher symptoms, diagnose perversions, and unearth causes and consequences in a systematic and coherent way (Roy Schafer, for example, has explored the narrative structures that subtend the interpretative discipline of psychoanalysis ["Narration," 25–49]). At this level, the feedback into the novelistic is complicated and subtle. Sexology lends to the novelistic a hierarchy of pathological states that locate the roots of (character) dysfunction in sexual disease and disorder. Like the sexological interlocutor, the narrator probes and exposes signs of malaise through coherent narratives of explanation that account for their causes. He tells stories of libidinal displacements—dislocations of erotic object and aim that issue in pathological forms of behaviour.

In its narratives of sexuality, *Women in Love* draws richly on the sexological, installing confession—self-revelation—as one of the primary modes for unearthing sexual secrets, while cultivating a pathology of sexual desire—sickness narratives that posit erotic dysfunction as the ultimate truth of identity. Through the characters Gerald and Gudrun, Hermione and Loerke, it produces a compendium of nineteenth-century pathologies of the sexual instinct—sadism, masochism, fetishism, inversion—theorizing desire as a lack, a functional disorientation that requires substitute objects and actions to gratify it.[9] Complicit with the ethos it loathes, *Women in Love* generates potent narratives of erotic "degeneration," stories of terminal decadence that feed off the very illnesses that keep them alive.

The teleology of sexological narratives is geared to the cure of pathological disorders: in redirecting the libido to more suitable objects and goals, it produces modified narrative accounts of the desire that engendered the illness. The cure, as it were, is a function of the ideology that originally reproduced the disease, foregrounding introspection, rational control and adjustment as its means to that end. In *its* cure, by contrast, *Women in Love* departs maximally from the sexological ethos from whose perspectives it diagnosed the disease. It purports no less than to shatter sexological constraints— the bondage of eros to time and to narrative sequence that it perceives as *the* symptoms of the disease sexology sets out to cure. In so doing, *Women in Love* reinscribes the two great Foucauldian procedures for eliciting the truth about sex, opposing a sexological theory of desire, based on an insatiable hunger and striving, to an *Ars Erotica* theory of pleasure, based on transcendent attainment. Focused entirely on Birkin and Ursula, and confined to one pivotal episode aptly named "Excurse," this *Ars Erotica* offers the protagonists access to a new plane of existence where states of transcendent pleasure supervene on those of sexological desire. In effect, *Women in Love* juxtaposes a subtle art of erotic initiation, a silent, essentially non-discursive practice opposed to introspection and narrative representation to a practice of sex that takes verbal confession as the sign of its truth, and that meshes desire indissolubly in narrative forms. The consequences for narrative are momentous: the *Ars Erotica* plot is contained within the diagetic space of one single episode, while the sexological plot expands to usurp the greater part of the text. It is to the agencies that collude in the takeover that we now turn our attention.

1. Sexological Narratives

What Foucault sees as the Western attempt to "annex sex to a field of rationality" and to subordinate the body to "a logic of concupiscence and desire" (*History* 78) has its analogue in Lawrence's critique of mentalized sex. Both Foucault and Lawrence expose the coercion involved in the compulsive need to rationalize, scientize, and narrativize sexuality—to assimilate eros to scientific and cultural norms in order to make sex speak the truth. In *The Crown*, for example, Lawrence links the post-Cartesian drive toward "conscious knowledge"—"scientific and introspective"—to the disintegration of the sexual instinct, i.e., its subordination to the chronologies and teleologies of representational form (1988, 281–284). Likewise, Lawrence's critique of Freud in *Psychoanalysis and the Unconscious* is based primarily on his sense that Freud identified the unconscious with the repressed contents of consciousness (1971, 204). Lifting repressions—exposing complexes to "full mental consciousness," as Lawrence puts it (1971, 200)—is thus a technique for verbalizing the unconscious, for transmuting sex into scientific "case-histories," subject to the same structural constraints and determinants as verbal narratives are.[10] Lawrence thus shares Foucault's characterization of Freud as the confessional master *par excellence*, the one who gave "a new impetus to the secular injunction to study sex and transform it into discourse" (*History*, 1981, 159),[11] reinforcing the repressions it purports to cure.

For Lawrence, by contrast, the unconscious escapes all determinisms—linguistic, scientific or cultural: "unanalysable, undefinable, inconceivable," it "bubbles up in us, prior to any mentality" (*Psychoanalysis*, 1971, 211, 212). Aligned to a theory of pleasure based on self-transcendence, similar to that which subtends the Foucauldian *Ars Erotica*, the unconscious is untamed by language, configurations, or symbols.[12] Bound to bodies and pleasures, it is mediated (in Foucault's words) through the "masterful art" that transfigures the "one fortunate enough to receive its privileges" (*History*, 1881, 58). As such it can never function as the domain of the narrative secret—the Barthesian, enigma founded on a predicative lack that demands resolution (*S/Z*, 1988, 107–108, 187–188)—precisely because it can never be finally known. It resists the subordination of eros to the epistemological enterprise, to a form of "knowledge-power strictly opposed to the art of (erotic) initiations" (*History*, 1981, 58).

In his cultivation of sexological narratives, the narrator of *Women in Love* exploits both the narrative secret of sex, and the knowledge-power strategies used to extract it. In relation to Gerald/Gudrun and Hermione/Loerke (*his* sexological pairs), he turns his knowledge of them into forms of absolute knowing, subjecting them to ruthless inquisitorial probings, extracting the secrets of their sexual psyches of which they themselves remain unaware. Through acute diagnostic analyses, intricate anatomizations of cause, ever more penetrating forays that link sexuality to a fundamental disease of consciousness, he transforms their erotic malaise into narratives of a personal decadence that ramify and divaricate with each successive recounting. Their dislocations of desire provoke his desire to unearth sexual etiologies to explain them. The first major exercise of such narratorial tactics, employed against Hermione at the start of the novel, is exemplary: it crystallizes the techniques that subsequent interventions will merely refine and make more exacting.

As Hermione walks to the church in the opening episode ("Sisters") to attend the wedding of Thomas Crich's daughter, the narrator, as silent interlocutor, uncovers the secrets of her sexual psyche through progressive exposures, positing ever more recessive levels of consciousness to dramatize their disclosure. The passage opens innocuously with the ascription to Hermione of a full conscious knowledge, the adequation of her social poise to the unrelenting gaze of the other (she knew that "her appearance was complete and perfect, according to the first standards"), before it unearths a deeper, subconscious condition, *its* secret poised uncertainly between Hermione's and the narrator's possession ("She always felt vulnerable . . . [there was] always a secret chink in her armour"). As if to resolve the ambiguity, and through an authoritative causal attribution, the narrator reveals the buried truth as *the* truth about sexuality of which Hermione is unconscious ("She did not know herself what it was . . . [there was] a deficiency of being in her . . . She craved for Rupert Birkin"). Diagnosed as a lack, a chronic libidinal hunger, sex constitutes the ultimate secret of selfhood, a challenge to truth-telling that the narrator's harsh interventions alone can resolve. It opens the possibility of ceaseless narrative reformulations, nuanced recountings of Hermione's histrionic behaviour which climaxes in a sadistic and near-lethal discharge—her attempted murder of Birkin. In a classic sexological procedure, etiology (the science of the cause of disease—Hermione's "craving" for Birkin) gives way to symptomatology, as the narrative cruelly transcribes some of the standard external tokens of female hysteria. Converting Hermione's inner paroxysms into somatic affects, it records with a keen sexological eye the uncontrollable "delirium" and the "convulsion[s]" that give her the look of a "demoniacal ecstatic" (17–22).[13] In representing Hermione as at once erotically charged but basically frigid, the narrator taints the language of traditional mysticism ("rapt," "ecstatic") with pathological suggestion in the manner sexological discourse was accustomed to do.[14]

If the psychopathology of Hermione's sexuality is exposed through a classic symptomatology, that of Gerald and Gudrun is disclosed mainly through the perversions. Put differently, the sexual drive is diverted away from the sexual object through a knowledge-power practice manifested primarily in sadism and masochism (the "most common and most significant of all the perversions," as Freud calls them [*Three Essays*, 1979, 70]). Assuming the same knowledge-power techniques he unearths in his characters, the narrator sadistically projects Gerald and Gudrun as the doomed objects of inquest and inquiry. Tightening the screws of the sexological, he reproduces in his analyses the same drive to mentalize sex that he uncovers in them.

In their first erotic encounter, Gudrun's protracted kissing of Gerald (under the same bridge where the miners kiss their sweethearts) constellates sexuality in a classic Foucauldian way, as "organised by power in its grip on bodies" (*History*, 1981, 155). Represented less as a negotiation of pleasure than an assertion of dominance, it enacts the continual conversion of erotic sensation into verbalized categories, the truth of pleasure translated into the potential pleasure of knowing the truth: "She wanted to touch him . . . till she had strained him into her knowledge. . . . Ah, if she could have the precious *knowledge* of him, she would be filled" (332). In the same manner that Gudrun obsessively "strains" Gerald into her conscious knowledge, displacing his erotic drives, scientizing his sexuality, converting her libidinal lack into a knowledge-power practice, so too the narrator "strains" Gudrun into his conscious knowledge, anatomizing her motives, verbalizing her desire, converting her erotic malaise into heuristic fictions that expose her sex-drive as a compensatory ploy.

In his role as pathologist, as diagnostician of the morbid, the perverse, and the aberrant, the narrator cultivates a hermeneutics of total exposure—a penetration into the intimate dynamics of the sexual exchange, disclosing its hidden mechanisms, diagnosing the orgasm itself as an organic dysfunction. In this process a pseudo-scientific rhetoric, endemic to sexological discourse, is displaced by (what one might term) a metaphorics of the perverse—extended analogies between the erotic exchange and the transmission of disease, through mutual contagion and contact. To adapt a Lacanian notion, metaphor behaves diagnostically to fix "in a symptom the signification inaccessible to the conscious subject" (166), making manifest precisely those connections that the protagonists conceal from themselves.[15] These extended metaphors generate their own special narrative program. The vehicles (the literal meanings of the words used metaphorically) combine together to encode ancillary narratives, secondary stories in the form of subtexts that compete with the main story of the lovemaking for dominance.[16] In the climactic encounter between Gerald and Gudrun (in "Death and Love"), they tell the story of the possessor of a deadly disease. (Gerald), who in the process of sexually contaminating the other (Gudrun) cures and restores himself (since the cure is a sexological one, it is, in the novel's terms, at once pseudo and temporary). Troped as a noxious expenditure, a poisonous dose that he injects into Gudrun, Gerald's spermatic effusion transmits his disease while causing her unbearable pain and discomfort. Reciprocally her orgasm is troped as a convulsive abreaction to his contagious discharge: "Into her he poured all his pent-up darkness and corrosive death, and he was whole again. . . . And she, subject, received him as a vessel filled with his bitter potion of death . . . in throes of acute, violent sensation" (344). Through a literal vocabulary drawn from biochemical medicine, the metaphorical vehicles in turn generate a "recovery" narrative (his "veins, that were . . . lacerated, healed softly"; "the

very tissue of his brain was damaged"; "the healing lymph of her ef-
fluence flowed through him" [344–345]). Essentially fraudulent, it
merely defers the manifestation of more serious symptomatic behaviour (Gerald's attempted murder of Gudrun) to a later occasion, whose violence lays bare the death-drive the erotic exchanges
concealed.

Such metaphoric narration is particularly well-adapted to un-
covering the secret machinations of incest—the "indispensable
pivot" (Foucault, *History* 109) around which sexological narratives
circulate and from which they draw sustenance. Rhetorically speaking, metaphor draws into dangerous proximity two terms which,
from the point of view of literal sense-making, should be kept
strictly apart: it tells the story of a transgression, a transport across
forbidden boundaries.[17] While in the Gerald/Gudrun exchange, the
tenor narrates the progress of the male/female sexual bonding, the
vehicles inscribe the progress of the son/mother one, in the process
blending, confusing and confounding them. In its identification of
Gudrun as all-encompassing mother, the narrative unearths incest
at the core of Gerald's erotic demand. It unfolds at two distinct levels: first, as the story of a nurturing mother, exhausted by her son's
insatiable hunger and greed ("Like a child at the breast, he cleaved
intensely to her, and she could not put him away"); second, as a tale
of regression to a pre-Oedipal paradise—non-differentiated, complete—analogous to the mother/child symbiosis ("like a sleep of fe-
cundity within the womb" [344–345]. In the Lacanian manner, a
metaphorics of the perverse exposes the truth of unconscious desire
through a continual substitution of the child/mother bonding for
the male/female one.

In the logic of sexological narrative, such perverse libidinal drives
have their aftermath in confession—in this case, Gudrun's protracted self-analysis as Gerald lies asleep by her side. Confession, as it
were, is drawn into the sphere of psychopathology. Situated strate-
gically after her lovemaking, it converts an inchoate sexual drive
into a coherent narrative of her own personal history, subjecting
"her childhood, her girlhood, all the forgotten incidents, all the un-
realised influences" to the laws of emplotment that grasp together
disparate events in order to master and integrate their affects: "It

was as if she drew a glittering rope of knowledge out of the sea of darkness . . . haul[ed] at the rope of glittering consciousness, pull[ed] it out phosphorescent from the endless depths of the unconsciousness" (346). Her subordination of desire to a narrative order is complicit with the narrator's desire to represent her as bound by that need. Seen in this light, Gudrun's self-psychologizing enacts a parodic rehearsal of Freudian, psychoanalysis in particular, and sexological discourse in general, at once in the sheer interminability of their verbalizations once the process has started ("she was weary, aching, exhausted, and fit to break, and yet she had not done") and, more insidiously, insofar as their lifting of repressions intensifies the very symptoms (the "violent active superconsciousness") it purports to cure (346).

In the psychopathologizing of the confessional act, sadism emerges as its most distinctive component—confession and torture constituting the "dark twins" that historically shadow and beget one another (Foucault, *History* 59). As one of the major preoccupations of sexological discourse from Krafft-Ebing's *Psychopathia Sexualis* and Havelock Ellis's *Studies in the Psychology of Sex* (Volume III), through Freud, down to Gilles Deleuze's *Masochism*, sadism feeds into the novelistic in the form of a sophisticated cruelty—the disciplined harshness exercised either by the narrator toward his characters, or by the latter toward one another or toward a surrogate object that mediates their sadistic desires, and that reinforces their "instinct for mastery."[18] If, as Laura Mulvey puts it, "sadism demands a story" (1993, 22), it is precisely because, in making something happen, it precipitates crises and confrontations, submissions, and oppositions, a grammar of active and passive positions that initiates strange narrative contracts and bondings. In addition (though Mulvey does not mention this), it induces painful self-revelations, exhaustive and exhausting confessions. In the structural sense, it produces powerful configurations—a constellation of images—through which the sadistic ritual is concretized in the process of its unfolding. In effect, sadism provides the mainspring of the narrative of the Gerald/Gudrun bonding.

It emerges less in the form of a dialogic exchange (though Gerald and Gudrun confess to themselves, they never confess to each other) than through large-scale public scenarios—theatres of action and self-revelation—which mediate their sadistic desires toward each other. Of the three major scenarios, however, only the third—Gerald's violent strangulation of Gudrun—conforms to Freud's simple definition of sadism as "the desire to inflict pain upon the sexual object" (*Three Essays*, 1979, 70). The first two, by contrast, triangulate the pattern, deploying surrogate objects—an Arab mare and a rabbit—which mediate the protagonists' self-recognitions. Since each scenario builds on the basis laid down by its predecessor, a law of narrative progression emerges: the more intense the chastisement, the more overt the erotic self-recognition. Thus while Gerald's disciplined cruelty toward the Arab mare (in "Coal-Dust") establishes at most an oblique link between torture and sexual stimulation (his action produces a brief sexual frisson in Gudrun [112–13], and his sado-aggressive maltreatment of the rabbit produces a "white-cruel recognition" between them whose specific content is left undisclosed (241–242), the third—Gudrun's strangulation—makes explicit the connection between pain and erotic arousal. Ventriloquizing Gerald's and Gudrun's perceptions, the narrator's verbal ejaculations mime their sexual ones in a dissimulated participation, which at once foregrounds their psychopathologies while it distances him from its affects: "What bliss! Oh what bliss, at last, what satisfaction, at last! . . . What a fulfillment, what a satisfaction! How good this was, oh how good it was, what a god-given gratification, at last!" (471–472). Insofar as its latent purpose is opposed to its manifest one, the text parodies the *jouissance* it pretends to incite, contaminating the sexological language of orgasm ("satisfaction," "gratification") through its incorporation into a context that radically compromises its meanings.

Broadly speaking, the sexological narratives I have just explored posit the unconscious as the source of pathological fictions—narratives of desire and repression, symptoms and substitutions, incest and prohibitions—the psychic blocking of satisfactions through deflections of desire onto surrogate objects. Such dislocations of desire, as we saw, paradoxically endow the narrative with its main motor-force, and with its potential to proliferate. At the same time, *Women in Love* exploits an alternative conception of the unconscious, op-

posed to the sexological one, and espoused by Lawrence himself in
Psychoanalysis and the Unconscious. As the pristine, primordial source of
libidinal energies, which flow spontaneously out toward their objects (eluding the displacements due to repression), *its* irruptions are
unmediated by a grammar of language or representational forms.
An index of liberation and plenitude, it points to an energy not yet
tied to a function, nor to pre-articulated satisfactions and goals. The
second section of this essay explores the problems posed for narrative by this displacement of a civilizing, though repressive, sexological force by an unconstrained, uninhibited erotic one (the *Ars Erotica*
practice evoked in "Excurse").

2. Ars Erotica

One of the major critical cruxes in *Women in Love* has centered on
locating "Excurse" within the precincts of the novelistic (the title
itself foregrounds its status as a digression) since both its mystical
eroticism and its esoteric psychophysiology place it outside the
bounds of traditional sexual narratives. (*Its* marginalization within
Women in Love paradoxically reproduces the marginalization of the
mystical, characteristic of sexological, and scientific, discourse in
general.[19]) In challenging the psychologization of the erotic, it also
challenges the constructions of sexuality worked out by sexology.
Its mysticism thus takes on the force of a radical dissent from sexological orthodoxies. In liberating narrative from its introspective
and confessional roots, it offers an experiment in erotic narration for
which no real precedent exists in the English tradition. Critics have
thus largely shied away from "Excurse," confining their analyses to
the Gerald/Gudrun affair or the Birkin/Ursula one before the
"Excurse" enactments, displaying the same negative fascination
with sexological "decadence" as the main narrative does. If its erotic
trances and transformations stretch critical credulity to its limits, its
radical stylization frequently appears as an infraction of style, pro-
voking censure and ridicule.[20]

  Critical disapprobation may have profounder roots, however, because in embracing the *Ars Erotica* vision, "Excurse" effectively un-

dermines the grounds of its own narratability. In gesturing toward a reality beyond time and becoming, where diachronic succession gives way to synchronic stasis, "Excurse" insistently pushes narration to the point of its own dissolution. Working against the narrative grain, it fissures the diegetic performance itself. In progressively distancing desire from its representations, it creates radical splittings or gaps—between description and action, event and interpretation, words and their conventional referents.

"Excurse" starts, however, with the staples of traditional narrative securely in place: rapid landscape vignettes, brief snatches of dialogue, plus the exchange of lovers' gifts mark the progress of Birkin and Ursula's car-drive deep into the countryside (302–305). The traumatic altercation that ensues signals at once a crisis and a denouement. It represents the last full-scale orchestration of sexological motifs (in relation to Birkin and Ursula)—a dialogic confrontation involving interrogation, confession, and the revelation of intimate secrets. Ursula's ruthless inquisition, her fierce accusatory tactics, expose Birkin's latent pathologies: "obscene and perverse," his sublimations—his pretensions to "spirituality"—have their roots in a coprophilic obsession that compounds together sex, "dirt, and death." Her aggressive denunciation in turn triggers his abject confession ("No doubt Ursula was right. It was true, really, what she said" [306–309]). In exorcising the sexological through a terminal showdown, the quarrel inaugurates a new kind of narrative, based on self-transcendence, that fractures the traditional link between storytelling and the dynamics of desire that sustain it.

In its initial manifestation, this involves a dramatic switch in narratorial posture and poise from a harshly judgmental to a deeply empathic narrator, from one who interrogates and unmasks to one who stands frankly in awe—the astonished witness to the quantum leaps he records but for which he possesses no adequate explanation. A language of biblical witness ("And now, behold") combined with a lexicon of the occult ("strange," "magical," "mystery" appear a dozen times in the space of three pages) create a hermeneutic fuzziness around the represented events (sexological discourse, by contrast, is ideologically wedded to hermeneutic precision and rigour). "Excurse" exploits, as it were, its absence of explanatory

force, translating narrator and reader into uncomprehending be-
holders of erotic transmogrifications whose purport resists hermeneutic appropriation.

Further narrative gaps are induced by those sudden,
unaccounted-for ruptures in character representation—abrupt,
unmotivated leaps from the mundane to the mystical, the personal
to the archetypal, the pragmatic to the transcendental. From being
a psychological subject, conditioned by time, place, and historical
circumstance, Birkin (for example) becomes an avatar of the uncon-
ditioned, escaping all character determinations—one of the "Sons
of God" (as he stands transfigured before Ursula at the inn of the
Saracen's Head), or an "Egyptian Pharaoh" (as he sits at the car
wheel in the late afternoon [312–313, 318]. While such iconographic
transfigurations are the stock-in-trade of *Ars Erotica* practice where,
as Mircea Eliade puts it, every "initiation presupposes passing from
one mode of being to another," and where, through ritual touchings and strokings, "the human couple becomes a divine couple"
(197, 221, 260), they are alien—even inimical—to novelistic narration where, even in modernist texts like *Women in Love*, character is
still constructed around paradigmatic attributions and traits, which
possess a relative stability, coherence, and integrative power. In their
deconstruction of the logic of motive, such leaps strike at the core of
sexological narration, which privileges a causal accounting for *its*
transformations, and confession as its chief method of verification.

Such narrative fractures are further exacerbated by a sexo-
mystical physiology, a cartography of erogenous zones that bears at
best a tangential relation to those featured in conventional sexual
narratives. Ursula's touchings of the back of Birkin's loins and thighs
evoke an extravagant rhetoric of interpretation—based on dark
mystical fires, electric circuits and currents, and irruptive fountains
and floods—which sever the normative link between erogenous
zones and their associated gratifications (while the sense of sight in-
cites the scopophilic and voyeuristic potential of story-telling,
touch, by contrast, depresses the narrative function). Such caress-
ings, in effect, combine a concentration of *Ars Erotica* practices—
awakening the deepest somatic source of libidinal energies located
at the base of the spine[21]—with a daring revision of sexological mo-

tifs. What appears from the latter perspective as pathologically anal, possessing the characteristics of exclusiveness and fixation that mark it down as a perversion (Freud, *Three Essays*, 1979, 75), from the *Ars Erotica* one becomes the source of transcendent bliss (in these love-acts, phallic aims are explicitly renounced and transcended).[22] A sex-ological grammar of gratifications is reinscribed through a metaphorics of "rapturous" states that unites the mystical and the physiological in unprecedented ways. The effect, paradoxically, is less to forward the narrative drive than to frustrate it through the generation of neologisms ("mystically-physically satisfying," for ex-ample) which fracture the kind of unities the text is inaugurating (314).

In its drive to replace a complex verbal communication with the "unspeakable communication in touch" (320), "Excurse" takes the *Ars Erotica* project to its logical end. The state of absolute plenitude to which both lovers accede—"[s]he had her desire fulfilled, he had his desire fulfilled" (320)—drains the narrative of desire, of its mo-tive force, establishing a transphenomenal, static condition of con-sciousness as its final attainment. The narrative impasse that such a concept of transcendence entails is nowhere more transparent than in the narrator's own compulsion to offer a verbal analysis of this essentially post-verbal state: "How can I say 'I love you,' when I have ceased to be, and you have ceased to be, we are both caught up and transcended into a new oneness where everything is silent. . . . [s]peech travels between the separate parts. But in the perfect One, there is perfect silence of bliss" (369). In this classic definition of mystical love, the distinction between one self and another—per-haps *the* basic precondition for generating the narrative contract—is abolished.

The subsequent story, however, does not conform to the logic of its own propositions and reduce Birkin and Ursula to silence. Though the "Excurse" enactments are not repeated (repetition en-tails precisely the lack or deficiency that "Excurse" repudiates), nev-ertheless the title of the episode implicitly acknowledges the need for the sexological to get the plot back on track. In effect, the final third of the novel is marked by a resurgence of sexological motifs, fuelled mainly by the introduction of a new character, Loerke, who represents a congeries of sexological traits, and who, as such, is the focus of the final section of this essay.

3. The Return of the Sexological

In the Barthesian sense, Loerke is a "proper name" (S/Z, 1998, 95), a mere nominal unit that attracts a compendium of sexological attributes. Constituted primarily through the accumulation of others' verdicts upon him, his subjectivity is overwhelmingly pathological. A catalyst for the fiercely judgmental assaults from the narrator, Birkin and Gerald—that mix together theories of cultural decline, racial degeneration and aesthetic decadence—Loerke represents a case history of all the standard perversions. His homosexuality (422), his fetishistic obsession with young girls (432), his sadism (433), his regressive anality ("mud-child" [427]), his masochism ("subjected being" [427]) constitute a ceaseless incitement to narrative, to provocative conflicts and confrontations (between Gudrun and Gerald, Ursula and Loerke). In effect, his representation revives the metaphorics of the perverse (temporarily suspended in "Excurse") employed to unearth pathological states, and transform latent desires into manifest symptoms (Birkin, for example, invents a narrative of progress down the alimentary canal to diagnose Loerke as anally fixated—living where "the river of the corruption . . . falls over into the bottomless pit" [428].[23]

Loerke's representation also resuscitates the theory of desire based on insatiable hunger and striving, reinstalling self-revelation as the technique for exposing its source in a lack. His abject confession to Gudrun, made against his own better judgment—"All his nature held him back from confessing. And yet her large, grave eyes upon him seemed to open some valve in his veins, and involuntarily he was telling" (425)—unveils an autobiographical narrative, rooted in youthful destitution and vagrancy (his begging and stealing in order to live), that links both his artistic and his sexual practices to an originary dislocation, displacement. Loerke, as it were, is the name for desires that elude their proper objects and goals. His storytelling techniques—communicating through "double-meanings . . . evasions . . .

suggestive vagueness" (453)—dramatize this elusiveness. As such they are paradigmatic of those major sexological narratives we have already explored which have libidinal displacements, deviations, and indirections at the core of their power to proliferate. As narratives of the perverse, they engage with the "foreplay" of meaning—with chains of pathological substitutions—instead of proceeding directly to the end-satisfaction of composed and completed significations (the analogy is with Freud's definition of perversion as "a lingering over the preparatory acts of the sexual process" [*Three Essays*, 1979, 132].

Given its intensifying sexological emphasis, it is entirely appropriate that *Women in Love* should end in a morgue—the pathologist's dream-chamber, the site of investigation, dissection, analysis, where lives are transposed into case histories and corpses are metaphors for reified desires. In his role as meta-physician, diagnostician and hermeneut, Birkin composes Gerald's life history retrospectively, unearthing the cause of the death-process in a petrified libido for which Gerald's "mute, material" body is the appropriate figure. Birkin's extended meditation—introspective, diagnostic, and confessional by turns—for which the death of desire is the pretext, highlights the same narrative contradiction we have already exposed. His analysis of desire as a lack, a slow congealing and petrification, usurps by far the greater part of the meditation, while his evocation of erotic transcendence generates only the briefest of references—his recall of a mysterious moment, never properly actualized, when Gerald clutched his hand "with a warm, momentaneous grip of final love," and then "let it go forever" (477–480).

Notes

1. Foucault later revised this particular listing, commenting that neither the Greeks nor the Romans had "any *ars erotica* to be compared with the Chinese *ars erotica*" (*Reader*, 1984, 347–348)—or with, one must suppose, the Indian one.

2. Though Foucault rarely makes explicit reference to Eastern systems of thought in his writings, nevertheless, as Uta Schaub observes, "[h]is surface text allows us to trace elements of Oriental philosophy, religion, and

kindred forms of Western mysticism and to assume that they constitute a generative code beneath much of his discourse" (1989, 307).

3. The Indian Tantric treatises, in particular, posit sexuality as the vehicle for escaping "the domination of time," destroying the basis of language in conventional reference, and for "attaining transcendence" (Eliade, 1970, 204, 250). Foucault contrasts the contemporary obsession with desire—in philosophy and psychoanalysis—with the total absence of concern with pleasure (*Reader*, 1984, 347).

4. Mircea Eliade gives an excellent account of these treatises, analyzing the iconographies (the mental images of the divinities), the physical postures, the body-touchings, the ritual sexual intercourse employed for attaining the "supreme truth" (1970, 200–273).

5. Stephen Heath, for example, defines sexology as the study of the conceptions and systematizations, both specific and historical, of sexuality—the representation of sex as a discursive entity. Such a study, he remarks, "goes back a little more than a hundred years" (1982, 11).

6. The critical corpus exploring the connection between narrative and psychoanalysis—perhaps *the* most significant branch of sexology—is already a large one. It includes two essay collections—*Psychoanalysis and the Question of the Text*, ed. Geoffrey Hartman, and *Discourse in Psychoanalysis and Literature*, ed. Shlomith Rimmon-Kenan—as well as large-scale works by Meredith Skura (*The Literary Use of the Psychoanalytic Process*), Daniel Gunn (*Psychoanalysis and Fiction*), and Donald Spence (*Narrative Truth and Historical Truth: Meaning and Interpretation in Psychoanalysis*). In *Reading for the Plot: Design and Intention in Narrative* and in *Psychoanalysis and Storytelling*, Peter Brooks explores the correspondences between psychic functioning, as postulated by Freud in *Beyond the Pleasure Principle*, and the dynamics of narrative functioning. See especially *Reading for the Plot* (1984, 99–112).

7. Foucault opposes a confessional literature in which one discloses "one's crimes, one's sins, one's thoughts and desires," to an oral literature "centering on the heroic or marvellous narration of 'trials' of bravery or sainthood" (*History*, 1981, 59).

8. While Krafft-Ebing's functional theory of the sexual instinct, for example, generates a sharp division between normal and pathological states (1965, 34–36). Freud's theory of the sexual drive, working out in the *Three Essays* (1978, 45–87), tends to blur the distinction between them. Nevertheless, as Arnold Davidson shows, Freud participates in the very system he criticizes, taking great pains to establish criteria that separate the perversions from normal sexual behaviour (1987, 252–277).

9. This is Krafft-Ebing's fourfold classification of the perversions (1965,

34–36). The argument of the present essay is not, of course, that *Women in Love* approximates to sexological discourse in its pretensions to scientificity, but that it co-opts some of its major motifs and strategies, adapting them to its own special narrative purposes.

10. Lawrence notoriously describes the Freudian unconscious as "the cellar in which the mind keeps its own bastard spawn" (*Psychoanalysis*, 1984, 204)—the kind of crude misapprehension that Freud corrects in the opening paragraph of his essay, "The Unconscious": "The repressed does not cover everything that is unconscious. The unconscious has the wider compass." The remainder of the essay goes on to explore the subtle complexities of the unconscious system, positing the existence of inherited mental formations in its constitution ("Unconscious," 1984, 167–210).

11. The Freud/Lawrence/Foucault triangulation is a tangled one, since Foucault associates Lawrence with Freud, both of whom he sees as caught up in the "complex deployment for compelling sex to speak" (*History*, 1981, 158). Foucault locates in Lawrence the same drive to verbalize sex that Lawrence locates in Freud. Lawrence's responses to Freud have been discussed by Elizabeth Wright (1984, 49–55) and Anne Fernihough (1993, 61–82).

12. While Lawrence's philosophical conception of the unconscious as the authentic source of creative activity has its roots in romantic theory going back to Schlegel and Schelling (Tzvetan Todorov has written a standard account of this theory [1982, 146–221]), his sexual conception of the unconscious as the erotically charged source of self-transcendence is derived from Indian (Tantric) sources. See Gerald Doherty's essay, which traces in detail the correspondences between the representation of *Ars Erotica* practices in *Women in Love* and Tantric erotic rituals of initiation (1984, 211–22).

13. The narrator's diagnosis of the cause of Hermione's behaviour in her repressed "craving" for Birkin bears an uncanny resemblance to Freud's characterization of female hysteria—"exaggerated sexual craving and excessive aversion to sexuality" (*Three Essays*, 1979, 79).

14. Michel de Certeau shows how nineteenth-century sexology in general, and J. M. Charcot in particular, linked together mystical perception and hysteria, diagnosing both as pathological phenomena (1982, 15–16). At this point, we may note that the narrator practices the same techniques of exposure on Gerald as on Hermione. Holding up a mirror in which Gerald sees his face, the narrator locates a major symptom to whose cause Gerald is blind (a "mortal dry fear, but he knew not what of"). The final diagnosis is a thoroughly Foucauldian one: before Gerald's sex-drive can find its ob-

ject, it must first be displaced, passed through the defiles of the knowledge-power complex ("He felt that his *mind* needed acute stimulation, before he could be physically roused" [232–233]).

15. For Lacan, the true speech of the unconscious, disclosed in the symptom, is articulated through the metaphorical process of substitution (1977, 164–71). Freud discusses the link between symptom and substitution in his essay "Repression" (1984, 154–158).

16. Luz Pimental offers a detailed theoretical account of metaphoric narration (1990, 9–33). In Lawrence's extended metaphors, the vehicles constitute secondary narratives with their own plots and time sequences (beginnings, middles, ends). They take on the status of virtual para-narratives.

17. Patricia Parker shows how the metaphorical process generates plots of deviation, transgression, errancy (1982, 143–147).

18. Freud's phrase (*Three Essays*, 1979, 110–111), which locates sadism in the pregenital organization of sexuality and in an essential blindness to the pain of the other.

19. De Certeau shows how, from the seventeenth century onward, the scientific world view increasingly isolates the mystical, defining it precisely by its degree of divergence from "normal or ordinary paths" (1992, 13).

20. F. R. Leavis rejects these scenes as "jargon-ridden," H. M. Daleski as "difficult" and puzzling, Emile Delaveney as "pretentious" and esoteric, Frank Kermode as inducing "strain" even in "sympathetic readers" (1978, 177, 176, 409–410, 74). Among the few critics who commend these scenes is Maria DiBattista, for whom "Excurse" is "one of Lawrence's most successful representations of a "generic" self-overcoming" (1985, 83)—a comment that points more to achieved thematic resolutions to erotic conflicts than to narrative ones.

21. Called "kundalini" in the Tantric treatises, this erotic energy is personified by a goddess. Awakened through ritual strokings and touchings, it ascends along the spine to the top of the head where it is transmuted into transcendent pleasure and bliss (Eliade, 1970, 245–249).

22. Since this source, as the text tells us, is "further in mystery than the phallic source" (314), it "ousts ... completely" the "normal sexual aim," thus defining itself (in Freudian terms) as a pathological symptom (*Three Essays*, 1979, 75).

23. If Birkin's metaphoric narration exposes Loerke as anal, Gerald's represents him as essentially oral, cannibalistic: Loerke incorporates women (especially Gudrun) into his system in the same way that a "little dry snake" ingests a bird, "gaping ready to fall down its throat" (454).

Works Cited

Barthes, Roland. *S/Z.* trans., Richard Miller. New York: Noonday Press, 1988.

Brooks, Peter. *Reading for the Plot: Design and Intention in Narrative.* Oxford: Clarendon Press, 1984.

Daleski, H. M. *The Forked Flame: A Study of D. H. Lawrence.* London: Faber and Faber, 1965.

Davidson, Arnold. "How to Do the History of Psychoanalysis: A Reading of Freud's *Three Essays on the Theory of Sexuality." Critical Inquiry* 13 (1987): 252–277.

de Certeau, Michel. "Mysticism." *Diacritics* 22 (1992): 11–25.

Delaveney, Emile. *D. H. Lawrence: The Man and His Work.* London: Heinemann, 1972.

DiBattista, Maria. "*Women in Love:* D. H. Lawrence's Judgment Book" in *D. H. Lawrence: A Centenary Consideration,* ed., Peter Balbert and Phillip Marcus. Ithaca: Cornell University Press, 1985.

Doherty, Gerald. "The Darkest Source: D. H. Lawrence, Tantric Yoga, and *Women in Love." Essays in Literature* 11 (1984): 211–222.

Eliade, Mircea. *Yoga: Immortality and Freedom,* trans., Willard R. Trask. Princeton: Princeton University Press, 1970.

Fernihough, Anne. *D. H. Lawrence: Aesthetics and Ideology.* Oxford: Clarendon Press, 1993.

Foucault, Michel. *The History of Sexuality: Volume 1,* trans., Robert Hurley. Middlesex: Penguin, 1981.

———. *The Foucault Reader,* ed., Paul Rabinow. New York: Pantheon, 1984.

Freud, Sigmund. "Repression." *On Metapsychology: The Theory of Psychoanalysis,* trans. James Strachey. Volume 11. London: Penguin, 1984, 145–158.

———. *Three Essays on the Theory of Sexuality. On Sexuality,* trans. James Strachey. Volume 7. London: Penguin, 1979, 31–169.

———. "The Unconscious." *On Metapsychology: The Theory of Psychoanalysis,* trans. James Strachey. Volume 11. London: Penguin, 1984, 167–222.

Heath, Stephen. *The Sexual Fix.* London: Macmillan, 1982.

Kermode, Frank. *Lawrence.* Suffolk: Fontana, 1973.

Krafft-Ebing, Richard von. *Psychopathia Sexualis, with Especial Reference to the Antipathic Sexual Instinct,* trans., Franklin Klaf. New York: Bell, 1965.

Lacan, Jacques. *Écrits,* trans., Alan Sheridan. London: Routledge, 1977.

Lawrence, D. H. "The Crown." *Reflections on the Death of a Porcupine and Other Essays,* ed., Michael Herbert. Cambridge: Cambridge University Press, 1988, 253–306.

————. *Fantasia of the Unconscious and Psychoanalysis and the Unconscious.* London: Heinemann, 1971.

————. *Women in Love,* ed. David Farmer, Lindeth Vasey, and John Worthen. Cambridge: Cambridge University Press, 1987.

Leavis, F. R. *D. H. Lawrence: Novelist.* Middlesex: Penguin, 1978.

Miller, D. A. *Narrative and Its Discontents: Problems of Closure in the Traditional Novel.* Princeton: Princeton University Press, 1989.

Mulvey, Laura. *Visual and Other Pleasures.* London: Macmillan, 1993.

Parker, Patricia. "The Metaphorical Plot" in *Metaphor: Problems and Perspectives,* ed. David S. Miall. Sussex: Harvester Press, 1982, 133–157.

Pimental, Luz Aurora. *Metaphoric Narration: Paranarrative Dimensions in* A la Recherche du Temps Perdu. Toronto: University of Toronto Press, 1990.

Ricoeur, Paul. *Time and Narrative.* Vol. 1, trans., Kathleen McLaughlin and David Pellauer. Chicago: University of Chicago Press, 1984.

Schafer, Roy. "Narration in the Psychoanalytic Dialogue." *On Narrative,* ed. W.J.T. Mitchell. Chicago: University of Chicago Press, 1981, 25–49.

Schaub, Uta Liebmann. "Foucault's Oriental Subtext." *PMLA* 104 (1989): 306–316.

Todorov, Tzvetan. *Theories of the Symbol,* trans., Catherine Porter. Oxford: Blackwell, 1982.

Wright, Elizabeth. *Psychoanalytic Criticism. Theory in Practice.* London: Methuen, 1984.

The Myth of the Fall in *Women in Love*

JACK F. STEWART

◆ ◆ ◆

T HE EXTENT TO WHICH the myth of the fall permeates
Women in Love[1] has not previously been recognized. The novel ex-
amines language, mythos, the whole logocentric tradition, revealing an underlying connection and a gap between the Biblical myth
of the fall, as expanded by Milton in *Paradise Lost*, and the modern
condition of alienation and *angst* that Lawrence diagnoses. At first
sight, references to the Fall in *Women in Love* seem marginal, even
clichéd. Displaced into fiction, the Genesis story that was imaginative and doctrinal truth to Milton bears uneasy and unstable relation to Lawrence's themes. But the theological concept of the fall
that Lawrence is intent on redefining is part of the novel's basic vision, which depends on recuperating as well as transvaluing the biblical source.

Theological and psychological accounts of the fall converge, as
Lawrence demythologizes biblical narrative and remythologizes the
modern world. The fall is a myth of origins, to which Lawrence re-
sorts because the causes of the modern dilemma are too complex to
trace through social history and because the myth focusses on a

spiritual condition. In one of his essays, Lawrence defines the prelapsarian condition: "While a man remains a man, before he falls and becomes a social individual, he innocently feels himself altogether within the great continuum of the universe. He is not divided nor cut off."² The condition Lawrence inscribes in the novel is a fall out of oneness and connection into separateness and division. The modern world is marked by the separate ego's alienation from Being and from others: relationships break down between man and God and man and woman, and a state of disintegration and corruption pervades society (the whirlpool, sewer, or vortex images). "The real trouble," Lawrence writes, "lies in the inward sense of 'separateness' which dominates every man. At a certain point in his evolution [equivalent to the fall], man became cognitively conscious: he bit the apple: he began to know. Up till that time his consciousness flowed unaware, as in the animals. Suddenly, his consciousness split."³

When Birkin switches on the electric light in Ursula's classroom it becomes "distinct and hard, a strange place after the soft dim magic that filled it before he came" (36). He has produced the conditions for his diatribe on the fall, in which electric light metaphorizes fallen mental consciousness. The schizophrenic Hermione inhabits a peculiarly modern, self-made hell in which the light is always blindingly on. Theologically, the fall cuts man off from God and self from other, leaving the subject in a state of solipsism.⁴ In his attack on one-dimensional knowing, Birkin inevitably refers to the Tree of Knowledge of Good and Evil in Genesis:

> "To know, that is your all, that is your life . . ." he cried. "There is only one tree, there is only one fruit, in your mouth."
>   . . . "What fruit, Rupert?"
>   "The eternal apple," he replied in exasperation, hating his own metaphors. (40)

Lawrence, like Birkin, seems to use the Genesis myth reluctantly.⁵ Fallen language, in which signifier is cut loose from signified, seductively offers an understanding that its divided nature withholds. "The belief that man fell from his primitive harmonious relationship with God"⁶ is displaced into fiction as the conviction that man and woman have lost their harmonious relationship with the cosmos and with each other. One recalls that there are *two* forbidden trees in Genesis, the other being the Tree of Life (2:9, 3:23–24); but the chief effect of the fall is dissociated "knowing"—objectifying what was originally, in the Edenic myth, natural and spontaneous.

Not wishing to "[come] out of the Christian Camp,"[7] Lawrence still depends on a revisionist theology, probing for buried truth in mythic paradigms. According to Joyce Carol Oates, he writes in a "chiliastic mood" of "prophetic eschatolog[y],"[8] while Frank Kermode sees the novel as "exhibit[ing] all the apocalyptic types in their Lawrentian version: decadence and renovation in a painful transition or crisis, elitism, patriotic fervour, sex and mystery."[9] I shall focus on Lawrence's rediscovery of "the fall" as universally articulated in mental consciousness, sexual conflict, alienation,[10] and entropy. Much has been written (by George Ford and others) on Lawrence's use of Genesis in *The Rainbow* and on his apocalypticism and revisionism in *Women in Love* (notably by Frank Kermode and Virginia Hyde). But the deep structure of fall myth, and its integration with the novel's themes, has not yet been exposed to view.

The myth has been fleshed out and culturally transmitted by Milton's *Paradise Lost*; while the core narrative of Genesis remains intact in the epic, it is continuously available for reinterpreting reframing, and refocusing—that is, for "displacement."[11] Such a myth, as Northrop Frye says, "presents [the novelist] with a ready-made framework . . . and allows him to devote all his energies to elaborating its design" ("Myth," 1963, 31). Used as an instrument of cultural analysis, the conceptual core is recharged with existential meaning. "A myth may be told and retold: it may be modified or elaborated, or different patterns may be discovered in it; and its life is always the poetic life of a story, not the homiletic life of some illustrated truism" (Frye, "Myth," 1963, 32). Reactivated myth provides structure and imagery through which the meaning of experience can be reconceived. It is a two-way process: mythic narratives absorb energy from human questing, expressing unconscious desires or dreads, and giving them manageable form.[12] Their deep structures *reverberate* (see Frye, "Myth," 1963, 37). While Lawrence alludes to the biblical/Miltonic myth, his radical reinterpretation of it, in light of contemporary social critique and apocalyptic prophecy,[13] is essential to the novel's themes.

As Lawrence sees it, the fall deflects energy from unconscious germination into self-conscious manipulation. "When we have knowledge, don't we lose everything but knowledge?" asks the masochistically self-accusing Hermione. "If I know the flower, don't I lose the flower and have only the knowledge? Aren't we exchanging the substance for the shadow, aren't we forfeiting life for this deadly quantity of knowledge?" (41). Her parroting of Birkin's doctrines exemplifies how Lawrence "sheds [his] sicknesses" (*Letters* 1981, 2:90) onto negative characters in novels. Hermione, who should know, articulates a fall into knowing that supplants being:

> "You don't want to *be* an animal [Birkin charges], you want . . . to get a mental thrill out of [your own animal functions]. It is all purely secondary—and more decadent than the most hidebound intellectualism. Passion and the instincts—you want them hard enough, but through your head, in your consciousness. . . ." (41)

The fall produces a schizophrenic split between the body that acts and the mind that pre-empts or "transmute[s]" (320) its sensations. In the fallen condition, alienated self-consciousness replaces spontaneous being.

The central symbol in this chapter is the mirror that reflects "purely secondary" images of the world, as in "The Lady of Shalott." The mind manipulates the body's primary sensations, mental images taking the place of reality: as Lawrence writes elsewhere, "[we must] shatter that mirror in which we all live grimacing: and fall again into true relatedness" (*Phoenix*, 382). Hermione dimly realizes as much, but she remains perversely locked into what she criticizes, "liv[ing] according to the picture" (*Phoenix*, 1972, 382). In her fall, she has substituted secondary reflection, that gives a fleeting illusion of control, for the "sensual body of life." "[Her] will and [her] conceit of consciousness, and [her] lust for power, to *know*" (42) have made her a radically divided self, with energy displaced upwards into superficial, nerve-driven consciousness.

Birkin reproduces the contradictions and hypocrisies of Hermione's character in oxymorons such as "deliberately spontaneous" and "deliberate voluntary consciousness." In mentally manipulating her sensations, she falsifies and contravenes her being. Intellectually she *knows* the difference between primary and secondary responses, correlatives of good and evil in a vitalist ethic. But instead of living "what she *is* as a phenomenon (or as representing some greater, inhuman will)" (*Letters* 2:183), she wants to transmute being into ideas that her consciousness can savor and manipulate: the apple of her tree of knowledge has a "strange sapience."[14] Such willed control inevitably alienates her from "real sensuality," as the "I" that knows must stand outside the "I" that acts and is known.

Birkin regards such detached knowing as an obscenity; like a Zen master, he wants to destroy Hermione's capacity for sublimating experience by "crack[ing] [her] skull" and releasing "a spontaneous, passionate woman . . ." (42). One-dimensional consciousness should not be mistaken for intellect, as genuine "Thought is a man in his wholeness wholly attending."[15] Mechanical processing takes the life out of experience; it is particularly evident in Sir Joshua Malleson's arid conversation, which presents knowledge "[in] compressed tabloids" (86).[16]

The fall causes a warping of intelligent being; sensuality, "innocent" in Eden, degenerates into pornography—"watching your naked animal actions in mirrors, so that you can have it all in your consciousness . . ." (42). Voyeurism directed at one's own acts, narcissism, and solipsism are symptoms of the fall in modern culture. To recover from it, Birkin recommends a return to "the great dark knowledge you can't have in your head—the dark involuntary being" (43). Only a death of the ego will allow "the coming into being of another" (43). Myths of flood and fall converge here, as only a flood of blood-consciousness can sweep away the ingrained habits of mental consciousness. Birkin calls for a change that would operate "[in] the blood . . . when the mind and the known world is drowned in darkness . . ." (43). As in Genesis, "the flood of destructive creation" (172) wipes out a fallen mode of being and replaces it with new life. Birkin's role as "Salvator Mundi," ironically invoked in "An Island," matches Lawrence's prophetic displacement of religious vision into writing. The novel, that "one bright book of life" which Lawrence explicitly compares with the Bible (*Phoenix* 1972, 535), is meant to become "the Word that reveals the Eden in the redeemable human soul, and so releases the power that leads to a new heaven and a new earth."[17]

In Birkin's philosophy, the Christian morality of good and evil has been transposed into a vitalist ethic, in which unfallen good is "the actual sensual being" and fallen evil is "the vicious mental-deliberate profligacy our lot goes in for" (44). ("Profligacy" is subliminally connected with the fall through Latin *profligare*, "to strike to the ground.") This perverse manipulation of the sensual recalls phenomena of the fall in *Paradise Lost*. As Birkin sees it, men and women must learn to live from a vital core of being, rather than ego-driven will. "You've got to lapse out before you can know what sensual reality is, lapse into unknowingness, and give up your volition. . . . You've got to do it. You've got to learn not-to-be, before you can come into being" (44). These are quasi-religious paradoxes that can only be resolved in a state of natural grace such as the lovers achieve in "Excurse." An effort of will is needed to resist the inertia of the fall, yet letting-go is the only way to recover spontaneity. Birkin's hectoring tone, as he struggles to verbalize his ideas in the threefold commandment, "you've got to," is amusingly out of synch with the blessed state he envisions.

Birkin significantly switches from second-person accusative to first-person confessional, when he says: "We'd rather die than give up our little self-righteous self-opinionated self-will" (44). His exasperation shows that he shares the effects of the fall that he diagnoses in others: he knows Hermione inside out because he has been entangled with her. In "Class-room," he introduces his peculiar and readily misunderstood cult of the demonic, and for his pains she calls him "a *dreadful* Satanist" (243). For Birkin, however, "the real devil [is the one] who won't let life exist" (43). He knows he is not exempt from the fall, and struggles to overcome its effects,[18] seen in a corrupted Tree of Life in "An Island" (126–127). Theologically, it is impossible to overcome the effects of the fall without God's intervention (see *Paradise Lost* 10.1086–1104); but in the novel, woman as Other largely takes the place of God (58).

Lawrence retains and redefines the biblical idea of a fall into knowledge.[19] His revisionist use of Genesis conveys Birkin's alienated consciousness as he struggles to cast off a dying culture and take root in Being. The Lawrencean fall is not so much into knowledge of *good and evil*, although Hermione, Halliday, Gudrun, Gerald, and Loerke display notable symptoms of perversity and corruption, as into all-absorbing mental consciousness. Birkin's desire to recover a premental state and "live in another world, from another centre," eschewing the prison of mirrors that entraps Hermione, parallels the mythic desire to recover a Lost Eden. To Ursula there is a residue of unfallen life in him, "a sense of richness and of liberty," that speaks "like another voice" behind his words, "convey[ing] another knowledge of him" (44). After he leaves the classroom, Ursula feels "lost" and weeps bitterly, "but whether for misery or joy, she never knew" (45). Her misery is for the loss of Eden, disclosed by Birkin, her joy for the discovery of a "Son of God," who has come to her like an annunciation from the unknown.

After the stale air and stridency of "Class-room," the sisters go for a walk on a "morning [that] was full of a new creation" (46). Vital sparks of being are alive in the sodden world, "tiny amber grains burning faintly in the white smoke of blossom" (46), like the "little red flames" of the catkins, so poignantly glimpsed by Hermione. Yet, as Birkin looks out of a train window, he sees evidence of the fall in the ruined Eden/Wasteland around him: "the earth [is covered] with foulness," and "life is a blotch of labour, like insects scurrying in filth . . ." (55).[20] Politically, he sees the moral corruption of the fall in the "strange, glistening malice" of Gerald's "plausible ethics of productivity" (56)—the enlightened self-interest of capitalism, masking a raw will-to-power.

The novel's working title, *Dies Irae* (Day of Wrath),[21] reflects Lawrence's apocalyptic vision, in which Birkin contemplates a Sodom-like destruction of mankind (59). Yet in the midst of gloomiest despair, he proclaims his faith in life:

"That which is expressed, and that which is to be expressed, cannot be diminished. . . . Let mankind pass away . . . The creative utterances will not cease, they will not only be there. Humanity doesn't embody the utterance of the incomprehensible any more. . . . There will be a new embodiment, in a new way." (59)

This selective quotation highlights the millennial aspects of Birkin's prophecy, in which a vital sense of *being there* and moving on with the unknown speaks out in the midst of industrial squalor and intellectual dispute.

Birkin articulates his faith in life (if not in humanity) in the midst of a period of mass destruction, in which "the bitterness of the war may be taken for granted in the characters" ("Foreword," *Women in Love*, 485). His quotation of Browning's "Love among the Ruins" is ironically appropriate to the fallen landscape, glamorized by sunset. Birkin tells Gerald: "I always feel doomed when the train is running into London. I feel such a despair, so hopeless, as if it were the end of the world" (61). His metaphysical anguish subsumes the fallen social world: London is a "centre of universal paralysis," like Joyce's Dublin, Eliot's London, or Dante's City of Dis. The train enters under an arch, into "the tremendous shadow of the town," as if passing through the gates of hell, and Birkin "feel[s] like one of the the damned" (61). In his soul, he seems to experience the evils that led to chaos and war in twentieth-century Europe.

The Café Pompadour, "this small, slow, central whirlpool of disintegration and dissolution" (380), is a cultural vortex at the center of a Dantesque hell. Gerald enters "the large, lofty room where the faces and heads of the drinkers showed dimly through the haze of smoke, reflected more dimly, and repeated ad infinitum in the great mirrors on the walls . . ." (62). In this "shadowy" world, symbols of the inferno are the disembodied quality of its denizens and the motifs of reflection, repetition, infinity, encapsulation. Gerald, stranger in Bohemia, "seemed to be . . . passing into an illuminated new region, among a host of licentious souls" (62). He is attracted to the Pussum, in whose look "flare[s] an unfathomable hell of knowledge," whose "burning, filmed eyes" have "a look of knowledge of evil, dark and indomitable," who is "confident in dreadful knowledge," and whose sexual aura is "like a magnetic darkness" (65, 69, 68, 71, 72). Gudrun later sees the bohemians as "creatures in some menagerie of apish, degraded souls" (380).

For Gudrun, the blackened mining countryside is a lurid, strangely seductive hell of lust and pollution, in which "the ugliness overlaid with beauty was like a narcotic to the senses" (115). She feels "a foul kind of beauty [in] this place" and a sordid glamor in the mass "of powerful, underworld men" (115). In this "mindless, inhuman," voluptuous, mechanical underworld, she responds to a "wave of disruptive force . . . given off from the presence of thousands of vigorous, underworld, half-automatised colliers . . . which . . . awk[es] a fatal desire, and a fatal callousness" (115–116). It is another displaced image of hell. As V. Sepũić observes, "Lawrence's landscape is diabolically alive and the human figures are assimilated to it. This world of mines and machines is an Underworld, a kind of modern Inferno. . . ."[22]

The very degradation of the mining countryside lures her on; rather than falling back in order to spring forward, as she claimed in "Sisters" (10), Gudrun is lapsing into "the single impulse for . . . mindless progressive knowledge through the senses" (253), oscillating violently with a destructive will. Stupefied by a "potent atmosphere of intense, dark callousness" (116), she feels a "nostalgia" for mechanized passivity and risks submerging her hard-won independence in order to enjoy the dark, unthinking power of mass-being. Although flaunting her colorful singularity in dresses as strident as a macaw, she is lured back from the city by the sinister otherness of the place. Conversely, her sensitivity is exacerbated by the "uncreated and ugly" environment, spread out around her like raw material for her active, yet parasitic, consciousness.

While the sophisticated artist experiences these effects of the fall self-consciously, the industrial magnate externalizes them, subsuming men and earth in a ruthless will-to-power that objectifies, alienates, instrumentalizes, until the miners voluntarily submit their being to the machine. Gerald's philosophy, in robbing them of freedom, resembles that of Dostoevsky's Grand Inquisitor. He can only *know* the will-to-power that dominates him by dominating others; he electrifies mines and organizes men as if their otherness were an extension of his own being. Translating will-to-being/*volonté de pouvoir* into will-to-doing/*Wille zur Macht*, and projecting it outside himself, he lets his vital core atrophy and die.

Gerald-the-industrialist's modernizing ethic resembles Gudrun-the-artist's modernist aesthetic. But while his will is monolithic, hers is ambivalent. She expresses her will-to-form in clearcut miniatures that fix and arrest the flux of being; yet she desires to yield up power over matter and fall back into a morass of sensation. She is tempted to exchange unstable freedom—"the goodness, the holiness, the desire for creation and productive happiness" (253)—for voluptuous enslavement. Struggling to preserve her balance, but attracted to a mindless, mechanical vortex, she "beat[s] her wings like a new Daphne, turning not into a tree but a machine" (116).[23] Having failed to take root in life, as Ursula does in *The Rainbow,* Gudrun is torn between conflicting impulses of sadism and masochism, control and abandon. Her metamorphosis signals a fall out of oneness with nature and being into the mechanized drift of cultural entropy.

The miners' voices, with their machine-like "resonance," are "a music more maddening than the siren's," tempting Gudrun to surrender to unconscious forces. Just as the individual feels herself turning into a machine, industrial culture systematically transmutes Eros into Thanatos. Gudrun's art, with its fixed images and closed forms, makes her vulnerable to a return of the repressed, so that the desire to sink back in a swooning lapse of will comes upon her with the force of an epiphany. (Gerald similarly lapses back in the boat, just before his descent into the underworld in "Water-Party" [178].) The voices of a "dangerous underworld" echo within her, "arous[ing] a strange, nostalgic ache of desire, something almost demoniacal, never to be fulfilled" (117). Responding to the seduction of the industrial wasteland, Gudrun attains a knowledge of evil that confirms her cynical outlook and corrodes her soul.

The refined artist Gudrun's attraction to inchoate mass-men might seem to parallel the intellectual Birkin's attraction to African fetishes and blood-consciousness. But while she gravitates knowingly towards the fall, he struggles for equilibrium. Suffering like Hermione from hyper-consciousness, Gudrun is "half in love with easeful death" (Keats). But, as Birkin says of fetish culture, "[there] is a long way we can travel, after the death-break: after that point where the soul . . . breaks away from its organic hold like a leaf that falls" (253). The fruits of the fall for Gudrun, her electrician boyfriend Palmer, and the miners are "a secret sense of power, and of inexpressible destructiveness, and of fatal half-heartedness, a sort of rottenness in the will" (118).

The question of where Gerald's "go go[es] to" is proposed in "Diver," where he dominates the surface of the water with a Nibelung-like mastery, and extended in "Water-Party," where he dives into "a whole universe . . . as cold as hell" (184). He has forfeited freewill and taken on the curse of Cain after "accidentally" shooting his brother. His attempt to rescue his sister from the underworld is an ironic anti-type of Christ's harrowing of hell.[24] Overwhelmed by failure and negative vision, he can only affirm the finality of death. The world of anti-creation he discovers parallels Milton's "region dolorous" of "Rocks, caves, lakes, fens, bogs, dens, and shades of death / A universe of death . . ." (*Paradise Lost*, 1993, 2.619, 621–622). His hand has been injured in machinery, symbolizing his impotence to give life (Birkin has to light the lanterns for him) or save life (he cannot rescue his sister). Gerald is driven by fate and a locked will to work out his own destruction. The fall is seen as enslavement to habit, exercising only part of one's being, exerting one's will at the expense of the unconscious. The only way to overcome the automatism of the fall, that draws energy from the ego as Satan does from pride (*Paradise Lost*, 1993, 1.314–30, 589–604; 4.75–86), is to recognize its effects on oneself and struggle to reverse them, by reorienting oneself to a power outside the ego.

Gerald fears a fall from illusory "harmony"—i.e., organization imposed by will on matter—into chaos and disintegration. Looking at his own masklike face in the mirror, "[he is] afraid that one day he [will] break down and be a purely meaningless babble lapping round a darkness" (232). There can be no fulfilment or equilibrium where there is no marriage of opposites, only domination or submission. Rigid with fear of the abyss, his will stretched to breaking-point, he looks for salvation to Birkin, whose "odd mobility and changeableness . . . [seem] to sustain the quintessence of faith" (232).

"In Rabbit," Gudrun's and Gerald's supra-carnal knowledge of each other constitutes another version of the fall: "it was as if he had

had knowledge of her in the long red rent of her forearm. . . . The long, shallow red rip seemed torn across his own brain, tearing the surface of his ultimate consciousness, letting through the forever unconscious, unthinkable red ether of the beyond, the obscene beyond" (242). The ether image, apparently derived from Anaxagoras,[25] signifies the chaos that would come again if concentric spheres of Aether and Air were to transgress their boundaries and mingle. The human order has been similarly violated: knowledge from the unconscious has hemorrhaged into consciousness, where it can be subjected to the gaze:[26] "Gudrun looked at Gerald with strange, darkened eyes, strained with underworld knowledge. . . . He felt the mutual hellish recognition" (242).

Birkin shows symptoms of the fall in "An Island," particularly the sense of sterility, the inability to grow; he is not yet rooted in Being like Ursula and "can't get [his] flower into blossom anyhow. Either it is blighted in the bud, or has got the smother-fly, or it isn't nourished. . . . It is a contravened knot" (125–126). His frustration with himself extends to others: in a fit of extreme misanthropy,[27] he refers to people as "apples of Sodom . . . Dead Sea Fruit, gall-apples . . . [whose] insides are full of bitter, corrupt ash" (126). According to legend, ash-filled apples grew on the site of the burned city of Sodom. They resemble those fruits of sin and corruption that delude Satan's legions in *Paradise Lost*:[28]

> . . . greedily they plucked
> The fruitage fair to sight, like that which grew
> Near that bituminous lake where Sodom flamed;
> This more delusive, not the touch, but taste
> Deceived; they fondly thinking to allay
> Their appetite with gust, instead of fruit
> Chewed bitter ashes, which th'offended taste
> With spattering noise rejected: oft they assayed,
> Hunger and thirst constraining, drugged as oft,
> With hatefulest disrelish writhed their jaws
> With soot and cinders filled; so oft they fell
> Into the same illusion. . . .
>
> (10.560–571)

For the embittered Birkin humanity is a Tree of Life corrupted into a tree of lies, on which "the most ghastly heavy crop of Dead Sea Fruit, the intolerable burden of myriad simulacra of people" hangs like a blight (126–127).

A problem with Lawrence's use of the fall myth is its duality: there are two kinds of fall in the novel—the pervasive fall out of nature into culture (recapitulating Genesis and *Paradise Lost*) and a rare fall out of culture back into nature, reversing the effects of the original fall and preceding "paradisal entry." The point becomes clearer if one contrasts negative and positive meanings of the word "lapse": to lapse (or relapse) into "the single impulse for knowledge in one sort" (253) is the syndrome of the fall into knowledge; to "lapse into unknowingness" (44) is a positive reversal of that fall. In the fallen world, culture is superimposed on nature in an entropic system to which individuals are enslaved by their own fallen wills (as the miners are to the mechanism of the mines). The result is a fractured reality: while the human world (like the blackened colliery district) is fallen, the unfallen world can be glimpsed in what remains of nature. A fortunate fall out of culture back into nature is posited in "Mino," as Ursula looks back to images of germination in *The Rainbow*. She has "fallen strange and dim, out of the sheath of the material life, like a berry falls from the only world it has ever known, down out of the sheath on to the real unknown" (144). By implication, the known is unreal, consisting of illusions, distortions, and mental deceptions. The unfallen state, to be regained by genuine *recul* or *ricorso*, is that of vital growth.

In the debate about sexual balance in "Mino," Ursula rejects Birkin's redefinition of *Wille-zur-Macht* as sophistry, asserting that it's simply "the old Adam."[29] "Oh yes," Birkin replies, "Adam kept Eve in the indestructible paradise, when he kept her single with himself, like a star in its orbit" (150). In *Paradise Lost*, Eve strays from Adam after extracting his reluctant permission and falls to Satan's wiles, consequently causing Adam to fall with her. Birkin, in his revision of Genesis, sees Adam and Eve before the fall as two single but mutually balanced beings, rather than "one flesh." He does not endorse Milton's sexual hierarchy nor go so far as his fallen Adam in claiming that the single male state was self-sufficient (*Paradise Lost*, 1993,

10.888–895). Birkin, for all his cursing of the Magna Mater and complaining that "[the] old way of love seem[s] a dreadful bondage" (199), still sees the necessity of balanced relationship with a woman.

Before stoning the moon's image on the dark pool in "Moony," Birkin muses: "There wouldn't have to be any truth, if there weren't any lies—then one wouldn't need to assert anything . . ." (246). Having rejected his own "Hamletis[ing]" as a lie (187), he deplores the knowledge of good and evil that condemns him to a dialectical treadmill. If one were released from the pressure of the fall, there would be no need for mind and will to assert themselves, so being could come more fully into play. Birkin angers Ursula by trampling verbally on her "female ego," so that she misinterprets his concept of "paradisal unknowing" as a covert power play. Having antagonized her with words, he realizes their inadequacy. How can he willingly destroy his own fallen will, or she give him a part of herself that she doesn't know? As long as they confront each other as self-insistent egos, they will be at loggerheads, as Adam and Eve were after the fall, when "high winds . . . /Began to rise, high passions, anger, hate, / Mistrust, suspicion, discord, and shook sore / Their inward state of mind . . ." (*Paradise Lost*, 1993, 9.1122–1125).

The fall is a lapsing out of the struggle for equilibrium within oneself and between self and others. In his reflections on entropy, Birkin defines the fall as a cultural and spiritual breakdown "between the senses and the outspoken mind . . . leaving the experience all in one sort" (253). All that is left is the craving for "mystic knowledge in disintegration and dissolution" (253), the rotten fruit of the Tree of Knowledge or falling leaves of the Tree of Life. The fall into fixed and false consciousness occurs at

> that point where the soul in intense suffering breaks, breaks away from its organic hold like a leaf that falls. We fall from the connection with life and hope, we lapse from pure integral being, from creation and liberty, and we fall into the long, long African process of purely sensual understanding, knowledge in the mystery of dissolution. (253)

Lapsing from the creative desire for fulfilment in an inner marriage of opposites brings about a fall into entropic sensuality or mentality, with inevitable corruption.[30] The fall is conceived as a living death, a descent into arrested, disintegrated, fetishistic, or parasitic "knowing." The "African process" is one of two polarized modes of the fall, the other being the Nordic way of "ice-destructive knowledge, snow-abstract annihilation" (254), that symbolizes mental consciousness and will.

The sisters, having crossed "over the border of evil" in mutual confidences, "[arm] each other with knowledge [and extract] the subtlest flavours from the apple of knowledge" (262). They enjoy a detached *sapience*, a taste for knowing in the head, that takes the place of being-in-touch. Their knowledge is curiously "complementary," with Ursula temporarily sharing Gudrun's capacity for critical dissection. But Gudrun's factual analysis is a lie, because it ignores the growing, changing, core of being. It is a reductive "diagram," like the "grotesque little diagram" (236) in which her pupil, Winifred, traps the essence of a pet pekinese.

In Birkin's "harrowing Hell" epistle, the fall is "the great retrogression, the reducing back of the created body of life, [in which] we get knowledge, and beyond knowledge, the phosphorescent ecstasy of acute sensation" (383). Gudrun's knowledge of Gerald follows this pattern and is associated with the fall in Genesis: "There seemed a faint, white light emitted from him, a white aura, as if he were a visitor from the unseen. She reached up, like Eve reaching to the apples on the tree of knowledge, and she kissed him, though her passion was a transcendent fear of the thing he was . . ." (331). She wants the forbidden knowledge that will give her power over her lover. Her violation of his being ironically parallels Birkin's penetration of it in "Gladiatorial," "always seizing with some rapid necromantic foreknowledge every motion of the other flesh, converting and counteracting it . . ." (270).

The two encounters are teleologically distinct, however. Birkin and Gerald's struggle is compared with Jacob's wrestling with the angel for a blessing (Genesis 32:24–30); Gerald and Gudrun's is marked by disequilibrium, lust for power, "transcendent fear," and fallen knowledge leading to destruction. Gudrun "encroach[es]" on her lover's being, as she traces his features with artist's fingers:

> Her soul thrilled with complete knowledge. This was the glisten-ing, forbidden apple, this face of a man. . . . He was such an unut-terable enemy, yet glistening with uncanny white fire. She wanted to touch him . . . till she had strained him into her knowledge. (332)

As her touch penetrates Gerald's defenses and lays bare his vulner-able core, she takes sensual delight in knowing "good and evil" in the vitality and corruption of his being. He seems to "materialize" under her touch as a complex battery of impulses, rather than a freely responsive partner. Knowing him, she knows death and the void, secrets of his fatalistic soul that Birkin also penetrates. Gu-drun's predatory appetite for knowledge is destructive of being and "a death from which she must recover" (332). In moments of inti-macy, she and Gerald remain radically apart, watchful, obsessed with gaining power over each other by transmuting sensations into knowledge. Gudrun has the capacity to release "the strength and the power of living desire" in Gerald (333), and he comes to depend on her for knowing this momentary surge of life in himself.

For Birkin and Ursula, who practice sacramental rites of touch, "paradisal entry" follows open conflict. In mutual consummation of being, they form "a new, paradisal unit regained from the duality" (369). The self-assertive, exclusive "I" is transcended and replaced by "something new and unknown" (369). Personal experience is sub-sumed in mystical, as marriage becomes Birkin's "resurrection and his life" (369). In "Continental," Ursula discovers a marriage of op-posites within her own being:

> In the midst of this profound darkness, there seemed to glow on her heart the effulgence of a paradise unknown and unrealised. Her heart was full of the most wonderful light, golden like honey of darkness . . . which was not shed on the world, only on the un-known paradise towards which she was going. . . . (388)

Her recovery from deathlike withdrawal in "Sunday Evening," and the breakthrough of "Excurse" with Birkin, lead to "paradise regained"; her experience typologically "identif[ies] her with the redemptive pattern for the 'new Eve' even while developing in her the instinctive qualities of the 'old Eve'" (Hyde, *The Risen Adam*, 1992, 110).

Birkin's "necromantic foreknowledge" of Gerald is the dark counterpart of Ursula's "ecstasy of bliss in foreknowledge" (388). He experiences a positive rite of passage from known to unknown, "falling through a gulf of infinite darkness, like a meteorite plunging across the chasm between the worlds . . . plunging like an unlit star through the ineffable rift" (388). There is an ironic, revisionist, echo of Satan's fall through space: "Him the Almighty Power / Hurled headlong flaming, from th'ethereal sky," or Mulciber's: "from morn / To noon he fell, from noon to dewy eve, / . . . and with the setting sun / Dropped from the zenith like a falling star . . ." (*Paradise Lost*, 1993, 1.44–45. 742–745). As Birkin willingly "[falls] into the unknown" (388),[31] the "unutterable peace of darkness in his [heart]" matches "the paradisal glow" in Ursula's. In their hierogamous marriage (cf. Hyde, 111) of "dark knowledge" with "golden light," they achieve a oneness that surpasses mere knowledge. Ursula's redemptive role, somewhat muted by Lawrence's revisions,[32] is consistent with Frye's account of the fall (very different from Milton's) as a fall out of matriarchy into patriarchy—into the world of Bismarck and the Industrial Magnate: "Man falls as woman, that is, as sexual being, hence woman would have to be the central figure in the restoration of the original sexual and social state" (Frye, *Words with Power*, 1990, 192.[33] But first they have to cross a deathly shadow zone: landing on the continent is "like disembarking from the Styx into the desolated underworld"; people glimpsed from the train are like "spectres" and Birkin "like a *revenant*" (389, 390). The new world can only be reached through the death of the old.

In contrast with Birkin and Ursula's "Paradisal entry" into new life, Gerald and Gudrun's "honeymoon before the wedding" (371) turns into a struggle to the death. Their relationship rapidly deteriorates from carnal knowledge to hatred and violence, because they remain "separate, like opposite poles of one fierce energy" (399). In their interdestructive passion, "one [is] destroyed that the other might exist, one ratified because the other was nulled" (445). Eros becomes deathly compulsion. Gerald suffers from "the constant passion, that [is] like a doom upon him" (401), an agony of desire that can never be sated. Contradictory effects of the fall are paralyzed numbness and painful awareness. As in Coleridge's "Dejection: An Ode," Gudrun is doomed to see and know natural beauty with all the more piercing clarity because she cannot feel or enjoy it: "She could *see* it, she knew it, but she was not of it. She was divorced, debarred, a soul shut out" (403).[34] Her spiritual condition is analogous to Satan's, as he looks in on the bliss of Eden from which he is forever debarred (*Paradise Lost* 4.205–392). Gudrun has forfeited joy through insistence on knowledge; she has alienated herself from Gerald by *knowing* and exploiting the sources of his power. She is too self-consciously proud of her knowledge to accept the "paradisal unknowing" that is bliss to Birkin and Ursula; she can only "env[y] them some spontaneity, a childish sufficiency . . ." (403).

Having crossed the "threshold" of knowledge and mocked and betrayed Birkin's notions of "*ultimate* marriage" and "Paradise" regained (289–90), Gudrun is left with the obscene mysteries of reduction and disintegration. She has made a trophy of Birkin's diatribe about "reacting in intimacy only for destruction,—using sex as a great reducing agent" (384), because it applies so well to her. Now she finds herself compulsively acting out the script and having it acted out upon her. As she approaches the end of her devious course, her state is already infernal; she is reduced to knowing, in the rhythms of her consciousness, the slow but inevitable mechanisms of the fall:

> "The world was finished now, for her. There was only the inner, individual darkness, sensation within the ego, the obscene religious mystery of ultimate reduction, the mystic frictional activities of diabolic reducing down, disintegrating the vital organic body of life." (452)

While she suffers this hell, the reborn and childlike Birkin and Ursula have left the snow-world behind and gained a sunny paradise that she, in her superior knowledge, scoffed at.

In terms of sinister "understanding," Loerke embodies the fall into knowledge: he is "the very stuff of the underworld of life. There [is] no going beyond him" (427). Birkin explains his attraction as that of "the perfectly subjected [fallen] being, existing almost like a criminal. And the women rush towards that, like a current of air towards a vacuum" (427). In Norse mythology, Loki is the spirit of negation or "World's Begrudger,"[35] just as Loerke is "a gnawing little negation, gnawing at the roots of life" (428). The "wizard rat that swims ahead" is a pioneer of evil, who thrives parasitically on a fallen culture and "lives . . . in the river of corruption, just where it falls over into the bottomless pit" (428)—an image that recalls the Eighth Circle, or Malebolge; of Dante's *Inferno* (Canto 18). Bat-like or rat-like, he represents a late stage in that process of corruption and deception whereby Milton's Satan metamorphoses into cormorant, toad, and snake.

The final fruit of knowledge for Gerald is to experience the death of the woman who has aroused and rejected his passion. Frye observes of Milton's Adam and Eve:

"After the fall . . . [appetite] ceases to be appetite and is transformed into passion, the drive toward death. . . . Passion operates in the mind as though it were an external force . . . and the passions of greed and lust have two qualities that the appetites do not have: excess and mechanical energy." (*Return of Eden*, 1964, 68–69)

Finding Gudrun in the snow with Loerke, Gerald reaches out eagerly to take "the apple of his desire," her throat, into his hands and strangle her—as she had taken "the glistening, forbidden apple" of his face in her fingers, to *know* his secrets. In a single convulsive image, Eros becomes Thanatos: he imagines her death throes as "her reciprocal lustful passion in this embrace . . ." (472). But it is Gerald who dies of a broken will, and after his "life-breath [has] frozen into a block of ice" and death has reduced him to "congealed, icy substance" (477, 479), "the cold devil of irony . . . [freezes Gudrun's] soul" (476). Whether physically or spiritually, they share the same fate, and Birkin's prophecy that "[the] white races . . . would fulfil a mystery of ice-destructive knowledge" (254) is made manifest in this couple.

The novel is a "Day of Judgment,"[36] extreme, eschatological, apocalyptic in its displacement of the myth of the fall. The industrial and social worlds in which people live and interact are a wasteland or inferno, as in Lawrence's painting, *Flight Back into Paradise* (1927), in which a Frieda-like Eve is breaking away from the industrial inferno, while a Lawrence-like Adam pushes back the sword of the angel at the gate.[37] Through mythic allusion and prophetic rhetoric, Lawrence offers a vision of the forces that lead to disintegration and despair, to the loss of paradise, in modern life. In this sense, the novel is a dark sequel to the integrative vision of *The Rainbow*. For the characters, who work out their destinies in relationships, there is only the fall (interdestruction, reduction, entropy) or regeneration (star equilibrium, paradisal re-entry). The deep structure of myth reveals universal spiritual patterns in an alienated and seemingly chaotic modern world.

Notes

1. *Women in Love*, ed. David Farmer, Lindeth Vasey, and John Worthen (Cambridge University Press, 1987).

2. "John Galsworthy," *Study of Thomas Hardy and Other Essays*, ed. Bruce Steele (Cambridge University Press, 1985), 211.

3. Review of *The Social Basis of Consciousness*, Trigant Burrow, in *Phoenix: The Posthumous Papers of D. H. Lawrence*; ed. Edward D. McDonald (1936; rpt. New York: Viking Press, 1972), 378.

4. The psychological condition is well described in Iris Murdoch's novel, *The Bell* (London: Chatto, 1958), as a "dreary trance-like solipsism" (192).

5. According to one commentator, "the roots of all subsequent revelation are planted deep in Genesis . . ." (*The New Scofield Reference Bible*, ed. C. I. Scofield [Oxford University Press, 1967], 1. Another commentator "suppose[s] that the [Hebrew] narrator created the tree of knowledge as a counterpiece to the tree of life" (John L. Mackenzie, S. J., *Dictionary of the Bible* [New York: Macmillan, 1965], 271).

6. Mackenzie, *Dictionary of the Bible*, 272.

7. *The Letters of D. H. Lawrence*, Vol. 2, eds. George Zytaruk and James T. Boulton (Cambridge University Press, 1981), 367.

8. "Lawrence's Götterdämmerung: The Apocalyptic Vision of *Women in Love*," in *Critical Essays on D. H. Lawrence*, ed. Dennis Jackson and Fleda Brown Jackson (Boston: Hall, 1988), 94.

9. "Lawrence and the Apocalyptic Types," *Critical Quarterly* 10 (1968): 21.

10. In Northrop Frye's biblical/cosmological scheme, "[the] physical environment we are born in [is] theologically a fallen world of alienation" (*Words with Power: Being a Second Study of "The Bible and Literature"* [Toronto: Penguin, 1990], 169).

11. Northrop Frye, in "Myth, Fiction, and Displacement," *Fables of Identity: Studies in Poetic Mythology* (New York: Harvest-Harcourt, 1963), defines *displacement* as "the techniques a writer uses to make his [mythic] story credible, logically motivated or morally acceptable—lifelike, in short" (36).

12. "Man lives," according to Frye, "within a mythological universe, a body of assumptions and beliefs developed from his existential concerns." (*The Great Code: The Bible and Literature* (Toronto: Academic Press Canada, 1983), xviii.)

13. Kermode compares Lawrence's and Milton's "typologising" of England's "renovation" and "decline," noting that Lawrence emphasizes decline.

14. Savoring the fruit of the fall, Eve hails the tree "of operation blest / To sapience," signifying a mixture of "sensual appetite," taste, and secret knowledge (John Milton, *Paradise Lost*, ed. Scott Elledge, 2nd ed., Norton Critical Edition [New York: Norton, 1993], 9:796–797, 809–810). Apparently alluding to *Paradise Lost*, Lawrence writes: "The serpent, with a crushed head, learned to brood along his spine, and take poison in his mouth. He has a strange sapience." ("On Human Destiny," *Reflections on the Death of a Porcupine and Other Essays*, ed. Michael Herbert [Cambridge University Press, 1988], 204; see also Daniel Dervin, *A "Strange Sapience": The Creative Imagination of D. H. Lawrence* [University of Massachusetts Press, 1984], 1–2).

15. *The Complete Poems of D. H. Lawrence*, ed. Vivian de Sola Pinto and Warren Roberts (Harmondsworth: Penguin, 1977), 673.

16. Malleson is a caricature of Bertrand Russell, whose intellectualism Lawrence attacked in a famous letter on blood-consciousness (*Letters* 2:470–471).

17. Northrop Frye, *The Return of Eden: Five Essays on Milton's Epics* (University of Toronto Press, 1964), 59. Cf. Lawrence's "New Heaven and Earth," in which he describes the experience of overcoming solipsism in marriage (*Complete Poems*, 256–261).

18. Cf. "Foreword": "Every man who is acutely alive is acutely wrestling with his own soul. The people that can bring forth the new passion, the new idea, this people will endure. Those others, that fix them-

selves in the old idea, will perish with the new life strangled unborn within them" (*Women in Love*, 485–486).

19. Lawrence expresses the concept clearly and colloquially in "Nathaniel Hawthorne and 'The Scarlet Letter,'" *Studies in Classic American Literature* (New York: Anchor-Doubleday, 1951): "When Adam went and took Eve, after the apple, he didn't do any more than he had done many a time before, in act. But in consciousness he did something very different. So did Eve. Each of them kept an eye on what they were doing, they watched what was happening to them. They wanted to KNOW. And that was the birth of sin. Not doing it, but KNOWING about it (94)."

20. This image of the Nordic/industrial world parallels the fallen world of the "African process," with its "knowledge such as the beetles have, which live purely within the world of corruption and cold dissolution" (253).

21. See George Ford, "Dies Irae: *Women in Love*," in *Double Measure: A Study of the Novels and Stories of D. H. Lawrence* (New York: Holt, 1975), 163–207.

22. "'Women in Love' and Expressionism (I)," *Studia Romanica et Anglica Zagrabiensia* 26 (1981): 426. P. T. Whelan, *Myth and Metaphysic in "The Rainbow" and "Women in Love"* (Ann Arbor: UMI Research Press, 1988), also relates the mining countryside to a mythic underworld (57).

23. Anne Fernihough, *D. H. Lawrence: Aesthetics and Ideology* (Oxford: Clarendon Press, 1993), notes that both Lawrence and Heidegger "develop . . . a myth of a 'fall' into our present, technology-driven condition . . ." (138).

24. Kermode observes: "Ritual descent into hell, followed by rebirth—that is the character of Lawrence's transitional period" (20). This descent matches Frye's mythic schema: "Below physical nature [is] the demonic world . . . [that] still exerts considerable power over the [physical dimension] as a result of the Fall" (*Words with Power*, 169). Gerald is an anti-hero, who cannot survive his knowledge of the abyss. Birkin, on the contrary, has faith in change and the power to blast through death to life: for him, "to know, to give utterance, [is] to break a way through the walls of the prison . . ." (186).

25. See "Explanatory Notes," *Women in Love*, 589.

26. Cf. Earl Ingersoll, "Staging the Gaze in D. H. Lawrence's *Women in Love*," Studies in the Novel 26 (1994): 268–280.

27. Oates remarks that "the vituperation expressed [in the novel] is perhaps unequaled in serious literature" (95): it is reinforced by Lawrence's prophetic use of the myth of the fall.

28. According to a note in the Norton Critical Edition, "Milton got the idea for the ironic apples from the well-known Jewish historian Josephus,

who claimed such fruit grew by the Dead Sea (*bituminous lake*, cf. 1.411), and from the myth of Tantalus . . ." (*Paradise Lost*, ed. Elledge, 244, n.).

29. See Virginia Hyde, *The Risen Adam: D. H. Lawrence's Revisionist Typology* (Pennsylvania State University Press, 1992), xvi, xx, 42, et passim, on the two Adams, type and anti-type.

30. Colin Clarke, *River of Dissolution: D. H. Lawrence and English Romanticism* (London: Routledge, 1969), argues in organicist terms the necessity of corruption and disintegration of reintegration and revitalization (an issue debated by Birkin and Ursula in "Water-Party") and claims that Lawrence affirms both poles equally. Oxymorons like "living disintegration" would seem to support his view, but within the mythic paradigm of the fall, with its dialectics of good and evil, corruption is clearly negative, stemming from a "death-break" or "lapse" (Latin *lapsus*, fall).

31. Cf. Ursula's confidence in her destiny: "If I were the moon, I know where I would fall down" (*The Rainbow*, 308).

32. See Pierre Vitoux, "The Chapter 'Excurse' in *Women in Love*: Its Genesis and the Critical Problem," *TSLL* 17 (1976): 821–836.

33. Lawrence, like Milton and the Blake of "dark Satanic Mills" and "England's green & pleasant Land," wanted to restore his fallen land and countrymen: "And I do so break my heart over England . . . And I am so sure that only through a readjustment between men and women, and a making free and healthy of the sex, will she get out of her present atrophy [the state of the fall]." (*The Letters of D. H. Lawrence*, vol. 1, ed. James T. Boulton [Cambridge University Press, 1979], 544.)

34. According to Sepŭić, "'Women in Love' and Expressionism (II)," *Studia Romanica et Anglica Zagrabiensia* 27 (1982), "[the] snow landscape . . . [is] presented . . . as a kind of counterpart to the Inferno of the 'Coal-Dust' chapter, as a kind of Paradise for the damned. . . . These inert, cold, levelling, life-denying expanses are significantly refracted through the consciousness of Gudrun; this is the landscape in which she reaches the final goal of her soul's journey . . ." (34).

35. William Morris, *Sigurd the Volsung*, cited in Ford, Double Measure, 196. Ford adds that "in some Norse myths Loki is the devil" (197). Birkin may seem "a dreadful Satanist" at times, but Loerke (his ironic counterpart) is the thing itself, in peculiarly modern form.

36. See Maria DiBattista, "*Women in Love*: D. H. Lawrence's Judgment Book," *D. H. Lawrence: A Centenary Consideration*, ed. Peter Balbert and Phillip L. Marcus (Cornell University Press, 1985), 67–90.

37. *Paintings of D. H. Lawrence*, ed. Mervyn Levy (London: Cory, 1964), Pl. 9, 45.

Totem, Taboo, and Blutbrüderschaft in D. H. Lawrence's *Women in Love*

CAROLA M. KAPLAN

❖　❖　❖

O N T H E S U R F A C E, D. H. Lawrence's *The Rainbow* and *Women in Love,* although they originated as a single fictional work, "The Sisters," appear to be two distinctly different kinds of novels: the first, a generational narrative, its roots in the nineteenth century; the second, an end-of-the-world vision, its nihilism forged by the nightmare of the Great War. Yet for all the apparent differences between the two books, their author insisted that they form "an organic, artistic whole." While conceding that the two novels are "very different," Lawrence maintained that *Women in Love* is a "sequel" to *The Rainbow* (quoted in Ford, *Double,* 1965, 164).

However divergent in tone and form, the two works are indeed united by a common purpose: that of diagnosing the ills of a culture and of proposing a new direction for men and women in the modern world. In this shared impulse, the novels are examples of a familiar Victorian and Edwardian fictional genre: the "Condition of England novel" (Lodge 1976, 113). Accordingly, *Women in Love* continues the diagnosis of England's ills begun in *The Rainbow.* Further, unlike such literary antecedents as C.F.G. Masterman's *The Condition of*

England and H. G. Wells's *Tono-Bungay,* Lawrence's text is not content with mere diagnosis but offers a prescription as well for a new social order. This utopian vision of the England that might be is inspired by non Western, nonindustrial cultures. Lawrence, like other artists of his generation, looked to "primitive" cultures,[1] in whose difference he saw both warning and blueprint for the West. His bifurcated conception of the primitive gave Lawrence a model for cultural regeneration through a new male-centered social order; but it also conjured up for him a nightmare vision of degeneration and eventual destruction through a female-dominated world of sensation seeking and unbridled sensuality. Thus Lawrence's primitivism was riddled with contradiction and his valuation of primitive cultures was undermined by ambivalence. As projection of both his deepest longings and his greatest fears, the primitive remained deeply troubling to Lawrence and proved ultimately futile in providing him with the sustained artistic purpose and redemptive social vision he had sought in it.

The purpose of this paper is to show how Lawrence proposes in *Women in Love* to furnish a cure for the otherwise terminal condition of England by way of entry into the primitive, but fails, through his cultural assumptions, historical placement, and unresolved psychosexual conflicts, to find in primitivism either instruction or corrective for modern ills. I will argue further that one specific primitivist text—Sigmund Freud's *Totem and Taboo* (1913)—provides both underlying meaning and narrative direction for the first half of Lawrence's novel. But Lawrence's vision is ultimately overridden by a powerful primitivist nightmare that triumphs in the last part of the book and destroys the earlier promise of social regeneration.

Continuing *The Rainbow's* narrative of the unraveling of English culture over three generations, *Women in Love* begins with a diagnosis of early twentieth-century malaise as proceeding from the loss of communal life and values. From the first, the text explores the possibility of forging a new community centered around a shared core of meaning. First it explores one counterculture community of artists in Bohemian London. Then, rejecting this world as a false alternative, the novel sets forth a utopian vision of a new social order, designed to compensate for the deficiencies of the modern world.

Early in the novel, the two central male characters, Rupert Birkin and Gerald Crich, discuss their longing for meaning in life but conclude that life "just doesn't centre" (58). Rupert expresses the hope that love for one woman may provide his life with "one *really* pure single activity" (57), but quickly adds the somber qualifier, "seeing there's no God" (58). The elegiac tone of this conversation is illustrative of Fredric Jameson's observation that "the very idea of value comes into being at the moment of its own disappearance . . . which is to say that . . . the study of value is at one with nihilism, or the experience of its absence" (251). *Women in Love* vividly illustrates Jameson's paradox that

> it is only in the most humanized environment, the one most fully and obviously the end product of human labor, production, and transformation, that life becomes meaningless, and that existential despair first appears as such in direct proportion to the elimination of nature and the prospect of a well-nigh limitless control over the external universe. (251)

Birkin epitomizes this dilemma when he enters London with only negative anticipations: "I feel such a despair, so hopeless, as if it were the end of the world" (53). London, to an even greater extent than the mining town of Beldover, exemplifies an overindustrialized society that, while apparently exerting a "well-nigh limitless control" over nature, makes its inhabitants feel that they are trapped and that their lives are devoid of meaning.

The theme of ennui and disaffection so extensively explored in the early part of the novel comes to a head in two interconnected scenes set in London, one in a café and the other in an artist's flat. The sequential chapters "Crème de Menthe" and "Fetish" paint a diagnostic picture of contemporary social malaise. In particular, they foreground the problems of class, race, and sexuality that Rupert and Gerald must confront. These problems, in turn, have their roots in the last half-century of British history, whose major events, trends, and intellectual currents appear in traces in these scenes. In particular, objects and events in Halliday's flat point to problems of

England at home and abroad: class differences; the emergence of the New Woman; the intensification of imperialism and its by-product, racism; fin de-siècle decadence; and Bloomsbury rebellion. In its symbolic contents, Halliday's flat is crowded, indeed.

At first glance, Halliday's lodgings and the London demi-monde he and his fellow artists inhabit are sites of freedom and unconventionality—classless, creative, sexually liberated. Yet Lawrence satirically demonstrates that these characters are more enslaved by conventions than the bourgeoisie they seek to defy. Appearances to the contrary, this Bohemian world is not an alternative space that repudiates the surrounding culture, but rather a microcosm of British society. The events and imagery of the scene suggest that this is but a particular rung in the general social hell of the modern world. The effect of Birkin and Gerald's sojourn in London Bohemia is to demonstrate the need to establish a radically different social order in contradistinction to a mere veneer of freedom that masks the underlying chaos.

If an alternative social structure is to offer real freedom, it must be based on solidarity, shared vision, loyalty, and friendship. The novel proposes that this alliance start with Birkin and Gerald. But there is an obstacle that the book must resolve in order to make their alliance possible: that of class difference. Existing class divisions would ordinarily make close friendship between Gerald and Birkin highly problematic, if not impossible. The novel—as exemplified in this London scene—works to resolve or deflect this problem with a variety of unconvincing and contradictory responses.

The text shows its anxiety about class in a number of ways: it places characters in a social hierarchy yet omits Birkin from this placement, it seeks to establish a new hierarchy based on innate superiority rather than birth, and finally it displaces class difference onto racial difference.

Clearly, Gerald and Birkin occupy different steps on the social ladder. Gerald, the heir to a mining fortune, belongs to a distinctly higher social stratum than Birkin, the school inspector (despite the fact that Birkin's social position is somewhat obscured by his enjoying additional income from an undesignated source). The class difference between them would be even more pronounced if Birkin, who otherwise shares a great many characteristics with D. H. Lawrence, were also to share Lawrence's working-class background as a miner's son who by dint of cleverness has worked his way up in the world. But the narrative is careful to avoid any social placement for Birkin: he is uniquely without family or social background, unlike all the other characters in the text.

The novel goes even further in removing from Birkin any hint of class placement. He is "not to be defined" (79) and, as Gerald puts it, "above the world" (209). Throughout the text, Birkin keeps his distance from the working classes; downplays the importance of breadwinning; and, more than Gerald, disparages the value of mere material comfort. Further, Birkin views manual labor with distaste, associating it with dirt and excrement. (Later, he will make a similar association between excrement and Africans, the manual laborers of empire.) Birkin protests, "we cover the earth with foulness; life is a blotch of labour, like insects scurrying in filth" (55).

Throughout, the text is irresolvably ambivalent about class. On the one hand, the text faults Gerald for his class-consciousness. When Gerald shows displeasure at learning that Ursula's father is a handicrafts instructor, Birkin jeers at him, "Class-barriers are breaking down!" (94). When Gerald later patronizes Will Brangwen at the Crich family's water-party, the narrator comments: "Gerald was so obvious in his demeanour" (160).

Further, the novel takes pains to demonstrate the superficiality of class distinctions in showing how easy it is to be fooled about class, as Gerald is by the aristocratic-looking Hindu servant: "He made Gerald uncertain, because, being tall and slender and reticent, he looked like a gentleman." When Gerald asserts, "He looks a swell" Halliday counters, "He's anything but a swell, really" (73).

Having gone to the trouble of showing that the conventional class hierarchy is based on flimsy criteria, the book works to prove that the important differences between people are intrinsic. According to this revised standard of class, Birkin tells Gerald, "Gudrun Brangwen . . . is your equal like anything, probably your superior" (209). As for Birkin himself, he is distinguished throughout the narrative by his innate superiority. In fact, in the scene in Halliday's flat, Birkin shows himself to be Gerald's superior in discernment and

cultivation. Gerald acknowledges Birkin's superiority in these crucial respects when he asks him how to interpret the African statue
in Halliday's flat. Without any specific knowledge of the culture that
produced the work, Birkin is somehow equipped to pronounce, "It
is art," and to understand intuitively the "complete truth" (78–79) it
expresses.

Finally, the text resolves the problem of class difference by displacing it onto racial difference. Thus Gerald and Birkin band together as exponents of English culture, asserting its social and racial
superiority to all other cultures. After all, when Englishmen deal
with the racial Other, class differences between them and within
British culture become so minimal as virtually to disappear. Unlike
the uncertain and equivocal hierarchy of class, the racial hierarchy
in the room is reassuringly clear. At the top are the white males;
below them, the Hindu servant; at the bottom, the black female as
represented in the African statue.

In this scene, all the white men band together to establish this
racial hierarchy. Collectively, they disparage the Arab, relying solely
on stereotypes in their assessment of him. In this way, the narrator,
Halliday, Maxim, Gerald, and Birkin describe him as inscrutable
(80), "very dirty" (73), static (80), dishonest (74), "half a savage" (73),
sporting a borrowed veneer of civilization (a gentleman's cast-off
clothing) but lacking underwear (showing that underneath, he is a
naked savage). He exists only to serve (conveniently disappearing
and reappearing to perform his job) and is abused for his efforts. Yet
this treatment is to be seen as his salvation, since Halliday boasts that
he picked the Hindu up by the roadside and thus kept him from
starving (73).

The ideas, actions, and dialog of this scene reproduce the racist
discourse of the late Victorian and Edwardian eras[2] during which the
intensification of the imperial enterprise in Arab countries, in the
West Pacific, and in Africa was justified by a British-produced colo-
nial view of natives as childish, savage, debauched, in need of moral
betterment and of useful work (to be specific, the menial work of
empire—serving its builders and maintainers). In reciting Gerald's
credentials, Birkin makes clear the connection between social ascendancy at home in England and racial ascendancy abroad: "He's a sol-

dier, and an explorer, and a Napoleon of industry" (64). Gerald's attributes—his status as a gentleman, his patriotism as a soldier, his
courage as an explorer, and his power as an industrial magnate—all
make evident his fitness to rule. The description of Gerald, who "explored the Amazon . . . and now . . . is ruling over coal-mines" (64),
recalls the nineteenth-century discourse about qualifications for
empire building.

Gerald's fitness to rule at home and abroad is further confirmed
by his response to Pussum's question "Were you ever vewy much
afwaid of the savages?" Gerald declares: "On the whole they're
harmless—they're not born yet, you can't feel really afraid of them.
You know you can manage them" (66). In these words, Gerald asserts his inherent superiority over the people of the Amazon, the
site of his explorations. This scene overtly sets forth overlapping assumptions about race, class, and nationality that confirm an Eng-
lishman's qualifications to rule at home and abroad.

Birkin shares with Gerald this assumption of cultural and racial
superiority, as evidenced in his assessment of the Hindu. "Birkin felt
a slight sickness, looking at him, and feeling the slight greyness an
ash of corruption, the aristocratic inscrutability of expression a nau-
seating, bestial stupidity" (80). Birkin associates the gray tone that
underlies the Arab's dark skin with death and "corruption." By contrast, in this scene, Birkin is twice described as "white." Thus common cultural and racial assumptions cement the friendship between Gerald and Birkin, taking precedence over the issue of class
differences within British culture, and the two men close ranks. Just
as Englishmen abroad are above all else Englishmen who must stick
together when engaged in the imperial enterprise, class differences
between Birkin and Gerald at home in England do not count when
compared with the abyss of difference that separates Britons
racially, culturally, morally, and—as we shall consider—sexually,
from other and lesser cultures.

These same assumptions aid the two men in declaring their ascendancy over women. Their shared sense of racial and cultural superiority assists them in asserting their sexual superiority as well.
They enact both their anxiety and their need to achieve mastery
over the female in their symbolic encounter with the African statue

of a woman in childbirth. In their detailed analysis of the meaning of the fetish, which they find both attractive and repugnant, they temporarily resolve their sexual conflicts and achieve a solidarity that will buttress them, for a time, in dealing with the two assertive and independent women with whom they are newly forming intimate relationships: Birkin with Ursula, Gerald with Gudrun. Their symbolic triumph over the female fetish does much to reassure them, at least temporarily, of their gender superiority and sexual ascendancy.

At first, the two men seem to disagree in their assessment of the meaning and value of the statue. In his role as art critic and cultural interpreter, Birkin praises the sculpture and attempts to allay Gerald's misgivings that it may be obscene. But Birkin's praise of the figure is so ambivalent and qualified that it seems as much criticism as admiration. He asserts of the statue, "It contains the whole truth of that state, whatever you feel about it" (79), thereby suggesting his own underlying negative feelings. Answering Gerald's objections that it cannot be high art because it does not come from a highly developed culture, Birkin maintains that there are "hundreds of centuries of development, in a straight line, behind that carving . . . it is an awful pitch of culture, of a definite sort" (79). His choice of words—"awful pitch"—suggests that this culture has developed in excessive and frightening ways.[3] Clearly, Birkin is both attracted and repelled by the instinctual and uninhibited sexual gratification the statue represents. As Hal Foster notes, "In this way the phantasmatic figure of the savage elicits an oscillation between esteem and disgust" (73–74).

At best, Birkin's admiration for the statue is double-edged. He praises it as representing "culture in the physical consciousness, really ultimate *physical* consciousness, mindless, utterly sensual" (79). Yet in applauding the woman's sensuality, he points out her lack of intelligence. By contrast, Birkin displays his exemplary intelligence throughout the scene: he triumphs through conscious knowledge; through his ability to describe, place, and judge the statue; to account for her through language. The fetish, voiceless and inert, is pure sensation as distinct from male cognition. The scene demonstrates that male cognition has the greater power.

Even the statue's sensuality has its disagreeable side. At first, she seems to embody the sensual knowledge for which Birkin has expressed longing: "It is a fulfillment—the great dark knowledge you can't have in your head—the dark involuntary being. It is death to one's self—but it is the coming into being of another" (43). Of course, this association of sensuality with death lends it an ominous as well as desirable quality. In addition, the fetish, while "rather wonderful, conveying the suggestion of the extreme of physical sensation, beyond the limits of mental consciousness," is also "strange and disturbing," and "looked almost like the foetus of a human being" (74). This description suggests that if she is highly developed in her sensuality, she is undeveloped in other important human characteristics. Further, since she comes from an ancient culture, she seems not so much to embody an early stage of human development but rather to be arrested in development.

But there is a yet more disturbing quality to her sensuality. The statue is linked with Pussum—and Pussum, with sexual corruption. Both the statue and Pussum are pregnant; the statue resembles a foetus and Pussum a child; the statue looks "tortured" (74) and Pussum's face is "masked with unwilling suffering" (80); the statue is characterized by extreme sensation and Pussum by sensation seeking; and Pussum's face, like the statue's, is "a small, fine mask, sinister too" (80). Gerald makes explicit the resemblance between Pussum and the statue: "It was a terrible face, void, peaked, abstracted almost into meaninglessness by the weight of sensation beneath. He saw Pussum in it. As in a dream, he knew her" (71). To the extent that the statue and Pussum resemble each other, the statue in her sensuality represents not sensual innocence but sexual dissoluteness.

The connection between Pussum and the African female has powerful historical antecedents in the nineteenth-century linking, noted by Sander Gilman, of two seemingly unrelated female icons—the Hottentot female and the prostitute (231). As in Manet's famous painting *Olympia,* the presence of the black female (the servant) points to the sexualized essence of the white female, whose apparent beauty masks her underlying uncleanliness and even disease. The utter Otherness of the black female, who is the antithesis of European sexual mores and beauty (Gilman 1986, 231), and the traditional association of blacks with concupiscence—an association going all the way back to the Middle Ages (228)—enable us to spot the Other in our midst—in the debased if apparently beautiful Pussum. This linkage between the prostitute and the Hottentot connects the sexualized female with deviancy and even disease, a yoking that reflects lingering traces of "the nineteenth-century understanding of female sexuality as pathological" (Gilman 1986, 235). In fact, *Women in Love* reveals an anxiety that all women are potentially prostitutes, as in the later scene in which two miners joke about purchasing Gudrun, one of them asserting that he would plunk down a week's wages for five minutes with her. Similarities between these two scenes—the scene in which Birkin and Gerald comment on the statue and the scene in which the miners comment on Gudrun—point out the novel's anxiety that an overt and aggressive female sexuality is essentially degenerate.

What makes Pussum and the statue so frightening to the men is the female sexual power they embody and its potential for destruction. As Birkin complains, "Woman was always so horrible and clutching, she had such a lust for possession. . . . She wanted to have, to own, to control, to be dominant. Everything must be referred back to her, to Woman, the Great Mother of everything" (192). Thus Gerald and Birkin fear that Woman, the Magna Mater, may gain control of them. And, in fact, Pussum as Magna Mater does take possession of Halliday, the father of her child: "She had got her Halliday whom she wanted. She wanted him completely in her power. Then she would marry him" (74). Thus, women are threatening not only because they literally have a power, reproductive power, that men do not have; but also because they can use their power as the givers of life to take life back, to recall men to the womb or tomb.

How are men to deal with such a threat? They must do as Birkin and Gerald do: unite to contain it. Thus, in their encounter with the fetish, Birkin's declaration of her aesthetic value is followed by Gerald's warning, "You like the wrong things, Rupert . . . things against yourself." Birkin heeds this warning by minimizing the statue's importance: "Oh, I know this isn't everything" (79). Whereupon Birkin turns away from her. Thus the discussion has come full circle. Birkin, having contained through language the power of the statue, joins Gerald in repudiation of her power over them and, by extension, of the power of all women over men. They forge an alliance to contain female force: This homosocial bond levels all differences between them, both of class and of ideology. As Eve Sedgwick describes such an enabling moment: "The spectacle of the ruin of a woman—apparently almost regardless of what counts as 'ruin' or what counts as 'woman'—is just the right lubricant for an adjustment of differentials of power between landlord and tenant, master and servant, tradesman and customer, or even king and subject," 1985, (76). In this instance, the adjustment of differentials of power serves to level the class differences between Gerald and Rupert. This scene prepares them to take the next step which the novel will go on to propose: to form a new, small, utopian community, centered on male power and brotherhood, that contains and controls women.

This scene raises the question whether another culture—especially a non-Western culture, as represented by the African artifact—can assume any importance or even serve an instructive function in the lives of men who are entrenched in the power structure of the West and deeply invested in retaining their position within it. Further, the reactions of the two men suggest that the female statue is too tainted by their Western cultural assumptions about power, race, and sexuality to enrich their lives.

Yet after the novel in this scene denies the value of the primitive as centered on female power, it turns its search for redemption to a primitivist society based on male authority. This vision of a male-centered community takes its inspiration from one specific primitivist text—Sigmund Freud's *Totem and Taboo.* In the first half of the novel, Freud's work provides both narrative direction and underlying thematic meaning (but in the second half of the novel, the denied and problematic side of the primitive resurfaces to doom Lawrence's project for social salvation).

Freud's account of the formation of society through patricide, fraternal alliance, and self-imposed sexual restrictions serves as protonarrative for Lawrence's vision of a new social order, expressed in Rupert Birkin's rebellion against modern life, in his proposed alliance with Gerald Crich, and in his hope for a new community and a new form of marriage. To read Lawrence's text in light of Freud's helps to explain some of the more puzzling aspects of the novel: to understand what Lawrence means by the carbon of character (Moore 1862, 2:183), an essential self that exists distinctly but relates communally; to see male-male relationship as central to the formation of social structure (and thus to understand the meaning of *blut-brüderschaft*); and, finally, to conclude that without a community centered on male alliance, marriage is unstable and incomplete (as is Ursula and Birkin's, at the novel's end).

In its account of the birth of civilization, *Totem and Taboo* serves as the protonarrative for the founding of a new social order to supplant the decay Lawrence observes in the modern world. According to Freud's narrative, civilization began when the sons of the primal horde rose up and killed their jealous father, devoured his body, and then felt remorse and belated affection for him. From their posthumous valuation of the father was born a sense of guilt that caused them to honor his memory in the worship of a totem animal who represented him. Henceforth they would refrain from killing this animal and, by forswearing the women of the clan who had belonged to the father, they would abstain from enjoying the fruits of the murder. They would therefore mate exogamously, finding women from outside the clan. From the killing of the patriarch there thus emerged the twin taboos that form the boundaries of civilization, murder and incest; and, with them, the beginning of social organization, morality, and religion.

In symbolic terms that recall Freud's narrative, *Women in Love* provides an outline for Rupert and Gerald to kill the father (as represented by Thomas Crich)—termed in the novel "the Patriarch" (224)—by repudiating his materialism, his hypocritical Christian charity, and his false marriage based on "acceptance of the established world" (353) to forge a self-chosen community. Asserting to Gerald, "two exceptional people make another world. You and I, we make another, separate world" (205), Birkin suggests that they form their own community, one reminiscent of Lawrence's proposed Rananim.[4] This community would proceed from their commitment to each other, "an impersonal union that leaves one free" (207). Repeatedly, the novel, through Birkin, postulates a new society that begins with a bond between brothers who pledge themselves to each other and who commit themselves to a new form of marriage. While Birkin's apparent parentlessness suggests his emancipation from patriarchal domination, for Gerald there is "no escape—he was bound up with his father" (321). Although inwardly in revolt against the Name-of-the-Father, his unexpressed rebellion having been displaced in childhood onto the brother he killed, Gerald is guilt-ridden, externally compliant, taking over the mines (although subverting the father's principles in doing so), playing host for his ailing father, implacably determined "to see him through" (321). Taking his model from his parents, Gerald sees marriage as "a doom": "He was willing to condemn himself in marriage, to become like a convict condemned to the mines of the underworld . . . like a soul damned but living for ever in damnation" (353). The antidote to this "seal of his condemnation" is the new pattern for marriage that Birkin offers him: "The other way was to accept Rupert's offer of alliance, to enter into the bond of pure trust and love with the other man, and then subsequently with the woman. If he pledged himself with the man he would later be able to pledge himself with the woman: not merely in legal marriage, but in absolute, mystic marriage" (353).

Even more important than the emancipation the proposed alliance offers Gerald is the freedom it offers to Birkin himself. The idea of *blutbrüderschaft* presents Birkin with a solution to his own most pressing personal difficulty: his powerful but to him unacceptable attraction to other men. The prologue that Lawrence later deleted from the published text explicitly discusses Birkin's dilemma:

> Although he was always drawn to women, feeling more at home with a woman than with a man, yet it was for men that he felt the hot, flushing, roused attraction which a man is supposed to feel for the other sex. . . . He kept this secret even from himself. He knew what he felt, but he always kept the knowledge at bay. He never accepted the desire, and received it as part of himself. He always tried to keep it expelled from him. (Prologue 107–108)

Since "Gerald Crich was the one towards whom Birkin felt most strongly that immediate roused attraction" (Prologue 111), the *blut-*

brüderschaft Birkin proposes offers him a way to resolve his ambivalent attitudes toward homosexuality by proposing a union with Gerald that is creative and life-enhancing—in fact, the fulcrum for an ideal community—while repudiating a homosexuality that is corrupt and degenerate, like that of Loerke and Leitner.

In Freud's scenario for the formation of a new society lies the meaning of the *blutbrüderschaft* Birkin proposes. The Freudian text seems to endorse, in sublimated form, homoerotic friendship and homosocial bonds. In stipulating the importance of male alliance in the formation of a new social order, *Totem and Taboo* offers support for the centrality of a male-male relationship, enacted not in directly sexual terms, but indirectly through affection, loyalty, and shared endeavors. Such an alliance the modern world considers, in Ursula's words, "a perversity" (481).

Not only does Freud's text prove useful in positing a male-centered society that sublimates homosexual desire and contains female power: it also recalls a society in which everyday human actions are charged with religious meaning and thus provides a center of meaning for the most intense portions of the novel. Since, as Lawrence sees it, the modern world is stagnant and incapable of movement, the narrative mirrors this stasis. In place of forward progression, the narrative offers charged individual scenes that serve as pockets of value and meaning. These scenes transcend symbolism into moments of numinous revelation through the presentation of totems, animals or objects charged with spiritual import.[5] Examples of such scenes are "Totem," in which the carved figure of a "savage woman in labor" reveals the mindless sensation-seeking of Minette; "Coal-Dust," in which Gerald's cruel subjugation of a mare reveals his sadistic will to mastery; "Mino," in which Birkin's approval of a male cat's cuffing a female reveals his own desire for sexual ascendancy; and "Moony," in which the moon reflected in water reminds Birkin of Ursula's aloof autonomy, which he would like to break, just as he shatters the moon's image by his stone throwing. In these scenes, the totemic animals or objects are extensions of individual characters, serving to reveal their true natures or essential selves. Thus the totems serve to reveal what Lawrence termed the carbon of character, the unrefined, unchanging being that underlies what is commonly called personality. As Lawrence maintains, in the oft-quoted apologia for *The Rainbow* that he sent to Edward Garnett:

> You mustn't look in my novel for the old stable *ego* of the character. There is another *ego,* according to whose action the individual is unrecognizable, and passes through, as it were, allotropic states which it needs a deeper sense than any we've been used to exercise, to discover are states of the same single radically unchanged element. (Like as diamond and coal are the same pure single element of carbon. The ordinary novel would trace the history of the diamond—but I say 'Diamond, what! This is carbon' . . .). (Moore 1962, 1:282)

Not only do the most intense scenes in the novel often focus on a totem, but they are themselves totemic, containing a ritualistic act or series of actions designed to lead the reader, as initiate, to a crucial spiritual recognition (Freud 164–94). Thus, in "Rabbit," first Gudrun's and then Gerald's brutal subjugation of a wildly resisting pet rabbit reveals the common element or carbon in their characters that prefigures their deadly sadomasochistic sexual relationship. The religiously charged language of the chapter reveals their spiritual affinity: "There was a league between them, abhorrent to them both. They were implicated with each other in abhorrent mysteries" (242). "There was a queer, faint, obscene smile over his face. She looked at him and saw him, and knew that he was initiate as she was initiate" (243). Their "smile of obscene recognition" (243) suggests the forbidden nature of their liaison. To apply the terms of J. G. Frazer's *Totem and Exogamy,* which Lawrence read (along with *The Golden Bough*) while writing the novel (Burwell 1982, 162), Gerald and Gudrun are members of the same clan, governed by the same totem animal. Their union is therefore incestuous rather than exogamous. Dark stars bound on a collision course, they form a taboo alliance that is the opposite of the pole star equilibrium that Birkin and Ursula struggle to achieve.

Yet, if primitivism—and, in particular, the primitivist scenario of *Totem and Taboo*—provides both a rationale for the proposed action of the novel and a retrieval of the numinous in scenes of modern life, the primitive remains a problematic source of meaning for Lawrence, fraught with ambivalence.⁶ As the novel proceeds, Birkin's underlying doubts about his masculinity and fear of female domination converge to undermine the reassuringly masculinist scenario for a new social order that structured the text's earlier primitivism.

In the second half of the book, the vision of the primitive originally gendered as masculine and characterized as regenerative is supplanted by a negative version of the primitive that is coded as feminine and associated with regression, loss of self, and taboo sexuality. This shift in the construction of the primitive is evident in the introduction of a second female African fetish that is much more ominous and threatening than the first fetish in Halliday's flat, over whose power and allure Birkin and Gerald had triumphed. That this second figure is more menacing and uncontainable than the first is evident in the fact that Birkin recalls her involuntarily and in isolation, and that he is unable to distance himself from her, but rather identifies her as "one of his soul's intimates" (253). Associating her "beetle face" and "protuberant buttocks" with a mindless anality and spiritual death, he projects onto her his own fear and desire: her beetle face, reminiscent of Pussum's fear of beetles, associates her with the sexual degeneracy of the prostitute, which is associated with dirt and excrement, the elements in which dung beetles live. Her protuberant buttocks serve as the stigmata of an excessive and aberrant sexuality, as identified in the Hottentot Venus and in the nineteenth-century penchant for classification, for medicalization, and for scientific information as ways of identifying, distancing, and protecting oneself from corruption by the degenerate Other (Gilman 1986, 232–38). Birkin, recalling the African statue, reflects that "[t]housands of years ago, that which was imminent in himself must have taken place in these Africans: the goodness, the holiness, the desire for creation and productive happiness must have lapsed, leaving the single impulse for knowledge in one sort, mindless progressive knowledge through the senses . . . mystic knowledge in disintegration and dissolution" (253).

This figure, onto which Birkin displaces his homosexual longing and his craving for mindless promiscuity, invites transgression but also threatens extinction. As he thinks about her, he feels frightened; and he responds to her in a variety of ways, all of them anxiety-provoking. In his identifying with her as passive sexual vessel—"She knew what he himself did not know" (345)—his masculinity is threatened. As he focuses on her "protuberant buttocks" (245), thus identifying with her implied male lover, he participates in a degenerate anality, "knowledge in dissolution and corruption" (253).

Even in attempting to distance himself from her—"How far, in their inverted culture, had these West Africans gone beyond phallic knowledge? Very, very far" (253)—his assumption of cultural superiority seems to point to an underlying sense of sexual inferiority. As Foster points out, the solitary female figure indicates the evacuation of the place of the African male so that the white subject may stand in for him, with an accompanying anxiety about inferiority to the figure he has displaced (1993, 99); much as the son in the Oedipal triangle fears the superior strength and prowess of the father he desires to supplant. In sum, Birkin's irresolvable ambivalence in this primitivist encounter, which he expresses in misogyny and racism, indicates areas of unacceptable Otherness that Birkin cannot acknowledge within himself.

For Birkin, the reappearance in his memory of the second African female fetish is a return of the repressed, precipitated by a sexual crisis in his life. This crisis has resulted from the failure of his efforts to contain the female and to sublimate his homosexual desire: specifically, from Ursula's resistance to his ascendancy over her and from Gerald's refusal of the *blutbrüderschaft* he proposed to him. As Foster points out, there is a crisis of masculinity in the primitivist encounter that is triggered by a crisis in the expression of genital sexuality that makes the subject regress to the pregenital order of the drives, especially to anal sadism and masochism (1993, 78).

Since the West, taking its cue from Freud, associates "tribal peoples with pregenital orders of the drives, especially oral and anal stages," it also correlates genital sexuality "with civilization as achievements beyond the primitive" (Foster 1993, 72). In light of this Western understanding of the hierarchy of sexuality, Birkin wishes to repudiate the allure of what he considers the regressive or taboo sexuality the statue represents to him. Torn between a desire to break down the cultural oppositions between European inhibition and primitive sensuality and an equally intense desire to strengthen his difference from the Other, Birkin runs away from this irresolvable conflict to his conventional heterosexual relationship with Ursula. In terror of succumbing to the sexual possibilities emblematically present for him in the African statue, Birkin takes refuge in monogamous marriage: "There was the other way, the remaining way. And he must run to follow it. He thought of Ursula. He must ask her to marry him. They must marry at once. . . . There was no moment to spare" (254).

After Birkin's wrestling match with Gerald in "Gladiatorial," he stages a similar retreat by turning away from Gerald, once more back to Ursula, a retreat that recalls Gerald's evasion of Birkin's initial proposal of *blutbrüderschaft* in "Man to Man." In "Marriage or Not," the ambivalence both Gerald and Rupert share about the future of their relationship receives final expression in Gerald's failure to respond to Birkin's offer of a " 'perfect relationship between man and man—additional to marriage' " (352). From "Gladiatorial" on, the novel abandons much of its earlier psychological and narrative complexity for a thin and tentative resolution to Birkin's psychosexual dilemma through his exclusive relationship with Ursula, in which anal sex, so the text asserts, merely serves as a means of eradicating sexual inhibition, a variation on, not a substitute for, conventional genital heterosexuality.

Thus Lawrence, through Birkin, manages to distance and to contain the lure of the primitive and its promise of sexual transgression, but only at considerable loss. This loss is enacted literally in the sacrificial death of Gerald, who becomes the repository for the novel's unresolved conflicts and contradictions. More importantly, this loss is evidenced structurally in the novel's gradual diminution of power, as talk and exposition replace dramatic action and numinous revelation. Finally, narrative movement subsides, or peters out—rather than culminates—in the novel's indeterminate, nostalgic conclusion.

Notes

1. For an extended discussion of the problematic nature of the term "primitive," see Torgovnick 1990, 3–41. See also Rubin 1984, 74.

2. For examples of late nineteenth-century rhetoric about the intellectual and moral inferiority, as well as sexual licentiousness, of native populations, especially in Africa, see Bolt, Brantlinger, Curtin, Gilman, and Hammond and Jablow.

3. In this scene, Birkin seems to intuit as well another meaning of this "awful pitch" of culture, that is, as awe-inspiring, although he overtly denies this interpretation. As Torgovnick points out, although Birkin insists that the fetish is "purely sensual," in her own culture "her function was probably not at all 'sensual,' was probably closer to the 'spirituality' he finds foreign to her" (1990, 162).

4. Rananim was Lawrence's name for the new society that he wanted to create. As he described his "pet scheme":

> I want to gather together about twenty souls and sail away from this world of war and squalor and found a little colony where there shall be no money but a sort of communism as far as necessaries of life go. . . . It is to be a colony built up on the real decency which is in each member of the Community—a community which is established upon the assumption of goodness in the members, instead of the assumption of [. . .] badness. (Moore 1962, 2:259)

5. I am using the term "totem" according to Freud's definition, which, in turn, is based on Frazer's:

> What is a totem? It is as a rule an animal . . . and more rarely a plant or a natural phenomenon (such as rain or water), which stands in a peculiar relation to the whole clan. In the first place the totem is the common ancestor of the clan; at the same time it is their guardian spirit and helper, which sends them oracles and, if dangerous to others, recognizes and spares its own children. Conversely, the clansmen are under a sacred obligation (subject to automatic sanctions) not to kill or destroy their totem and to avoid eating its flesh (or deriving benefit from it in other ways). The totemic character is inherent, not in some individual animal or entity, but in all the individuals of a given class. From time to time festivals are cel-

ebrated at which the clansmen represent or imitate the motions and attributes of their totem in ceremonial dances. (Freud 1989, 5)

While Lawrence clearly interprets totems and totemic rituals to suit his own artistic purposes, at times he seems to subscribe quite literally to Freud's definition; for example, when Gudrun observes of Gerald, "His totem is the wolf," and of his mother, "His mother is an old, unbroken wolf" (9).

Relevant to the argument of my paper is the fact that Lawrence, in the course of his extensive revisions of *Women in Love,* alternately gave the title "Totem" and "Fetish" to chapter 7. Both titles appear in the variant versions of the book as currently in print.

6. Throughout, the language of *Women in Love* records Lawrence's ambivalence about the primitive: on a positive note, for example, Hermione describes Gudrun's carvings as " 'perfectly beautiful—full of *primitive* passion' " (32; emphasis added); negatively, Ursula maintains of Gerald's accidental shooting of his brother, " 'This playing at killing has some *primitive desire* for killing in it' " (42; emphasis added).

Works Cited

Bolt, Christine. *Victorian Attitudes to Race.* London: Routledge, 1971.

Brantlinger, Patrick. *Rule of Darkness: British Literature and Imperialism, 1830–1914.* Ithaca: Cornell University Press, 1988.

Burwell, Rose Marie. "A Checklist of Lawrence's Reading." *A D. H. Lawrence Handbook.* Ed. Keith Sagar. New York: Barnes & Noble, 1982.

Chamberlain, Robert L. "Pussum, Minette, and the Africo-Nordic Symbol in Lawrence's *Women in Love.*" *PMLA* 78 (1963): 407–416.

Curtin, Philip D. *The Image of Africa: British Ideas and Action, 1780–1850.* 2 vols. Madison University of Wisconsin Press, 1964.

DiBattista, Maria. *"Women in Love:* D. H. Lawrence's Judgment Book." *D. H. Lawrence: A Centenary Consideration.* Ed. Peter Balbert and Phillip L. Marcus. Ithaca: Cornell University Press, 1985, 67–90.

Ford, George H. "An Introductory Note to D. H. Lawrence's Prologue to *Women in Love.*" *The Texas Quarterly* 6 (1963): 92–97.

————. *Double Measure: A Study of the Novels and Stories of D. H. Lawrence.* New York: Holt, Rinehart, and Winston, 1965.

Foster, Hal. " 'Primitive' Scenes." *Critical Inquiry* 20:1 (1993): 69–102.

Frazer, J. G. *Totemism and Exogamy.* 4 vols. London: Macmillan, 1910.

Freud, Sigmund. *Totem and Taboo.* Trans. James Strachey. New York: W. W. Norton, 1989.

Gilman, Sander L. "Black Bodies, White Bodies: Toward an Iconography of Female Sexuality in Late Nineteenth-Century Art, Medicine, and Literature." *"Race," Writing, and Difference.* Ed. Henry Louis Gates, Jr. Chicago: University of Chicago Press, 1986, 223–261.

Hammond, Dorothy, and Alta Jablow. *The Africa That Never Was.* New York: Twayne, 1970.

Kessler, Jascha. "D. H. Lawrence's Primitivism." *Texas Studies in Literature and Language* 5:4 (Winter 1964): 467–488.

Lawrence, D. H. "Prologue to *Women in Love.*" *The Texas Quarterly* 6 (1963): 98–111.

————. *Women in Love.* 1920. Middlesex, Eng.: Penguin, 1995.

Lodge, David. "*Tono-Bungay* and the Condition of England." *H. G. Wells: A Collection of Critical Essays.* Englewood Cliffs, N.J.: Prentice-Hall, 1976.

Moore, Harry T., ed. *The Collected Letters of D. H. Lawrence.* 2 vols. New York: Viking, 1962.

Morris, Inez R. "African Sculpture Symbols in *Women in Love.*" *College Language Association Journal* 28:3 (March 1985): 263–280.

Rubin, William, ed. *"Primitivism" in 20th Century Art: Affinity of the Tribal and the Modern.* 2 vols. New York: Little, Brown, 1984.

Ruthven, K. K. "The Savage God: Conrad and Lawrence." *Critical Quarterly* 10: 1–2 (Spring and Summer 1968): 39–54.

Sedgwick, Eve Kosofsky. *Between Men: English Literature and Male Homosocial Desire.* New York: Columbia University Press, 1985.

Stewart, Jack F. "Primitivism in *Women in Love.*" *The D. H. Lawrence Review* 13 (1980): 45–62.

Torgovnick, Marianna. *Gone Primitive: Savage Intellects, Modern Lives.* Chicago: University of Chicago Press, 1990.

Widmer, Kingsley. "The Primitivistic Aesthetic: D. H. Lawrence." *The Journal of Aesthetics and Art History* 17:3 (March 1959): 344–353.

Zytaruk, George J., and James T. Boulton, eds. *The Letters of D. H. Lawrence.* 7 vols. Cambridge, Eng.: Cambridge University Press, 1981.

Entrapment and Escape in D. H. Lawrence's *Women in Love*

BETHAN JONES

◆ ◆ ◆

IN A LETTER TO Catherine Carswell on 11 October 1916, Lawrence referred to *Women in Love* as a novel that had enabled him to take one stride toward freedom: "I have knocked the first loophole in the prison where we are all shut up."[1] The imagery employed here, asserting the need for the breaking of bounds, the flight from imprisonment, is characteristic of Lawrence's language in *Women in Love*, which draws heavily on images of entrapment and escape. Terms such as *constraint, bondage, bounds, closed, shut, escape, release*, and *freedom* in conjunction with images of nets, prisons, chains, traps, spells, and snares are prevalent throughout the novel. Such images are used to reveal the constricting, repressive nature of physical locations, from the mining countryside of the Midlands to the snowscape evoked in the final chapters. The sense of constraint extends to the lives of the novel's protagonists, who identify entrapment in their own circumstances and articulate potential ways of breaking free. Yet entrapment is more pervasive still: it is evident in the interrelation between characters, in the subjugation of one by another, sometimes with violent results. This article will consider the role of entrapment and escape as it functions in the aspects of the novel specified above.

It is significant that imagery and terminology of entrapment is associated in the novel with every location or context in which the protagonists are situated, including, ironically, those to which they have turned in the hope of escape. With regard to the portrayal of Beldover and the mining countryside in general, this language is frequently indistinguishable from imagery linked to industrialization: the endless repetition and monotony of the mechanized way of life stems from and, in turn, provokes the restraints imposed on and by the landscape. The black path on which Ursula and Gudrun walk in the opening chapter, for instance, referred to as "trodden-in" by the feet of the "recurrent colliers," is "bounded from the field by iron fences" (11–12²). Throughout the novel, the term *bound* indicates more than a mere boundary, demarcating the division of land; it is indicative of compulsion, restriction, or constraint. In this case, the blackness and reiterative tramping are separated by iron from the natural field. The iron fence suggests a kind of imprisonment—a restriction imposed; a freedom of straying prevented.

The sense of Beldover as inherently closed in, creating its own claustrophobic yet compelling unity, is evident in Birkin's vision of the town as he sees it in the distance on his return from the woods in the chapter "Moony":

> He saw the town on the slope of the hill, not straggling, but as if walled-in with the straight, final streets of miners' dwellings, making a great square, and it looked like Jerusalem to his fancy. The world was all strange and transcendent. (255)

The language employed here is interesting, and incorporates the ambiguity often evident in Lawrence's portrayal of the mining countryside. Frequently in the novel, imagery associated with being "walled-up" is solely negative, indicating, for instance, a cloying psychological restriction imposed on one character by another, and resulting in a need to break out, even through employing violence. Here the term "final," in conjunction with "walled-up," might appear to imply an undesirable rigidity or stasis. Yet the image also suggests neatness or self-containment, an almost magical quality that paradoxically facilitates imaginative liberation. Such ambiguity, frequently evident in Lawrence's evocation of the industrial landscape, extends to the portrayal of the workers reliant on the mines for their livelihood. Often seen as cogs in the wheel of the vast machine, these workers are also able to identify "a sort of freedom, the sort they really wanted" (231), even in the most rigorous and harsh conditions imposed by Gerald once he assumes power.

The ambiguity that arises from the portrayal of a location as restricting and/or liberating, is often attributable to the shifting narrative perspective. The novel is fundamentally dialogic,[3] so that the act of perception is filtered through the consciousness of each particular character without the intervention of a presiding authoritative narrator. This is evident, for instance, in the portrayal of Breadalby, which is described in disparate circumstances through the narratives of both Ursula and Birkin. Ursula sees the house as an *enclosure*, yet employs this term entirely in a positive context, identifying "a magic circle drawn about the place, enclosing the delightful, precious past, trees and deer and silent like a dream" (84). Birkin analogously identifies "the lovely accomplished past" in the place, yet perceives its power of entrapment as destructive:

> And then, what a snare and a delusion, this beauty of static things—what a horrible, dead prison Breadalby really was, what an intolerable confinement, the peace! Yet it was better than the sordid scrambling conflict of the present. (97)

It is ironic that Birkin is here attributing the horror of constraint to something he perceives as "static," when he has previously indicated the paradoxically liberating, transcendent quality in the "final" miners' dwellings cut neatly into a square.

So Breadalby is seen as a "prison"—an image that is enforced when Lawrence describes Hermione's party guests as "feeling somehow like prisoners marshalled for exercise" (87) when she places a compulsion on them to accompany her on a walk. The role of Hermione is, of course, significant when considering how the image of Breadalby is filtered through Birkin's narrative. By this time he has come to associate Hermione with restriction and compulsion, and his narrative is therefore infused with language of entrapment in responding to her house. Birkin's perception of the house is also inevitably bound up with the theory he is formulating and articulating in particular in "Excurse," in which he voices the need for freedom beyond the conventional attachment to a specific, claustrophobic location.

Ursula and Gudrun identify their childhood home as analogously claustrophobic, although it is significant that the imagery of entrapment is employed mainly in retrospect, when the house has been stripped bare:

> Everything was null to the senses, there was enclosure without substance, for the walls were dry and papery. [. . .] They went to the drawing room. Another piece of shut-in air, without weight or substance, only a sense of intolerable papery imprisonment in nothingness. (372–373)

The terms *enclosure, shut-in, imprisonment, null,* and *nothingness* give a forcible impression of something vacant and vacuous: a space that traps you within while remaining oddly sketchy and insubstantial. The clarity of perception evident here suggests that once the junk and trimmings have been cleared from the rooms, the empty space can respond by affording an epiphany, an apotheosis of the previous feelings of constraint that the sisters have suppressed to a degree when the house was a home. The sense of imprisonment results in part from their psychological re-engagement with a past that they have wilfully rejected, a feeling that is given substance through transferral to a physical location shutting them in.

While entrapment characterizes the house and countryside associated with the sisters' youth, it is also omnipresent in the places that appear ostensibly to afford escape. For instance, in the chapter "An Island," when Ursula travels with Birkin to the island, she moves from the initial experience of delight and excitement to a state of mind in which she is "afraid of being any longer imprisoned on the island" (131). Here the feeling of captivity seems occasioned by her sense that "some sort of control was being put upon her" by

Birkin's assertions. It is significant, also, that Ursula is unable to leave the island without the compliance of her companion, so the sense of constraint is physical as well as psychological. The would-be haven thus forfeits its potential magic and becomes merely a place from which to run.

London is another location seen as offering an escape from the limitations of the mining landscape, yet appearing flawed and undesirable as an alternative. When Birkin and Gerald travel to London on the train and approach the outskirts, the locomotive is described as running through "the disgrace of outspread London" (61). The passengers are alert, "waiting to escape," yet paradoxically Birkin feels the need to "shut himself together" before contemplating emerging, as though escape itself necessitated self-protection or self-enclosure. The negative aspect is given voice more powerfully through Birkin's dialogue and the ensuing narrative that continues to convey his perspective: " 'Don't you feel like one of the damned?' asked Birkin, as they sat in the little, swiftly-running enclosure, and watched the hideous great street" (61).

The train embodies the paradox of being both in motion ("swiftly-running") and binding ("enclosure") while its purpose seems nullified by the fact that its destination is epitomized by the term *hideous* (suggesting physical ugliness), and by Birkin's analogy with hell (suggesting pain and perhaps moral degeneracy). London is seen throughout the novel to possess a surface glamour—an artistic allure—yet one that is, at root, as insubstantial as the crumbling walls of Ursula's childhood home. This is exemplified in a conversation between Gerald and Birkin, in which the former is enquiring about the lifestyle and circumstances of Birkin's Bohemian friends. In response to Gerald's question "All loose?" Birkin replies, "In one way. Most bound, in another. For all their shockingness, all on one note" (60). The apparently liberated set are seen here to possess the predictability of routine, and are hence no more free than those "bound" by the mechanistic principle. Their lives only glisten with the surface tint of spontaneity, lacking the flair to improvise or entertain.

The final example given here of a location that ostensibly offers release yet merely exerts another kind of entrapment, is the snowy environment portrayed in the chapters "Snow" and "Snowed Up." Here, a narrative offering Gerald's perspective gives the following evocation:

> [. . .] the cradle of snow ran on to the eternal closing-in, where the walls of snow and rock rose impenetrable, and the mountain peaks above were in heaven immediate. [. . .] He saw the blind valley, the great cul de sac of snow and mountain peaks, under the heaven. And there was no way out. (401)

The language harbours the ambiguity referred to earlier. The term *cradle* suggests a protective enclosure that nurtures rather than destroys, while the connection established between the mountain peaks and "heaven" implies a landscape that is transcendent in its power. Yet the snow runs on to an "eternal closing-in," as if its end or purpose (seemingly an act of conscious intent) is that of suffocation, while the terms *blind*, *cul de sac*, and *no way out* create the sinister image of ultimate entrapment and perhaps death. Gerald, of course, finds "no way out" of the snowy impasse, as this is the place in which he finally settles to sleep—creating a neat, ironic cyclicity in which birth (the snow-cradle) and death are brought into proximity through the use of these images of entrapment.

I have considered ways in which language and imagery of entrapment, in conjunction with dialogic narrative, are employed in the portrayal of specific locations. I will move on to discuss various kinds of psychological entrapment, focusing on the way in which the protagonists have come to perceive their lives as dead ends or culs-de-sac, without the apparent possibility of development, release, or escape. Gudrun, for example, asserts in the opening chapter that "Nothing materialises!" and explains her return to Beldover as simply a regression in order to effect a more complete and successful escape, or "reculer pour mieux sauter" (10). The fact that her return imposes on her an unbearable constraint is emphasized by the way in which she is constantly seen to be "grasping at release" (12)—finding ways to imagine herself out of a situation by placing a limit on the period of imprisonment—and by the way in which she is compelled to keep her mouth "shut close" in order to preserve her integrity and sanity in this context.

Birkin refers to Gudrun as a "restless bird" (94), identifying a characteristic that is emphasized in Gudrun's reiteration of the phrase "one must be free" in the chapter "Flitting." Here, Gudrun's repulsion at the repressive nature of her emptied house (described earlier) provokes a strong psychological reaction: the need to escape such constraint through voicing alternative methods of self-definition. She acknowledges a necessity articulated elsewhere by Birkin, that of avoiding being labelled merely according to the number of a house or street to which you become arbitrarily attached. Freedom, by implication, is defined by the avoidance of a fixed residence and certainly avoidance of an imprisonment at Shortlands through marriage to Gerald.

Gerald possesses an analogous fear of being constrained, which is in his case articulated in physical terms. When asked by the Pussum whether he is afraid of anything, he replies: "Yes, I'm afraid of some things—of being shut up, locked up anywhere—or being fastened. I'm afraid of being bound hand and foot" (66–67). This is, perhaps, a soldier's way of voicing fear of capture; a throwback, also, to Gerald's childhood when he sought a "savage freedom" (221) and was prepared to fight to attain it. Yet Gerald is portrayed in the novel as lacking the wherewithal to acquire freedom; of all the protagonists he seems most tightly and fatally bound. A further image is employed during the period of limbo that drives Gerald to Gudrun in an attempt to rescue his self-sufficiency: "for another night he was to be suspended in chains of physical life, over the bottomless pit of nothingness" (337). This metaphor is conveyed through Gerald's narrative, indicating that he has reached a psychological state that is directly equivalent to his worst physical nightmare: that of being bound hand and foot. Here, however, the image is made more horrifying by the sense that escape from the chains will precipitate only an endless fall into "nothingness" rather than any kind of release.

In Birkin's narrative, Gerald's inability to be free is attributed to a psychological malaise: in his opinion, "Gerald could never fly away from himself, in real indifferent gaiety. He had a clog, a sort of monomania" (207). Birkin is suggesting that Gerald is too hidebound, laden with self-consciousness, in a way that inhibits or even prohibits the spontaneity that Birkin identifies as liberation. Previous interpretations of *Women in Love* have attributed the lack of spontaneity evident here to Gerald's "role" as embodiment of the mechanistic principle. Another possible perspective would derive from Gerald's fatalistic sense that something in his lineage has resulted in a curse or flaw of inherent entrapment. Cage imagery permeates Lawrence's portrayal of the relationship between Gerald's mother and father, in which "she had beat against the bars of his philanthropy" and sunk into silence "like a hawk in a cage" (215). This image of subjugation through entrapment results in the following interesting formulation:

> By force of circumstance, because all the world combined to make the cage unbreakable, he had been too strong for her, he had kept her prisoner. And because she was his prisoner, his passion for her had always remained keen as death. He had always loved her, loved her with intensity. Within the cage, she was denied nothing, she was given all license. (215)

Here, "licence" defines the illusion of luxury afforded to the being encaged within a restricted space; while the position of prison-warder is seen to be the overriding principle that conditions obsessive love: the love of that which is subjugated. Gerald instinctively places the encaging rituals of love and marriage within the context of the mining world about him, expressing at one point a willingness "to become like a convict condemned to the mines of the underworld, living no life in the sun, but having a dreadful subterranean activity" (353). Marriage is perceived by him to inflict a tighter bondage, rather than affording liberation. In the narrowness of this definition, Gerald both conforms to and differs crucially from Birkin's assertions regarding the nature and possibilities of marriage.

While Gerald's sense of physical and psychological entrapment infiltrates and dominates him emotionally, resulting in fear and depression—a sense almost of real, palpable bonds—Birkin's relation to such imagery and language is usually intellectualized and articulated as part of a developing, shifting theory. His metaphors are frequently overstated to the extent of implausibility or even absurdity in his attempt to voice these hypotheses. His starting-point is an acknowledgement that life, as he experiences it, is inherently limiting; that he fails to make "a success of [his] days" because "one seems always to be bumping one's nose against the blank wall ahead" (125). This image is extended later in the novel in the assertion made (within Birkin's narrative) that a movement forward requires that "one must break away through the walls of the prison, as the infant in labour strives through the walls of the womb" (186). Prison for Birkin is not a question of his own set of circumstances; it represents the whole of society—the pattern of life as he knows it—which must be destroyed. In a conversation with Gerald, he asserts the need to "bust [life] up completely, or shrivel inside it, as in a tight skin" (54), due to its inability to expand.

Imagery associated with constraint is employed on numerous occasions by Birkin when categorizing and rejecting the "old way of love." In one such formulation, old love becomes "a dreadful bondage, a sort of conscription" (199), indicating that war language has filtered into Birkin's prose as well as that of Gerald. Later, the "Dionysic ecstasy" approach to love is referred to as a "squirrel cage" (251), a pattern of endless repetition reminiscent of the false freedom given to Mrs. Crich when portrayed as a caged hawk. Also, Birkin's narrative alludes to the "yoke and leash of love" (254), which must be surpassed in order for a condition of "freedom together" to be attained. His narrative defines his conception of star-equilibrium against the terrestrial constraints listed here, cleverly adopting a rhetoric in which the position advocated is placed starkly against a backdrop of images portraying prison walls, ropes, and bars. The dialogic narrative debunks the theories, through Ursula's satire and Gerald's scepticism, but the backdrop remains omnipresent and hard to ignore.

Ursula offers a conflicting perspective to Birkin in which love is synonymous with freedom: a position dismissed by the latter as "sentimental cant." Yet the language of entrapment is most striking within Ursula's narrative when he is exerting a direct influence upon her, particularly in moments of crisis or despair. At these points, her conception of life-as-prison resembles Birkin's, showing, perhaps, a concordance within their portrayed sensibilities, and/or suggesting a process of linguistic borrowing in which Birkin's language starts to penetrate Ursula's own: "Everything was gone, walled in, with spikes on top of the walls, and one must ignominiously creep between the spiky walls, through a labyrinth of life" (193).

Prison imagery is employed strikingly here to articulate Ursula's deep psychological disillusionment. As in Gerald's narrative, the psychological suffering provokes a vivid picture of physical constriction. In Ursula's narrative this strand moves outward in two directions—to a direct allusion to the mechanistic monotony of the passage of time, and to an analogy derived from her own experience to serve as an illustration. It is within her narrative that a direct parallel is drawn between life as "prison" and as "rotary motion, mechanised" (193). This idea is given another altered formulation in the phrase "The terrible bondage of this tick-tack of time, this twitching of the hands of the clock, this eternal repetition of hours and days" (464) from which there is "no escape." The term "tight horror" is used to express the sense of restriction occasioned by this meaningless sequence of repetitions. However, the language is perhaps most vivid when it derives from Ursula's direct experience. She employs an analogy in which the experience of modern-day imprisonment is seen to resemble the experience of her schoolchildren, who look through the window and glimpse "perfect freedom" outside. The analogy becomes bleak in that the adult perspective results by contrast in the knowledge that "the soul was a prisoner within this sordid vast edifice of life, and that there was no escape, save in death" (193). The childish vision is one that is forfeit with the onset of knowledge.

Ursula's perspective here is bleak, but it is characteristic of the dialogic nature of the novel that her nihilistic conception of the world oscillates with moments of adventure or happiness. These times are often identified as "freedom," such as the moment in which she and Gudrun "escape" from the water-party and run naked on the island (165). This experience is described directly as a return to the naive perspective of childhood (in a manner previously denied): "And this was one of the perfect moments of freedom and delight, such as children alone know, when all seems a perfect and blissful adventure" (165).

The apparent incongruity in Ursula's oscillation between the delight of innocence and the despair of experience results, in fact, from a consistency of characterization. Ursula is unique in the novel in that the ambiguity of her character is directly stated: she is described as possessing "that strange brightness of an essential flame that is caught, meshed, contravened" (9). She is given the attributes of a natural or elemental force that is nonetheless captured, yet, unlike Gerald or Gudrun, her "escape" is portrayed as inevitable. She is merely "suspended," while "in the darkness, something was coming to pass" and she has "an intimation of something yet to come" (9). Lawrence employs metaphors of growth in order to counteract the negative implications of Ursula's despair in which her school week seems the be-all and end-all of her existence: "Her spirit was active, her life was like a shoot that is growing steadily, but which has not yet come above ground" (52). Entrapment, in Ursula's life, is always perceived as a transient condition, with inevitable escape.

As well as conveying ways in which characters identify or escape entrapment within their lives, Lawrence uses such imagery and language in order to reveal the various ways in which characters create a sense of constraint or compulsion in their interaction with others. For instance, the dialogue in the novel's opening chapter results in Gudrun causing "a constraint over Ursula's nature, a certain weariness," after which Ursula's narrative articulates the desire to be liberated from "the tightness, the enclosure of Gudrun's presence" (13). Such an experience may be transient, provoked by a specific jarring moment of dissent in which a "friction of dislike" occurs, or it may be wider reaching, voicing a crucial impasse within a relationship. Later in the novel, Ursula speaks in an emotional way that puts "a constraint" on Birkin, as though a character's freedom of thought and speech may be impaired not only by the words of the other but by the manner in which these words are spoken.

Constraint may also be occasioned by the process of subjugation through which a character gains ascendancy over another, which is expressed in this novel through references to compulsion, possession, the casting of spells, and the setting of traps or snares. Gerald, in his struggle with the Arab mare, experiences a surge of pride at the impression he gains that Gudrun is "compelled by him" (120). Gudrun's narrative echoes this sense of compulsion in which she responds to his physical beauty "as if in a spell" (120). When finally she transfers her allegiance from Gerald to Loerke, one spell seems to have been annulled and another cast, for when Loerke talks and Gudrun listens without comprehension of the actual meaning, she is "spell-bound watching him" (406). While Gudrun is in the grip of a "spell" she is also capable of casting spells on others, as is evident when she dances before the cattle in the chapter "Water-Party." She moves "as if in a spell," yet her dancing results in Ursula being "spell-bound" in her continued singing, and in the cattle huddling in a "little, spell-bound cluster higher on top" (168). The term *spell* seems an attempt to define a compulsion that is unconscious or unwilled by implying an outside force—magic of a sort—that is responsible for exerting a powerful influence.

Another way of envisaging this compulsion is through the term *possession*. A character may be possessed by the presence of another, or by a residual emotion occasioned by the prior existence of that presence. The term seems to have sinister resonance when applied to the influence of Hermione on Birkin as he becomes "neutralised, possessed by her as if it were his fate, without question" (22), before he finds a way of breaking loose. A more interesting use of the term occurs later when Ursula is consumed by a feeling of utter hatred for Birkin, and is entirely dominated by this feeling: "[. . .] she was translated beyond herself. It was like a possession. She felt she was possessed. And for several days she went about possessed by this exquisite force of hatred against him" (197–98). Notably, the force of hatred is "exquisite," suggesting that the possession is not to be seen as a negation but as an intensification of living, in which she is able to "fly" beyond herself in a way that Gerald fails to do.

In addition to the casting of spells and the possession of one being by another—implying a process that is intangible, occult, and beyond our conscious control—other more physical images are employed in defining the instinctive interrelation between characters. Watching Birkin as he articulates his ideal regarding manly love, Gerald is "deeply bondaged in fascinated attraction" (207). Gerald's attraction for Gudrun is articulated in analogous language in which he suffers and delights in the experience of subjugation: "He groaned inwardly, under its bondage, but he loved it" (456).

While Gerald feels bound by Gudrun and "writhed under the imprisonment," her narrative expresses a similar sense of constriction—she is "caught at last by fate, imprisoned in some horrible and fatal trap" (325). The terminology associated with Gerald throughout the novel suggests that he derives fulfilment through the subordination of others, so that (for example) the Pussum becomes "slave-like" while "absorbed by him" (67). By contrast, Birkin is offered as a potentially liberating force, in that Ursula's response to his quick and attractive form "gave such a sense of freedom" (129). At the time when Ursula watches Birkin turning the handle of a sluice, "winding heavily and laboriously, bending and rising mechanically like a slave"(185), she is compelled to turn away, recognizing the incongruity of the situation and reacting violently against his position of subservience. Entrapment is portrayed as a powerful force that binds the protagonists of this novel into coexistence, and I will now examine the consequences of a situation in which the characters exert themselves in order to break out, freeing themselves from constraint. The attempt may be violent and devastating, as in the first example, in which Hermione strikes Birkin with a ball of lapis lazuli in the chapter "Breadalby." It is notable that the tension building up to bursting point within Hermione prior to the attack is provoked primarily by Birkin's non-involvement in the "struggle"—his denial of the entrapment she wishes to create through being "unconscious" of her and apparently immersed in his reading, with his back turned. Yet, paradoxically, this act of non-participation is itself seen as a kind of bondage, in which he is "closed within the spell [. . .] motionless and unconscious" (105). In this episode, the experience of intensifying suffering through exclusion is described as follows:

> [. . .] she felt as if her heart was bursting. The terrible tension grew stronger and stronger, it was most fearful agony, like being walled up.
>
> And then she realised that his presence was the wall, his presence was destroying her. Unless she could break out, she must die

most fearfully, walled up in horror. And he was the wall. She must break down the wall—she must break him down before her, the awful obstruction of him who obstructed her life to the last. (104–105)

The images of constriction create the sense of a physical obstacle which must be broken down, and correlate strikingly and ironically with Birkin's assertions regarding the necessity of breaking through walls to establish a new path onward. Oddly, the intensity of Hermione's experience of constriction precipitates a situation in which Birkin is in turn constricted, closed in, and rendered physically immobile. In becoming "the wall," Birkin seems to forfeit the ability to function according to the uniquely human dictates of sentience and personal freedom. Constriction and entrapment are evident in other moments of violence, even when one of the combatants is nonhuman. In the chapter "Rabbit," Gerald combats the writhing and vicious twisting of his bestial adversary by finding a method of physical restraint: "It made one immense writhe, tore his wrists and his sleeves in a final convulsion, all its belly flashed white in a whirlwind of paws, and then he had slung it round and had it under his arm, fast. It cowered and skulked" (241). Conflict, in both passages above, is seen to entail an imbalance, in which one participant in the struggle is perceived as obstacle or victim to be secured faster or closed in—resulting either in the cowering of a defeated prey, or the recoil exemplified in Birkin's escape into the forest.

It is revealing, however, to consider the way in which entrapment, often functioning as a negative force within conflict, also becomes a key element in the "Gladiatorial" scene. Birkin, previously trapped within Hermione's spell, here seems to cast one of his own: "Birkin had a great subtle energy that would press upon the other man with an uncanny force, weigh him like a spell put upon him" (270). Birkin's apparent dominance (here seen as almost supernatural) is echoed in a passage that employs further imagery of entrapment or containment:

It was as if Birkin's whole physical intelligence interpenetrated into Gerald's body, as if his fine, sublimated energy entered into

the flesh of the fuller man, like some potency, casting a fine net, a
prison, through the muscles into the very depths of Gerald's
physical being. (270)

It is interesting that, while the prison image is ostensibly pejorative,
the terms *potency, fine sublimated energy, fine net*, and later *fine grip* seem to
suggest a desirable bondage, while the term *interpenetrated* hints at a
deep-rooted reciprocity rather than the dominance of a single ego.
Birkin wrestles with Gerald's body "as if to bring it subtly into subjection" (270), yet perhaps the assumption is that such subjection is
not the true aim: the aim is inherent in the struggle itself. It is notable that one powerful image of imprisonment or confinement encompasses both men as they wrestle: they become "a tense white
knot of flesh gripped in silence between the walls of old brown
books" (270). The knot image implies a coherence, an inseparability,
and is in fact employed a second time, when Lawrence describes the
intertwined bodies as a "white, interlaced knot of violent living
being that swayed silently" (270). The term *violent*, through its juxta-
position with *living*, clearly emphasizes the potency or vitality of the
struggle, suggesting a mutually enriching conflict.

   I have indicated, above, that imagery of entrapment and escape
pervades *Women in Love*, and is crucial to the portrayal of setting and
character interaction within the novel. The images are diverse,
drawn from many areas of experience, employing terminology
from several discourses. Chains, walls, bars, and prisons have their
origin in language both of war-time and of criminality; traps and
snares have an agricultural derivation; while possession and spell-
casting carry the association of magic and superstition. The dialogic
nature of the novel weaves a rich textual fabric in which these terms
and images coexist, often engendering contradiction and ambiguity.
The prevalence of such imagery indicates the centrality of
Lawrence's preoccupation with the breaking of bounds; with the
need to move beyond established patterns of living in order to create
new avenues of possibility. To adopt terminology derived from the
essay "Chaos in Poetry," it is necessary for the visionary to slash
through the simulacrum-parasol that has been erected between our
safe, constricted little world and the chaos beyond, opening out a

"window to the sun." Yet he also acknowledges the implications of this newfound freedom to be catastrophic, for "man cannot live in chaos."⁴ *Women in Love* remains caught within this paradox: it is claimed as the first loop-hole in our ambient prison, yet its language relentlessly asserts the inevitability of ubiquitous entrapments, and the futility (as well as the desirability) of any attempt to find lasting release.

Notes

1. George J. Zytaruk and James T. Boulton, eds., *The Letters of D. H. Lawrence,* vol. 2 (Cambridge University Press, 1982), 663.

2. All citations from the novel are derived from *Women in Love,* eds. David Farmer, Lindeth Vasey, and John Worthen (London: Penguin, 2000).

3. David Lodge gives the "Class-room" chapter as an example of dialogic prose, alluding to the "fluid, flexible handling of point-of-view" in the novel. He provides the following definition, which is relevant here: "What makes this scene dialogic in the ideological as well as the purely formal or compositional sense (i.e., containing a lot of direct speech) is that the narrator never delivers a finalizing judgemental word on the debate or its protagonists. The narrator also 'circulates' between them. The narrator seldom speaks in a clearly distinct voice of his own, from a plane of knowledge above his characters: rather, he rapidly shifts his perspective on their level, and shows us now what Ursula is thinking of Birkin, now what Birkin is thinking of Ursula, now what Hermione is thinking of both of them, and they of her." [David Lodge, "Lawrence, Dostoevsky and Bakhtin: Lawrence and Dialogic Fiction," in Keith Brown, ed., *Rethinking Lawrence,* Milton Keynes and (Philadelphia: Open University Press, 1990)].

4. D. H. Lawrence, "Chaos in Poetry" in *Selected Poems,* ed. Mara Kalnins (London: Dent, 1992), 271.

Violence in *Women in Love*

MARK KINKEAD-WEEKES

◆　◆　◆

LAWRENCE IS AN UNCOMFORTABLE WRITER who often
forces us to face up to ourselves in ways that we would rather
avoid. This may offend what in us is sentimental, fashionable, or dishonest; and nowhere more so than in his exploration of violence.
We are repelled by violence, afraid of it, yet fascinated, vicariously
avid, as so many of our entertainments bear witness. But we insulate
ourselves from ourselves in comforting ways. Some people argue
that domestic violence is essentially a male phenomenon. Anthro-
pologists and politicians differ about whether violence is innate or
the product of conditioning, social class, or deprivation. Most of us
would like to think that it can be contained by improving social organization and welfare. We suppose ourselves to be peaceable and
that what we read in the newspapers is about people quite other
than ourselves, if perhaps less fortunate.

What horrified critics and policemen of all kinds about *The Rainbow* in 1915 however—after which the novel was banned for a
decade—was more than the "obscenity" of treating sexual relationships with newly daring openness. The reviews reveal a deeper hor-

ror. It seemed wholly unacceptable to show civilized human beings as impelled by forces far below the level of awareness and choice. Critics refused to see themselves as unstable and governed by subterranean impulse. They resisted the idea of flux and change as a principle of life. Most felt threatened, even outraged. Very few early readers understood the religious dimension announced by the novel's title and biblical symbolism, or the deep seriousness of its exploration of the forces in human beings that helped to make them creative or destructive. What was perhaps most shocking of all was the potential for destruction as well as development in the novel's increasingly emancipated women, though this revealed itself with psychological rather than physical force.

The effect on Lawrence himself of what happened to *The Rainbow* was traumatic. From the beginning, he had reacted to the outbreak of world war and the eagerness of Englishmen to enlist in it, with mounting horror. The destruction of his essentially religious novel seemed further evidence of a world gone mad. It brought his rejection of his country to a head. He tried to leave England for America at the end of 1915 but did not obtain the necessary endorsement to his passport,[1] so he did the next best thing and isolated himself as far away as possible near the tip of Cornwall. It was there in 1916, the most terrible year of the most terrible war mankind had ever seen, that he began to write *Women in Love* with at first no idea of publication. From feeling himself a writer at the height of his powers, confident that he had lifted his art a dimension above *Sons and Lovers* and sure that he had written a great work of religious imagination and struck a blow for the inner emancipation of women, he became a writer who had lost his audience and felt totally alienated from his society. He began without any reader in mind, indeed in a state of hostility: "it is beyond all possibility even to offer it to a world, a putrescent mankind. I feel I cannot touch humanity, even in thought, it is abhorrent to me. But a work of art is an act of faith, as Michael Angelo says, and one goes on writing, to the unseen witnesses."[2] In that final sentence we see the Lawrence that matters. Successive drafts show him struggling with misanthropy, contempt, and his hatred of the world, which the first version put in the mouth of Birkin. Lawrence had spoken earlier (about *Sons and Lovers*) of how one might "shed one's sickness" in a book, presenting it in order to get beyond it.[3] But this means that the narrator of *Women in Love* is no wise soul helping us to share his complex vision. He is *agonistes*, inside the conflict he creates, fighting to recover his own equilibrium in a world Lawrence thought was bent on destruction.

Indeed, one of the most important things about *Women in Love* is that it is a war novel, even though its society is apparently at peace and its date left deliberately vague (485:5–6).[4] For violence—now unmistakably physical and potentially lethal—wells up in most of the characters. Though Lawrence wished to trace its sources in a world apparently at peace, he clearly saw something apocalyptic about what had happened to his world in the year of the Somme and Verdun. He thought of calling the novel *Dies Irae*—Day of Wrath and Last Judgement—and though he significantly decided against that, the book remains an apocalypse of a kind. Things are falling apart. This creates great difficulty since the art, in form and language, must be such as can render and explore violence, disruption, excess, and anarchy without itself becoming anarchic. The most crucial question we have to decide is whether it is a destructively violent and excessive work, or a diagnosis of violence, enabling its author and its readers to "come through"? Above all, what does the novel reveal about the causes, sources, and significance of the violence pent up within its people?

That Lawrence thought something potentially lethal had now spread throughout his society first becomes clear in "Breadalby" (chapter VIII). The old house, beautiful product of past Enlightenment but also "complete," "final" in more than one sense like an old aquatint (82:29), belongs to a woman of high culture. Her country-house weekends gather together no mere decaying aristocracy but a group of intelligent, educated, and sophisticated people. When Hermione tries to smash Birkin's skull with a beautiful ball of lapis lazuli, therefore, the novel's first shocking blow to complacency insists that murderous violence can well up nowadays, not only in a woman, but in a soul devoted to beauty and within the very heart of "civilization." It is not the first act of apparently gratuitous physical violence in the novel (which came when the Pussum suddenly jabbed a knife across the hand of a young man in the Pompadour

[70:38]). Yet that was less shocking than Hermione's act. It is no great surprise when tipsy Bohemians behave with anarchic license, obeying whatever impulse comes uppermost. Pussum acts from uninhibited annoyance, like a cat clawing and drawing blood. Soon we shall learn to see her as corrupt in ways no animal could be; but though her sadomasochism will acquire greater significance when we come to realize both its bearing on Gudrun and its radical difference from the cat behaviour in "Mino" (chapter XIII), it is not lethal in itself. Hermione is.

How and why? Where does such violence spring from in a person of the highest "civilization"? The first feature of Lawrence's diagnosis is that the source lies in an *absence*, a hollowness. From the beginning (16:17–17:15) we are made aware of how—great lady and spiritual and cultural aspirant though she may be—Hermione's entire sense of herself is dangerously dependent on endorsement from outside herself, pre-eminently from Birkin. Without this, increasingly, there is a sense of drowning, of hopeless nullity, of torment and shame. But the second element we come to recognize is a counterforce of will that is finally seen to approach insanity. She tries to bully what she wants into existence, unable to accept either the truth about herself or the independent being and feeling of the "other" on whom she so depends. So when she forces Birkin to explain his response to a Chinese drawing of a goose, his perceptiveness is unendurable. She cannot but see a truth to *herself*, and one more fundamental than his previous attacks on her lack of spontaneity and sensuality, her bullying will, and her overweening desire to know, possessively (41:30–42:38).

For what Birkin intuits in the drawing, and voices in a language as peculiar as it turns out to be precise (89:17–21), comes home to Hermione as a devastating exposure. What the Chinese artist has captured is, first, an impression of the goose's "centrality", a creature centred in its own being and its world, in cruel contrast with the uncentered emptiness within herself. But its kind of vitality (all Hermione can aspire to?) is also inseparable, like a lotus, from the cold flux of water and mud in which it exists. Though the goose is warm-blooded, its blood will seem unwholesomely alien ("bitter," "stinging," "corruptive") to a being of a different kind. Birkin's rapt language may sound absurd; and the novel will have to struggle to articulate and justify it. But in the unconscious of Hermione it rings instantly and horribly true of herself. She feels a sick dissolution setting in: "he caught her, as it were, beneath all her defenses, and destroyed her with some insidious occult potency . . . She suffered the ghastliness of dissolution, broken and gone in a horrible corruption"(89:28–34).

From *Sons and Lovers* onward, Lawrence had made his readers sharply aware that there is a violence of the tongue that is no less wounding, damaging, and destructive than the violence of the fist. What Birkin says may be true—we wait to see—but it is also "hard and vindictive" (89:38). As the weekend goes on, he awakens in Hermione an answering inner violence, less and less controllable. On the surface this is a response to her horror of rejection. In the "irresponsible gaiety" of his dancing he shows himself a creature of change—hence "treacherous" to her dependency (92:24–42)—and she becomes more and more aware that she cannot hold him. But when her murderous violence breaks out, it is not sufficiently explained by that, or even by his vehement rejection of her liberal ideas about equality, though this brings "violent waves of hatred and loathing of all he said" (104:10–12). For these waves are "dynamic . . . coming strong and black out of the unconscious," far below the level of ideas, or even of relationship. She tries to kill him because her unconscious identifies his continued existence as a lethal threat to her own being. Psychologically, it is an act of self-defense. But it is also—as an expression of what she profoundly wants, needs, and desires from the depths of herself—a tremendously voluptuous and ecstatic act.

Murderous impulse has sprung from hollowness, lack of center, dependency, rejection, until finally the "other" is perceived as a lethal threat. We are far more ready than readers in the early twentieth century to accept how the causes of murderous violence may lie in the unconscious of the individual. But Lawrence also brings perspectives to bear which take us beyond the individual to the representative. As the concussed Birkin strips naked, and seeks to cleanse and heal himself in a wet world of natural growing things, the scene seems to emphasize the unnaturalness of what has hap-

pened. But Birkin is a sick soul too, and there is surely a question
mark about his simplistic contrast of vile humanity with clean nature, however understandable that is in the light of what has happened. We have no idea, yet, what "the lotus mystery" (89:21) might
be. But surely the flux of cold water with mud, the elements of both
cold lotus and hot-blooded goose, is no less natural than the soft
vegetation Birkin finds so healing? Moreover, if there is some link,
however obscure as yet, between the "corruption" perceived by the
Chinese artist from a decadent Mandarin culture, and the state of
Hermione's soul in a decadent modern Europe, the diagnosis is also
of something *in the times*, with perhaps some bearing on their murderous violence, and not merely in Hermione.

Some readers might now and again have shared the impulse to
"biff" Birkin the preacher (108:34). Yet the way he accepts what has
happened as *right* for Hermione is oddly sympathetic. If she were to
recognize and come to terms with her state of soul and the significance of her own violence, might that be the beginning of healing
for her? But she sets her will against any such recognition.

At the railway crossing (chapter IX) a peaceful scene—a hand-
some man on a beautiful Arab mare, waiting at the gate—erupts
into another kind of violence, appallingly rendered in industrial-
mechanical cacophony, implacable human will, and sensitive animal terror. Behind this, there is again a question about man and nature—How far may it be "natural" and justifiable for man to impose
his will on other creatures for his own ends?—a question reaching
uncomfortably beyond the obvious cruelty of the bloody spur in the
side of the terrified horse, however inclined a reader may be to share
Ursula's simple horror and hatred. But it is the effect on Gudrun, as
opposed to her sister, that is the scene's major significance. In Gudrun's imagination afterward the event is transformed into a sexual
experience, in which she imaginatively identifies herself with the
mare, sensing the "indomitable soft weight of the man, bearing
down . . . the strong indomitable thighs . . . a sort of soft white magnetic domination from the loins and thighs and calves, enclosing
and encompassing" the female into "soft blood-subordination, terrible" (113:30–36). Terrible, but also magnetically attractive? What was

in her high witch scream, "I should think you're proud" (112:35), as she opened the gate to him? Excitement? Defiance? We are dealing with the terrible attraction, and the danger, of violence between man and woman that is potentially inherent in the sexual act itself.

It is clear now that the structure of the novel works by isolating two or three characters in the presence of some catalyst that brings out their being (see the chapter titles) and then by collecting at intervals a whole party together, so that we are led to compare and contrast more widely and to see what is happening as a dimension of society. In terms of individual psychology, "Water Party" (chapter XIV) focuses what has gone before and prepares for what is to come. But when violence comes to the party and shatters the festivity, we are also led to see something more widespread, antisocial, and rebellious.

Here is a society apparently at peace and at play. Since this is class-ridden Britain however, the "open day" on the Crich estate is not open to everyone; there is a policeman at the gate. Class tensions show themselves. William Brangwen, not a gentleman, is ill at ease. Though his daughters have also been invited as teacher and artist, they reveal kinds of defense and aggression about their situations as women. Hermione, the aristocrat, feels free to inspect others. Birkin, the more diplomatic inspector, is never quite right socially. Gudrun despises "the crowd," and remembers with horror her trip up the Thames when fat bourgeois men threw coins for ragged urchins to scrabble for in the appalling mud. So tensions in the body politic are registered, though (so far) they may seem containable within the festivity over which Gerald presides. Gudrun, for all her sophistication, both becomes childlike with him and seems to make "the blood stir in his veins, the subtle way she turned to him and infused her gratitude into his body" (163:12–14). Lawrence's new subterranean insight is at work, showing how being impacts on being sexually, without touch and below conscious awareness. But what she is grateful for is help in opting out of a social situation; and her female submissiveness to the dominant male may contain more than meets the eye.

Having been entrusted with a canoe, the sisters escape into a pri-

vate world where they can be themselves, naked and free (as Gudrun complained in "Diver" that women couldn't be). When Ursula begins to sing, the differences which have been emerging since
the beginning become suddenly clearer: how Ursula, for all her uncertainty, lives "at the centre of her own universe" (165:28–29),
while Gudrun always has to demand that the "other" be aware of
her—a link with Hermione. As Gudrun begins to dance, she unin-
hibits and reveals her inner self in an unconsciously suggestive exposure: her urge, first to free herself from repression, then to express herself, and then unmistakably (with the arrival of the
Highland bulls) to define and assert herself *against* the other, the
male. Behind the submission to the attractive alpha male, it turns
out, lies a strongly reactive female counteraggression. Previous hints
gather into revelation: the fascinating first glimpse of Gerald whose
"totem is the wolf" (14:40); the taking to herself by Gudrun of his
domination of the mare, and her ambivalent gull-scream; the impulse to be childlike and suppliant that links her with the Pussum,
but also the perception now that this too is a mode of power which
can swiftly turn into aggression. When Gerald substitutes himself
for the bulls, the hidden violence in this pattern of submission/ag-
gression spurs out in spite of herself in an instantaneous blow
across his face, and the prophetic dialogue that shows both of them
shocked into sudden awareness of their sex relation as (in its way) a
war. "Why *are* you behaving in this *impossible* and ridiculous fashion?"
(171:11–12) is the reaction of her conscious mind, but the Gudrun-
ness of Gudrun has been exposed on a deeper level, as has the question of whether the man or the woman will ultimately prove the
stronger.

Yet "love" as a kind of war—in terms of domination and submission, defeat or victory—is not the only possibility open to Gerald
and Gudrun. Nothing is determined yet. As they set out on the lake
together in the frail canoe, the mode of their love suddenly becomes quite different. There is space between them and, with that,
they seem able both to be themselves, balancing each other, and to
see a magical beauty in the other without wanting to possess or to
dominate. Gudrun may feel at first she has Gerald at her mercy, but
she is soon overcome by the beauty and mystery of his otherness, his

maleness now a wonder not a threat. And he, who always keeps so tight a grip on himself, begins for the first time to let go, to become "lapsed out" into his surroundings (178:11), not trying to control or impose himself on them. Now there is an extraordinary new peace and beauty. For this couple there are two quite different ways of being a woman or a man "in love." Which way will they go?

Meanwhile Birkin has danced *his* sardonic little dance, which Ursula doesn't like because it combines self-abandon, which attracts her, with mockery and distance. The novel is also structuring itself by constant parallel and comparison. Later, he preaches a sermon drawn from *The Crown.* Written between *The Rainbow* and *Women in Love,* these essays had re-cast the former's central insight, the creativity of a marriage of opposites, in the light of a world given over to destruction. Now we discover the import of the "lotus mystery." We think of life as creative; but there are times—and for Birkin this is one of them—when the cycle of creation comes to an end and everything is given over for a while to destruction.[5] Individuals, and indeed whole societies, may be caught up in a death process, a dark "river of corruption" (172:29) in which things fall apart into their elements. Birkin feels that it is *fin de siècle* now and that they may all be "flowers of dissolution" (173:3). But though he voices ideas that Lawrence had written, it is clear that he is less than his author now. For Ursula will have none of his acceptance of deathliness (however necessary before new creation can come about). *She* isn't a flower of dissolution, but feels herself a rose, warm and flamy with life. She detects a death wish in him, a sickness which she must fight. Sermon turns into drama.

It is time to light the lanterns and see deeper. They are rose and primrose, or blue; they suggest a life above the surface and below, a cool dark vitality, and a warmer, flamier life. The greatest beauty appears however when they set each other off, in contrast and in balance. Yet Gudrun is afraid of the underworld, and makes her sister take the cuttlefish lantern. We shall see its white writhing creature again, but the question for now is what might be involved in rejecting it. Was Blake right, for instance, that everything that lives is holy, all energy eternal delight?[6] Or are there subhuman modes of being that should be rejected and denied?

They set out on the lake, these two pairs "in love," the different lanterns adding beauty to the night, the lights reflected in the dark water. But people are subject to their social world. The magic is violently shattered by an "accident," which results in the drowning of Gerald's sister Diana and the young doctor who dived to save her. But was it accident? Twice already the question has arisen of whether things do happen accidentally, or whether there was secret impulse when the child Gerald shot his brother (26:10), or when Birkin drank his champagne at the wedding "accidentally on purpose" (30:34)? Diana's voice was heard at the wedding, the voice of the rebel (27:31–32). Why was she dancing on the roof of the steamer? Was it not the stimulus of rebellion, the excitement of danger, the frisson of risk? Something that has quickly proved lethal connects Diana with Gudrun, and with Gerald who becomes a "Diver" now in a much darker mode than the glad naked freedom of chapter IV. Below the surface lies a whole dark, cold, deathly world—water and mud—which seems bigger and more real to Gerald than the one up above; and he is dangerously drawn to it. There might be two kinds of "lapsing out," one suddenly sees: into unity with a living universe, or a letting go into nothingness, a death wish, a desire not to be. Birkin struggles against this in his friend, as Ursula had struggled against nihilism in him. The pairs are not only "in love," whether in tender or aggressive ways, they are also poised at crossroads between modes of deathliness and possibilities of new life, and this would seem to be the case more widely, too, in their world.

In three crucial chapters at the centre of the book, the characters begin to give intimations of the ways they might go, and violence lies at the heart of all three.

In "Rabbit" (chapter XVIII), Gudrun and Winifred set out to sketch the Looliness of Looloo the Pekinese. Winifred produces a wicked little "diagram" or caricature, which nevertheless is very "like." She's an apt pupil to Gudrun, who likes to pin things and people down, to grasp them once and for all: Gerald as wolf, birds as little Lloyd Georges (264:3), her own sculpted creatures that can be held in the hand. Art, for her, is a means of knowing-as-possession, exerting a kind of power over its object, which is why the drawing does the little dog "some subtle injury" (236:6). But it is one thing to sketch Looloo, and quite another to haul the great buck rabbit Bismarck out of his cage by the ears in order to do the same. For Bismark has power of his own, and reacts against the attempt to "grasp" *him* by instantaneous violence, a tempest hardly controllable. This in turn brings welling up in Gudrun a "fury," a "heavy cruelty," as her wrists are clawed and she battles to subdue the "bestial stupidity" (240:30–32). To hear her high voice "like the crying of a seagull, strange and vindictive" (241:2) is to be reminded of the scene at the railway crossing—especially when Gerald takes over the struggle. But the response of violence to rebellion is heightened now, as the man's hand comes down on the rabbit's neck like a hawk. The animal screams in the fear of death, until, with a final writhe and tearing, it is mastered. As the scene with the highland cattle re-orchestrated the one at the railway crossing, so "Rabbit" takes us another stage deeper into the potentialities of sexual war between Gerald and Gudrun. The action has been wholly realistic. But now, from behind the realism, the new art begins to open up once more a dimension undiscovered in earlier fiction: for "the scream of the rabbit . . . seemed to have torn the veil of her consciousness" (241:20–21), and what can lie behind the veil in Gudrun and Gerald is revealed to them both, beyond disguise.

The language shows the strain of having to put into words something that, by definition, is almost beyond articulation. Gudrun looks at Gerald with eyes "strained with underworld knowledge" (almost a contradiction in terms) "like those of a creature which is at his mercy," an expression caught in the eyes of rabbit and girl alike, "but which is his ultimate victor" (241:40–242:1) unless he could treat her as he has treated Bismarck. He feels a "mutual hellish recognition" (242:2) because she seems a willing, even mocking, "recipient of his magical, hideous white fire" (242:4–5) of cruelty. As she shows off the red gash in her white flesh, there "was a league between them, abhorrent to them both. They were implicated with each other in abhorrent mysteries" (242:22–24). There follows perhaps the most absurd-sounding sentence Lawrence had ever written: "The long, shallow red rip seemed torn across his own brain, tearing the surface of his ultimate consciousness, letting through the forever unconscious, unthinkable red ether of the beyond, the obscene beyond" (242:34–37).

Yet this is by no means unintelligible. Staring into the bloody redness opened up by violence, Gerald can momentarily sense his way through its medium into his own psyche and hers, to be enveloped and overcome by what comes welling out of the sight: the fascinating *excitement* of violence and of power, whether for sadist or masochist. *The Rainbow* had made it clear that sex is always, for Lawrence, going beyond one's ordinary self and old consciousness into a new mode of being. But here the mode is "hellish" and "obscene" because its "ether"—the supposed medium in the space beyond the normal atmosphere (within the self now, rather than above)—is *pleasure* in violence, whose final frisson may be death. Bismarck then gets rid of his distress and frustration by tearing round and round in meteoric frenzy, seeming mad but perhaps just according to his nature. (Again, however, what is "natural" in animal or man? Is violence, death dealing, and war, natural or denaturing?) As the lovers exchange suggestive hints of the possibilities their subconscious has suggested, they show a readiness to offer and accept rabbit sexuality and animal violence that may even now be "shocking" in its "nonchalance" (243:28–29).

Yet the final sentence of the chapter (243:33–4) is a sudden reminder of the path not taken since "Water Party." For Bismarck is not the power wielder and warmonger of his name. In truth he *is* a mystery, a wonder, like Gerald in the canoe when seen with reverence for his otherness rather than with the urge to dominate—whether by Winifred's fantasy and mothering, or Gerald and Gudrun's power struggle (perhaps even to the death).

The second scene shows how much there is that is violent and deathly in Birkin and Ursula too. Yet the crucial discovery of "Moony" (chapter XIX), challenging sentimentalists, is that there is a kind of violence that can heal, as well as the kind that brutalizes and destroys. The changeability of this pair has been evident since "Water Party." Birkin has become sickly and withdrawn again. Ursula has been repelled anew by what she sees as his sickliness, and feels a kind of pure hatred for his very being, oppressive to her ego. As she wanders through the dark trees she is in a mood of almost nihilistic repudiation, hating the brilliant moonlight which makes everything definite and visible to consciousness, and drawn to the darkness in which one can lose oneself. Yet there by the pond is Birkin, a shadow, muttering to himself so ludicrously that she wants to laugh. The husks he drops in the water recall the flowers scattered on the pond in "An Island," when they first admitted their love, now gone dead and dry. Birkin's muttering suggests that any relation with women has become for him an antiphony of lies. Indeed the moon now suggests a horrible female power, like that of the Syrian goddess who emasculated her acolytes. So it seems in hatred of woman that he begins to stone the moon's reflection. But when it is over he will ask, "Was it hate?" (248:33). However much it may be (both in Birkin and the watching Ursula) a working off of anger, dislike, and frustration, it seems also deeper than that. What actually happens to dark water and white moon, and in the minds of the watchers?

The impact of the first stone makes the moon's reflection look like a writhing cuttlefish, and with a second stone the moon explodes. Waves of darkness run into the centre, but after near destruction the moon re-forms. Again, with stones close together, Birkin's explosions momentarily obliterate the moon, but again it re-forms. Then he throws stone after stone after stone. This, if we submit imaginatively to the language and the rhythm, is an extraordinary experience of violence. Yet after and through it comes a strange peace and tenderness, in which words of simple truth can be spoken. Neurosis, hatred, deathliness have vanished (though they may come back). Moreover, after the apparently annihilating violence, the moon looks different. It no longer seems hard, triumphant, a thing of power. It has become a rose, constellated in the dark water. We are reminded of Ursula's rose (no *fleur du mal*) against Birkin's dark river of dissolution, and of how the rosy lantern balanced and harmonized with the dark one and its writhing sea creature. It is not the rose alone, but the rose constellated in darkness that becomes the symbol of love. What has happened in the pool and in the subconscious of the lovers seems to be a mode of love in which relationship can come through intense clashes of personality, even violent conflict, to wholeness, harmony, and peace. In *The Rain-*

how, sex had been seen as a kind of death and rebirth, a loss of consciousness and an experience of oblivion at the hands of the "other"
(as in the first stoning here), which opened up a new life beyond.
Then however, as the Lawrence of 1915 rewrote his philosophy in
The Crown, he had seen that there might be times when violence and
destruction have to go very far indeed before new creation can
begin. The subconscious may need to be broken open and neurotic
consciousness almost disintegrated, before a new integration can
come about and the whole self become calm and composed, at
peace. Yet it comes about experientially here, because neither of the
opposed forces overcomes the other. Out of the writhing polyp, the
crashing noise, the broken water, the splintered light, the shattering
violence, come healing, peace, and tenderness. "There is a golden
light in you, which I wish you would give me" says Birkin (249:15)—
that is, something more than merely personal.

As soon as they begin to speak, however, misunderstanding flares
and conflict begins again. Ursula thinks Birkin is demanding male
supremacy, that she should submit and serve, and he is far from
clear about what he does want. He is also infuriated by the Magna
Mater (the great Female and Mother) in her and by her assertive will
and self-insistence—as against his, of course. Yet what they reached
for a moment is real, and will come again when the words and the
self-conscious "old stable ego"[7] give way. Afterward, Birkin is able to
clarify to himself the different "ways" in which modern men and
women can go. Halliday's African statuette seems to embody a
mode of being which—no longer fusing body, mind, and spirit—
has given itself over entirely to experiencing and knowing through
the senses. This is a kind of "disintegration and dissolution" (253:22)
because it is a falling apart of unified being, a reduction of wholeness
to only some of its elements, though Birkin admires its culture,
which has gone much further down the road than his own. (Dissolution, "corruption," may be *necessary* before a new integration can
begin.) But there is also an opposite "Arctic" way of disintegration
and reduction, when life is wholly dominated by mind and will, the
gleaming white life we have seen in Gerald and the pale Hermione.[8]
But now the Birkin who preached about the "river of dissolution"
has been brought by Ursula and the experience of the pond to see

that there is a third way (though it will prove ironically premature
to call it "paradisal"). There is a violence and disintegration that can
heal, a conflict after which the "opposites" can regain themselves,
but constellated together now in new peace and beauty of being and
relationship. He goes off impulsively to ask Ursula to marry him—
comically, because he doesn't yet understand what he has intuited,
and because Ursula has changed again so that another row ensues.
But there has been a glimpse of a way through and beyond sex war
for them.

   The third key scene (chapter XX) focuses on violence between
men. When Birkin meets Gerald in the library after his row with Ursula, he is quietly furious and Gerald is in a nihilistic state. Having
given himself to a machine world of mind controlling matter, Gerald finds—when work stops and he is left to himself—that inside
him there is a void, as though his blue eyes were bubbles stretched
over nothingness. So an inner violence springing from anger, hollowness, and frustration finds a "Gladiatorial" outlet in a "friendly"
wrestling match, naked, and ironically surrounded by the books of
civilization. But as the writhing "underworld" creature appears
once more in the shape of the white bodies wrestling with increasing
violence, "Rabbit" and "Moony" should have taught us to compare.
Is this about sublimated homosexuality, as has sometimes been
claimed? That hardly seems the essence of the scene, though the
young men are physically attracted to each other.[9] Is it, as in "Rabbit," a power struggle for dominance? Or is it, in the end, like
"Moony," a Blakean conflict of opposites out of which comes
growth, so that opposition proves true friendship?[10] Certainly the
quick "physical intelligence" (270:21–22) of the wiry dark one and
the massive power of the blonde one seem equally matched, and
wrestle each other into oblivion. Both of them "lapse out" into unconsciousness, but when consciousness returns there is (again)
peace, wholeness, and reintegration, and a new tenderness. Words
can be spoken that would normally be difficult for Edwardian
males: "I think also that you are beautiful" (273:2)—compare
"There is a golden light in you." In the instinctive handclasp and intimacy—and the suggestion that there can be a relationship between men, too, that leaves them individually separate but with the

possibility of permanent commitment, a kind of blood brotherhood—it seems possible for males to relate in the same sort of "way" that Birkin and Ursula found in "Moony." The way, indeed, seems more important than the gender.[11] The novel is showing us how to read. But it is only when one grasps in these central chapters how there may be a creative and healing as well as a destructive kind of violence, that one will see how and why the characters' paths proceed to divide more and more, in opposite directions of life and death, as if on some last Judgment Day.

Then "Excurse" (chapter XXIII) translates the violence of "Moony" into more realist terms, in a flaming row between Ursula and Birkin over Hermione and other things. The engagement rings he has bought are signs of the commitment he wants; and being red, dark blue, and primrose, remind us of the lanterns and the challenge to harmonize oppositions in human beings and relationships. But Ursula's resistance to commitment is fueled by jealousy and her sense of being undervalued, while Birkin is infuriated by the way she makes everything personal. As used to happen between Lawrence and Frieda, to the scandal of more inhibited and conventional friends, the row gets out of hand. It culminates in Ursula not only flinging his rings in Birkin's face but denouncing his very being as foul, corrupt, split between false spirituality and dirty sex—until, comically, she is forced to be silent while a cyclist pedals by. (Lawrence is sometimes accused of being humorless, but even in this dark novel there are several moments of pure comedy.) Once again, however, violence and seeming hate can be healing if they can be accepted and gone through. For—unlike Hermione—Birkin is able to take denunciation on board and to see that there is truth in it, if not the whole truth. Above all, under its stunning impact, oblivion comes over him again. The "knot" of his conscious mind is broken, he is "dissolved in darkness" (309:40), aware only of his need for her to come back. And she does, with a flower for him, the violence having blown itself quite away and cleaned the air as after a thunderstorm, so that everything has become simple and clear and loving.

Then over tea in a public place, Lawrence tries to embody (literally) the essential condition for what Birkin had called the third, paradisal, way of "love," though that word can mean such different things that he is loath to use it. If violence springs from uncentered hollowness, what is the precondition of wholeness? When Ursula puts her arms round his loins and thighs she makes an extraordinary discovery. There is a charisma in him, a force, "the strange mystery of his life-motion" (313:17–18). As her sense of mystery increases, the language struggles again to find terms to express it. The moment is clearly vitally important; but what exactly is the experience? Why the particularity of the touch just there? Why the bizarre metaphor of dark, fluid electricity? Why the religiosity of seeing him as "one of the Sons of God" (313:35)? Even some admirers of Lawrence have felt embarrassed. But though the strain on language is at its maximum hereabouts, one can see something of what Lawrence is trying to articulate, almost beyond the reach of words, and why he takes such risks.

In his sickness, Birkin had brooded over the fact that the genital front of the human body seems to proclaim its incompleteness, the need for a complementary other half. It is conversely at the base of the spine that people hold themselves upright, moving with their own independent motion, pivoted on the fulcrum of their limbs. Here is the locus of self-balance. So, in the first place, Ursula is touching the source of Birkin's independent and spontaneous self-existence and otherness, something deeper and more important than his "phallic" manhood (314:34) and nothing to do with the will. Indeed true individuality, she now sees, is a divinely creative life force, and Birkin is a "Son of God" because he manifests that energy of God in him. She has been waiting for such a man since the breakdown that followed her unhappy affair with Skrebensky at the end of *The Rainbow*. Like all truly living and individual things Birkin is a mystery, a wonder, to be reverenced. (Lawrence is careful later to reverse the positions in "Flitting," chapter XXVII. The wonder and mystery of Ursula is just as important and life giving.) Paradoxically their "way" of love has required oblivion of the conscious self, yet a kind of rebirth has given them back to themselves with increased individuality and vitality. By contrast, it was their hollowness and consequent dependence on some other, coupled with the will to find selfhood in dominating others that has made Hermione, Gerald and Gudrun so dangerous. The vitality Ursula is touching, moreover, is physical as well as psychological and mystical. Individual 'otherness' is not an idea, it is something forcefully *there* (like Bismark); not merely palpable, but only fully experienced in the flesh. But how then produce a language of touch, subconscious and not idea, that can convey the sense of energy, of force? One sees now why Lawrence was driven to a kind of imagery (Futurist, and theosophical)[12] for a "power" that is invisible but very real, and "dark" because nothing to do with the conscious mind. It is "in" the person, but also impersonal and transcendent, just as electricity flows through a cable but is not defined by it. And the experience, finally, is of the essence of liberating sexual relationship as Lawrence now conceives it: the coming together of individuals who neither dominate nor serve each other, and certainly never merge into one flesh. It is like a passing away, a death, and then a rebirth, the discovery of wonderful new life. Once that comes right (and a touch of fingers in a public place is enough) then all else can follow: the joy in radiant light *and* the full sexual relationship in the dark of Sherwood forest, the ability to give and take in every mode, including all parts of the self. This "love" has managed to combine forceful individuality with commitment and indeed abandonment to the other. We lay hold of what Birkin's image of "star equilibrium" had been trying to grasp[13]: how two individual and separate beings can, without losing their own momentum, be bound to and balanced by each other, so "constellating"—the word releases its full meaning—their oppositions in relationship. This will not put an end to conflict, but Ursula and Birkin have definitely found their way beyond violence and deathliness, toward new life.

The contrast with the other couple grows clearer, now. The title of the corresponding chapter for Gerald and Gudrun is "Death and Love" (chapter XXIV)—and it is darkly ambiguous. It seems simply to foretell how Gerald will go from his dying father to kiss Gudrun under the bridge, and then from his father's grave to her bed. It actually hints at how this pair of lovers seem to be setting their feet on a path opposite to that of Ursula and Birkin, a different kind of "love" which may indeed become deadly. The dying of Thomas Crich shows the horror of dissolution for a man who had willed to live only what he thought the higher and Christian life of mind and

spirit (with disastrous effects on his wife), but who is now imprisoned in his dying body, and terrified to let go. Gerald's fascination
with death, which we saw in "Water Party," keeps him at the bedside
and feeds his nihilism. But for him, too, love seems to offer, wonder-
fully, a path away from death to life. He and Gudrun walk to the
bridge, balanced in dual motion. When they kiss it is a kind of oblivion and a kind of perfection. It is a hair's breadth away from the
mode of love that heals and gives life—as in the language of Last
Things the path to death and hell is said to open at the very gate of
heaven. At first it looks just the same. But it differs radically, and the
divergence gets ever wider. For all the glamour, Gerald seems to
drink Gudrun into himself in his power and mastery; and when she
is gone she is gone in him, so that *he* is perfected. Moreover when
her fingers wander over his face it is with an excitement not of reverence but of *knowing*—we think of Birkin's denunciation of
Hermione—gathering Gerald in by touch, wanting to have him in
her hands, possessing (excitedly) a dangerous enemy. When in desperation he comes from the grave to Gudrun's bed, the difference
becomes still clearer. As he now takes her fully, sexually, it is to pour
into her as into a vessel "all his pent-up darkness and corrosive
death" (344:11), and to feel himself dissolved, warmed through,
healed, as though with sunshine, or healing water in a bath or
womb. He falls asleep like a child, but she is left terribly wakeful,
"destroyed into perfect consciousness" (345:20), hearing the hours
strike, endlessly drawing a rope of consciousness out of the sea of
her unconscious. The crucial difference, then, is that "love" for
these two is always one-sided: one dominant and the other submissive or rebellious; one taking all what the other has to give; one ex-
citingly held off while the other enjoys the frisson; one reduced to
the object of the other's knowledge. The "and" of the chapter title is
in fact a hyphenation. Even now there is something deathly in this
"love." Seeds of the future are here already.

Quite how far the different ways of love will diverge however,
only becomes clear in the final section of the novel, where the
Alpine snowscape becomes a kind of scanning chamber, focussing
intensely diagnostic light on the two pairs of lovers and their condition.

First, however, the Bohemians in the Pompadour (chapter XXVIII) are allowed to ridicule an old letter from Birkin about the "Flux of Corruption," to paradoxical effect. On the one hand this is a Birkin (and a Lawrence) the novel has outgrown. Ursula, indeed, has been a fierce critic of the preacher and would-be savior in him. Yet the residual truth of Birkin's intuitions, behind the rhetorical striving for expression, has come home to us in dramatized experience since "Water Party." The rhetoric served a purpose on the way—but we are well beyond it now, and Lawrence can enjoy parodying his protagonist (and his own 1915 self) with a zest no other mocker could rival. Yet the letter also reminds us of important perspectives before we reach the snow. What we will see may begin in the souls of individuals; but may also be part of the times in which they find themselves. It is all the more important, then, that Birkin's letter should point not only to *fin de siecle* "dissolution" and "reduction," but also to the possibility of ending, indeed transcending those processes in the self.

For Birkin and Ursula indeed the journey to the Alps involves a shaking off of the past, and a projection into new life. They are not at all idealized. In them, too, the light of the snow shows up continuing flaws. There is something falsely sentimental in Ursula. She too enjoys asserting her female power, and never quite gives all of herself. There is an element of bestiality in Birkin's love, and Ursula will never be all-in-all to him. But in their courage of commitment to marriage, their uprightness in themselves and acceptance of the otherness of each other, and their loving tenderness, they seem to have found a way beyond the violence and the malaise of their former selves. The snow for them is an experience to pass through, to somewhere where growth and flowering may be possible.

Violence grows steadily however in Gerald and Gudrun. In the snow their glamour is intensified, but also shadowed with more and more foreboding as they become *aware* of what has hitherto been unconscious, and come to intend, indeed fiercely to will and desire, what was before still only a potential. The snow intensifies certain tendencies we have seen before but, as a kind of disintegrative element, like radium, it also burns away everything else. They have been complex people with multiple possibilities. Now complex

selves become steadily narrowed to obsessiveness; and complex relationship gets reduced, step by dramatized step, to acknowledged enmity and final, fully lethal violence.

We are given a last reminder by Gudrun in "Snow" (chapter
XXX), all the more effective for coming so late, of the charisma and
the stature of Gerald: his male beauty, his business intelligence and
huge organizing ability, his whole-hog approach to things, his real
potential greatness. He is tremendously sexy and athletic. It is all the
more tragic that previous hints of a hollowness beneath the apparent power become intensified in the snow. He can find no sufficiency
in himself, or his work in which he has lost all interest now. He cannot stand alone. He may reap the maidens, but cannot finally commit himself to any "other," without which is no abiding love. His
sexuality is all male ego and power play, cloakng inadequacy, neediness. That neediness has now concentrated his whole being on Gudrun. His craving for her as prop and stay has become obsessive, and
everything else unreal. But Gudrun's vision of snow slopes and twin
peaks outside her window comes as a new revelation: an image of
the beauty of her own body, a powerful symbol of femininity. She
begins to change before our eyes, shedding the submissiveness that
had been a mode of power over him, and rebelling more and more
against his attraction for her which now seems a treason to the new
image of herself—with which she communes alone. And though
we see with new intensity in their first embrace in the Alps how her
submission can strengthen Gerald's sense of maleness and power, a
new awareness gradually dawns in him too: how his desire for her
"would destroy him if he were not fulfilled" and more, how he
"would destroy her rather than be denied" (402:12–15).

"Sex war" ceases to be at all metaphorical as the risks in their relationship visibly increase. Now that Gudrun has resolved to fight
his power over her, it can suddenly almost paralyze her with fear to
be alone with the Wolf, even though he is making no move. On the
other hand there is a new exhilaration in extreme risk, when Gerald
takes her on the toboggan to the brink of death, swerving aside only
at the last moment. This soon translates into the excitement of real
danger in resisting, and then in torturing him, seeing how far she
can go. For Gerald, their "love" becomes a withering of his con-

sciousness, a blasting of his mind, but one he must go on with to the end because his need of her is so imperative. The more beautiful and goodly that need makes her seem to him, the more this nullifies *his* defect of self. When she forces him to admit that he does not love her, and is indeed incapable of love, his heart whispers to him "If only I could kill her—I should be free"(442:39–40). As she tortures him she pretends to pity, but really her deepest motive now is hatred and fear. She seems to have killed something in him as he stumbles inertly into bed and unconsciousness; but to revive him as a demonstration of her power is to bring his passion back in all its strength. Now it is she who feels that she is being killed, by a sexuality "ghastly and impersonal, like a destruction, ultimate" (444:29–30). The die is cast. If they stay together we can see that it may in sober truth come to "kill or be killed."

A significant difference becomes apparent. Gudrun may seem the stronger because she is able to harden herself on herself, increasingly impervious like a stone. Under the influence of Loerke moreover, her cynicism, irony and mockery increase. She sees herself again as 'the artist' free to shape her own reality; a modernist (and even post modernist) kind of art owing no allegiance to any truth to life. Indeed she and Loerke assert their critical ability to play with past and present, reducing all to the terms of their own knowingness. (For Ursula, this is a disintegrative process, reductive to both art and life and negating their essential relation.) Another dangerous element of contempt and jealousy has entered the relationship between Gerald and Gudrun, and it proves the last straw. Loerke is struck aside like a straw man. Gerald's hands close around Gudrun's throat, as they had closed around the rabbit. But as he strangles her, Gudrun strikes the last blow—to Gerald's heart—as she had prophesied she would.

But why does Gerald not go through with killing her? Is this weakness, or a kind of nobility? Was it really a strength that Gudrun should so have hardened herself to herself? Or is Gerald's willingness to keep open the rent in his being and to accept the truth of himself even to final dissolution, a kind of integrity and endurance? He proves able to limit his violence, and to refuse to burden his soul with the guilt of Gudrun's murder. But his path of life becomes a blind staggering to self-extinction in the snow. Question marks coil around a huge irony. The apparently submissive and weaker maiden has killed the magnificent stallion, reduced him to a block of insensate ice—and has also, to all vital intents and purposes, killed herself, become cold, barren, incapable of relationship. And there is a tragic sense of waste that Birkin's lament for Gerald brings out—for it did not have to happen.

Violence has its sources it seems both in hollowness and dependency, *and* in egotism and self-assertion. Conversely, the way through violence to new life demands apparent opposites: the ability to stand alone *and* the ability to give oneself to an 'other' to the point of self-oblivion, in order to find oneself renewed. Gudrun becomes all ego, hardened to herself, incapable finally of relation or giving—and hence reducing time to mere succession, bereft of living purpose. Gerald cannot risk standing alone even when he sees very clearly that he ought to leave her. All he can do, finally, is walk into an oblivion that is without any hope of new life. It is the final and most caustic irony that he should see the crucifix, with its message of resurrection through death—the essential truth of which in daily life and sexuality *The Rainbow* had tried to reinterpret—as a murder of the self, a horror.

Notes

1. After the passage of the Derby Act it was necessary for travelers abroad to attest their willingness to serve King and country, if called. Lawrence was so strongly opposed to the war that, although he stood in a queue for some time, waiting to attest, he could not bring himself to do so.

2. To Barbara Low, 1 May 1916, *Letters* ii, 602.

3. To A. W. McLeod, 26 October 1913, *Letters* ii, 90.

4. All page references in the text are to the Cambridge edition ed. David Farmer, Lindeth Vasey, and John Worthen (Cambridge, 1987)

5. The essay entitled "The Flux of Corruption" in *The Crown* cites water plants and birds, warm-blooded or sun-colored above but with feet in the cold below, as symbols of such a phase. See *Reflections on the Death of a Porcupine and Other Essays* ed. Michael Herbert (Cambridge, 1988), 270 ff.

6. William Blake, "Proverbs of Hell," *The Marriage of Heaven and Hell* (1790).

7. In his letter to Edward Garnett, 5 June 1914, *Letters* ii, 182–83, Lawrence explained how his new concept of character was attempting to subvert nineteenth-century ideas of character as stable and consciously analyzable

8. Lawrence anticipates the ideas of the later "Negritude" movement, especially the contrast between "white" and "black" in the writings of Leopold Sedar Senghor.

9. Birkin confessed to having experienced erotic feelings for men in the original Prologue, which Lawrence decided to discard. In chapter XVI "Man to Man," however, the physical attraction of Birkin and Gerald for each other is clear, though Gerald is uneasy about any commitment to the offer of blood brotherhood.

10. "Proverbs of Hell," op.cit. note 6.

11. See also the two different types of homoerotic feeling in the discarded Prologue.

12. On the Futurists—who were much concerned with power and energy—see the letter to Garnett referred to in note 7. "Excurse" also shows the influence of J. M. Pryse's *The Apocalypse Unsealed* (1910), which recalling Hindu mystical neurology, held that cosmic energy "lies at the base of the spinal cord and is the start of the central current."

13. See 143–7; 150:34–40; 254:25–31; 290:30–31; and 319:36–8.

The Dialogue with the Avant-Garde in *Women In Love*

GINETTE KATZ-ROY

◆　◆　◆

A New Era

In his autobiography, Wyndham Lewis evokes the drastic changes that occurred in Europe just before World War I in these dramatic terms: "Europe was full of titanic stirrings and snortings—a new art coming to flower to celebrate or to announce a "new age."[1] Those were the days when T. E. Hulme, under the influence of Wilhelm Worringer's theories on primitive art and inorganic forms,[2] advocated a new anti-humanist art in Alfred Orage's socialist magazine, significantly called *The New Age*.[3] Those were the days when Ezra Pound proclaimed: "I want a new civilization."[4]

In the spring of 1914, Wyndham Lewis founded "The Rebel Art Centre," which promoted revolutionary art ideas and nonrepresentational art. The years 1913/1914, during which Lawrence wrote the first drafts of *The Rainbow* and *Women in Love*, were crucial in the history of the European avant-garde movements. England witnessed the first Imagist publications, Roger Fry's break[5] with the more radical Wyndham Lewis, Pound's split with the Imagists, the new alliance Pound/Lewis which led to the creation of the Vorticist movement and its magazine *Blast* (1914/1915) in the wake of the "Rebel Art Centre," and also the Vorticists' quarrel with the Italian Futurists. This chaotic situation bespeaks a tremendous desire for novelty that Pound expressed rather crudely in these terms: "To the present order of things, we have nothing to say but *merde*."[6]

One may wonder whether Lawrence was drawn into the vortex of modernism or tried to avoid its lure. Ezra Pound, one of the most prominent avant-gardists, passed such fluctuating judgments on him that we may suspect the answer is not an easy one. In a letter to Harriet Monroe dated March 1913, Pound said of Lawrence's poetry: "I think he learned the proper treatment of modern subjects before I did."[7] One year later, he still considered him to be one of the best prose writers of the new generation, on a par with Joyce. After 1917, he changed his opinion radically. It is true that some of Lawrence's contemporaries seemed to be much more innovative in style and technique than Lawrence, notably those writers who had participated with Pound in the short-lived Vorticist venture from 1914 to 1916: Wyndham Lewis, T. S. Eliot, and Joyce. Yet, even if Lawrence never belonged to any avant-garde movement, he was inevitably in contact with modernism, given his curiosity and the fact that he was acquainted with some of its eminent representatives, particularly during the period when he was writing the first drafts of the Brangwen saga.

Several scholars have mentioned or studied in broad outlines Lawrence's interest in some of the modernist trends of the period, often taking into account the whole of his work, including his writings on art. This is the case, for instance, of Emile Delavenay in his essay entitled "Lawrence and the Futurists."[8] Since none of Lawrence's novels is more obviously based on a dialogue with the avant-garde (and not only with Futurism) than *Women in Love*, it may be interesting to carry the investigation further in the context of this specific work.

Modernism

Modernism is a somewhat elusive notion. Malcolm Bradbury and James McFarlane see the modernist era as a period of increasing relativism and cosmopolitism in which "all frontiers were in vital and often dangerous flux."[9] The first two decades of the twentieth century were a period of intellectual effervescence on philosophical and aesthetic problems and of formal research in the visual arts. In *Women in Love*, two characters, Gudrun and Loerke, are artists, Birkin is an art lover, and several chapters are devoted to London Bohemia (just as Wyndham Lewis's novel *Tarr*, 1918, is about the Parisian Bohemian milieu). There are few direct allusions to modern art. All we know is that there are two Futurist paintings in Halliday's flat and a Pissarro in the Brangwens' house. But the debates on art—art and life, art and industry, art and truth—are central to this work just as they were at the centre of the intelligentsia's preoccupations. In the novel, the starting point of a character's meditation on art is always a picture or a sculpture—never a book.

From the turn of the twentieth century on, artistic movements succeeded one another or overlapped, most of them having a common aim: that of breaking with nineteenth-century realism, including Impressionism, and even with the illusionistic art of the Renaissance or the Graeco-Roman period. The neo-impressionists (Seurat, Signac) had already rejected pure mimesis. A new relationship was established between man and object and there emerged, roughly speaking, two great tendencies: some artists tried to recreate the outer world in a geometric or semi-abstract way like Cézanne or, later, the cubists; others expressed a personal relation to the world stressing its spiritual, even occult, dimension, as in Symbolism, or giving voice to their emotions and their deeper selves, as in Expressionism. About 1910, the expressionist and formalist trends met in Futurism, in Italy, and in Vorticism, in Britain. The debate between Loerke and Ursula about the equestrian statuette in the "Snow" chapter mirrors the opposition between a formalist approach and a psychologizing expressionist one. Loerke insists that "that horse is a certain form, part of a whole *form*. It is part of a work of art, a piece of form" (430)[10] For Ursula, the statuette reveals mostly the sculptor's psyche, what he projected of his own ego onto the subject he was treating: "The horse is a picture of your own stock stupid brutality, and the girl was a girl you loved and tortured and then ignored" (431).[11]

Thanks to the famous exhibition organized by Roger Fry, called "Manet and the Post-Impressionists," in London in November 1910, the English public had discovered, much later than elsewhere, Cézanne, Gauguin, and Van Gogh, (i.e., the recreation of forms, primitivism, and exoticism). Lawrence discovered them still later, since he did not see this exhibition (he mentions Van Gogh for the first time in a letter dated 1 March 1915). He also missed the "Second Post-Impressionist Exhibition," (1912) which showed works by Picasso and Matisse and presented both French formalists and expressionists to the public. Nevertheless, Lawrence came to know other forms of expressionism while he travelled on the continent: the Vienna Secession, *die Brücke*, which developed in Dresden between 1905 and 1913 (it is there that, at the end of *Women in Love*, Gudrun hopes to find an artistic environment that suits her) and *Der Blaue Reiter* (1911–1912), founded in Munich by Kandinsky who eventually practised a totally abstract expressionism. Let us note that, in his peregrinations, Loerke, like Lawrence, had travelled to Munich (426). In 1913, the novelist wrote to his friend Ernest Collings: "I hate Munich art. But yet it is free of that beastly, tight, Sunday feeling which is so blighting in England."[12] Another ironical passage in his essay "Christs in the Tirol" reveals that he hated the violence of German expressionism as much as the lack of vigour of English art:

> I, who see a tragedy in every cow, began by suffering from the Secession pictures in Munich. All these new paintings seemed so shrill and restless. Those that were meant for joy shrieked and pranced for joy, and sorrow was a sensation to be relished, curiously; as if we were epicures in suffering, keen on a new flavour. I thought with kindliness of England, whose artists so often suck their sadness like a lollipop, mournfully and comfortably.[13]

In Italy, Lawrence learnt about Futurism, an art movement founded in 1909 to glorify the "universal dynamism"[14] of the mechanical and industrial world. For Marinetti, "a roaring car that seems to ride on grapeshot is more beautiful than the Victory of Samothrace."[15] Futurism was an unstable blend of cubism, symbolism, and neo-impressionism. In "Study of Thomas Hardy," Lawrence comments on a Futurist sculpture by Boccioni, *The Development of a Bottle through Space*, criticizing it for showing a lack of balance between the masculine and the feminine principles, between the intuitive approach and the scientific one. Two letters also reveal his new interest in this avant-garde movement which was the most boisterous of the time. On 2 June 1914, he wrote to Arthur McLeod: "I have been interested in the Futurists. I got a book of their poetry—a very fat book too—and a book of pictures—and I read Marinetti's and Paolo Buzzi's manifestations and essays—and Soffici's essays on cubism and Futurism"; but he asserted that, globally speaking, he was hostile to their theories. This did not prevent him from telling Edward Garnett three days later that the new novel he was writing was somewhat Futuristic: "I think the book is a bit Futuristic—quite unconsciously so"[16] and he quoted sympathetically a passage from the "Technical Manifesto of Futurist Literature" published on 11 May 1912. It is obvious that he was as fascinated by Futurism as he was repelled by it.

Even if Lawrence did not see the exhibitions organized by Fry or witnessed the stir caused by the numerous lectures given by the noisy Futurist leader Marinetti between November 1913 and June 1914, he could not possibly have remained unaware of the passionate debates on art that were going on among avant-garde circles since, on his return to London, he met such artists as Amy Lowell, Richard Aldington, and Wyndham Lewis, among others.

Contacts with the Avant-Garde

Ezra Pound, whom he had known since 1909, had created Imagism in the spring of 1912 to promote a type of poetry based on visual images (Lawrence contributed a few poems to the Imagist anthologies). In T. E. Hulme's definition of this new technique, the stress was clearly put on the alliance of the visual arts and literature: "This new verse resembles sculpture rather than music; it appeals to the eye rather than to the ear. It has to mould images, a kind of spiritual clay, into definite shapes."[17] In June 1914, Pound broke with Imagism and founded Vorticism with the painter and writer Wyndham Lewis. This movement was formed as a reaction against related rival groups: Imagists, Futurists, and "the Omega Workshops" created by Roger Fry, a member of the Bloomsbury Group, who promoted a modern form of primitivism inspired by Chinese and African motifs. A letter to Arthur McLeod proves that Lawrence met Wyndham Lewis in July 1914 and had "a heated and vivid discussion" with him:[18]

Vorticism, friend and foe of Futurism, was a kind of cubo-Futurism which drew its inspiration from mechanical forms but questioned the new sort of realism advocated by the Futurists, their "automobilism," their love of movement, and their political commitment. This is how Pound defines Vorticism: "expressionism, neo-cubism, and Imagism gathered together."[19]

As for the Bloomsbury group, Lawrence was quite familiar with one of its meeting places, Garsington Manor, the home of Lady Ottoline Morrell, the prototype of Hermione in *Women in Love*. He was in contact with this circle from 1914 to 1916. There he met Bertrand Russell with whom, for a short period of time, he made enthusiastic plans for social reforms. Bloomsbury was not a real avant-garde movement but could more or less be considered as such in so far as it gathered artists who challenged Victorian conventions. Among its members, there was the eclectic Jewish painter Mark Gertler, whose painting "The Merry-Go-Round" largely inspired Lawrence's description of the frieze carved by Loerke for a factory in Cologne, and other artists like Clive Bell, Roger Fry, and the painter Duncan Grant, who were closer to the modernist trend. In a letter to Lady Ottoline Morrell, Lawrence judges Grant's experiments in the field of abstraction very severely. He is convinced that the underlying structure of a picture may be abstract but not the finished product:

> The architecture comes in, in painting, only with the suggestion of some whole, some conception which conveys in its own manner the whole universe. Most puerile is this dabbing geometric figures behind one another, just to prove that the artist is being

abstract, that he is not attempting representation of the object. The way to express the abstract-whole is to reduce the object to a unit, a term, and then out of these units and terms to make a whole statement. *Do* rub this into Duncan Grant, and save him his foolish waste.[20]

In avant-garde art, representation was affected by distortion or even rejected in order to render the tension between subject and object. At the level of form, the most anti-realist modernists chose a type of stylisation inspired by primitive art or geometric constructions—or a mixture of both. The main problem was the relation of art to the real world or the validity of abstract or semi-abstract art—a problem that literature could not solve in the same way as the visual arts. There is no debate on purely abstract art in *Women in Love*, and this may be due to the difference between the novelist's approach and that of the painter or sculptor.

To what extent does *Women in Love* fit into this complex panorama? First, it is valuable as a testimony and a critical assessment of the avant-garde; second, it takes up themes which were common at the time to many British art movements; last, its structure and style owe quite a lot to avant-garde theories and practice. The period during which Lawrence began to write this novel was marked by the impact that the new ideas in the visual arts had on literature, particularly in such movements as Imagism, Futurism, and Vorticism.

In 1912, Wyndham Lewis had painted a picture called "Kermesse" that the British public had thought as revolutionary as Picasso's "les Demoiselles d'Avignon" (1907). This work, now lost, represented in almost abstract fashion three festive characters taken in a whirl of pleasure. The second and last issue of *Blast* (1915) contains a drawing by Wyndham Lewis, also entitled *Kermesse*, which may give us a fairly good idea of what this picture looked like. The theme (*une kermesse* is a fair), the contorted bodies, these inhuman figures given grotesque geometric forms, inevitably recall Loerke's frieze which is "a representation of a fair, with peasants and artizans in an orgy of pleasure [. . .] whirling ridiculously in roundabouts" in a "frenzy of chaotic motion" (423). Lawrence may have seen a copy of *Blast* since the magazine was popular among his friends.[21] What is certain is that

Pound had noted down Lawrence's name on the list of people who were to receive publicity for it; this note is now kept in the Wyndham Lewis Collection at Cornell. If Lawrence never saw or heard about *Kermesse*, it remains that the coincidence is striking.

In Kensington, in Ford Madox Ford's circle, Lawrence also had the opportunity of meeting the Vorticist sculptors Jacob Epstein, whom he mentions in one of his letters, and Gaudier-Bzreska. Gaudier had produced small carvings of men or animals, that looked rather primitive with their simplified forms, much like Gudrun's miniatures, of which Gerald says: "I thought it was savage carving again," and which Birkin describes in these terms: "animals and birds, sometimes odd small people in everyday dress, really wonderful when they come off" (94).

Representation and Criticism of the Avant-Garde Movements in *Women in Love*

Women in Love is not the faithful reflection of a life-experience nor does it reveal very precise influences. The novel gives us a synthetic idea of the artistic context. We can perceive a streak of modernism in a number of characters. Loerke might be Mark Gertler; Wyndham Lewis; or a member of the *Deutscher Werkbund*, which advocated the functional integration of sculpture into architecture, or any Futurist, given his discourse on the necessary subservience of art to industry:

> "Sculpture and architecture must go together. The day for irrelevant statues, as for wall pictures, is over. As a matter of fact, sculpture is always part of an architectural conception. And since churches are all museum stuff, since industry is our business, then let us make our places of industry our art—our factory-area our Parthenon—ecco!" (424)

In the first "Manifesto of Futurism" (1909), Marinetti declares: "We will sing of the great crowds agitated by work, pleasure and revolt; [. . .] the nocturnal vibration of the arsenals and the workshops beneath their violent electric moons." Loerke's speech is almost a parody of these words: "the acts of labour are extremely, maddeningly beautiful" (424). In spite of the sculptor's reservations about Futurism, his glorification of mechanical movement borders on the absurd: "What is man doing, when he is at a fair like this? He is fulfilling the counterpart of labour—the machine works him, instead of he the machine" (424). Gudrun resembles Gaudier, without his talent and fame. She and Loerke hate the Yugoslav sculptor Mestrovic, like the Vorticists who blacklisted him in their magazine in a series of virulent "Blasts,"[22] but both love the eighteenth century like the members of the Bloomsbury group. How can we label Birkin, who is curious about everything from primitive art (the African statuettes), Asian art (the Chinese drawing in the "Breadalby" chapter), eighteenth-century art (the chair in chapter 26), impressionism (we have seen that he admires a Pissarro painting at the Brangwens')—everything except abstract art, unless the change from Pissarro to Picasso in one of the 1916 typescripts—TSIb—indicates a new interest in something more modern? Should we try to identify Barnes and Olandese of Florence in the chapter "Woman to Woman" ("Barnes is starting a school of aesthetics and Olandese is going to give a set of discourses on the Italian national policy—" [298] or take them as inventions, even if it is true that Italy was awakening to aesthetic and political problems? As a matter of fact, Barnes was the name of a pro-fascist political theoretician living in Florence whom Lawrence had met in Italy in January 1914. To hide this reference, Lawrence uses a simple trick: he attributes political interests to the other man cited in the sentence.

Without naming any individual or group precisely, Lawrence fiercely denounces the sterility of the Garsington crowd, the sophisticated eclecticism of Bloomsbury, the inane theory of the upholders of "significant form," and the Futurists' fascination with the machine. Contrary to Marinetti, who extols urban civilization, Lawrence has a very gloomy view of the modern world: in London, Birkin feels "doomed" (61); when Ursula and Birkin arrive in Ostend, it is for them "like disembarking from the Styx into the desolated underworld" (389); in "Coal-Dust," the train is compared to "a disgusting dream that has no end" (111). Birkin does use a car but, ironically enough, in it he reaches a state of perfect stillness: "He sat still like an Egyptian Pharaoh, driving the car [. . .] like the immobile, supremely potent Egyptians, seated forever in their living, subtle silence" (318). Yet, this recalls Wyndham Lewis's description of the vortex: "At the heart of the whirlpool is a great silent place there all the energy is concentrated. And there at the point of concentration, is the Vorticist."[23] The whirlpool of modern life justifies the quest for a fixed center.

The society in which the characters of the novel move is organized in coteries like the intellectual and artistic circles of the period, but fictional ones. There is, on the one hand, the Breadalby circle, with Hermione Roddice—who is ironically presented as "a social artist" (300) among her uninspiring intellectual friends—and, on the other hand, in London, a group of degenerate artists who meet at the Café Pompadour (alias, the Café Royal, a favourite haunt of Lawrence and avant-garde artists). Finally, there is the suggestion of a potentially more rewarding association around Birkin, whose desire to flee from England with a happy few recalls Lawrence's utopian dream of founding a small community named Rananim somewhere in the world.

In spite of all the meditations the book contains on the two artistic tendencies that come together in the twentieth century—i.e., primitivism and modernism—this work finally proves to be less concerned with a reflection on art than with the quest for an art of living. Birkin definitely prefers "being" to "having"—even having an elegant period chair or any other object of beauty. The hero of the novel is not an artist, which is meaningful. In fact, he seems to share Soffici's view that "art, as an individual product, no longer has its *raison d'etre*, simply because the expression on which it is based has passed from individual works into the acts of life."[24]

From Destruction to Recreation

In the "Technical Manifesto of Futurist Literature," Marinetti declares: "Each day we must spit on the Altar of Art."[25] Lawrence participates in this desacralization of art, even if, in his novel, some works of art bring about epiphanies that shape his main character's personality. Birkin finally asserts (under the influence of Ursula, who hates old things whatever their artistic value): "one can't go on living on the old bones of beauty" (356). Beyond this rebellious attitude, what Lawrence has in common with most avant-gardists—and particularly the Futurists and the Vorticists—is an apocalyptic vision of our decadent civilization, a call for the destruction of the old order, a mistrust of intelligence and education, the valorization of instinct, the habit of opposing Southern races and Northern races, elitism, fits of prophecy, and a mixture of scientific and irrationalist themes. All these artists drew their inspiration from the same sources: Schopenhauer; evolutionist theories; Nietzsche; Bergson; and, sometimes, Cesare Lombroso; Mme Blavatsky; Otto Weininger; Edward Carpenter; Havelock Ellis; T. E. Hulme; etc. Without going through all that period's history of ideas, we may notice a wavering between scientism and subjectivism both in philosophy and in the arts.

The term *avant-garde*, with its militant connotations, suited Marinetti's propagandism and bellicosity very well. To destroy the existing world in order to turn man into a superman was the aim that he expressed early in his career in a poem like "Destruction" (1904) and in his reflections on the war as "the world's only hygiene."[26] Wyndham Lewis, who was definitely against the war, believed nonetheless that starting from a *tabula rasa* again was a necessity. It is sad to note that his friend Gaudier-Bzreska, who was to die in the trenches in 1915, sent a text for *Blast* n 2 in which he proclaimed: "This war is a great remedy."[27] This destructive mood is that of the Halliday clique, of which Birkin says: "They are really very thorough rejecters of the world—perhaps they live only in the gesture of rejection and negation—but negatively something" (60). There is a lot of violence in *Women in Love*, particularly between Gerald and Gudrun, Birkin and Hermione (Marinetti too speaks of "the war of the sexes" and advocates "scorn for women" in his 1909 Manifesto), between Gerald and Loerke, between men and animals, even between two animals (for instance in the "Mino" chapter where the he-cat plays a macho game with the she-cat and cuffs her). Gudrun and Loerke never speak of the future "except one laughed out some

mocking dream of the destruction of the world by a ridiculous catastrophe of man's invention [...]" (453) and Birkin, an utter mis-
anthropist, confides to Mrs Crich: "Not many people are anything at
all [...] It would be much better if they were just wiped out" (25).
Speaking to Gerald, Birkin exclaims: "Let mankind pass away—time
it did" (59) or "Man is a mistake, he must go" (128). In "The Crown,"
an essay written at the same time as the novel's composition (1915),
Lawrence, in spite of his well-known hatred of the war, calls the
spirit of destruction "divine" and offers this comment: "The war is
one bout in the terrific, horrible labour, our civilization labouring in
child-birth, and unable to bring forth."[28] Thus, all the characters are
caught in the "flux of corruption." Birkin asserts that "Dissolution
rolls on, just as production does [...] It is a progressive process—
and it ends in universal nothing—the end of the world, if you like"
(173). Disintegration is most suitably represented by the mud
image—both deadly and regenerative mud. This can be found several times in the book, for instance, in the reference to the mud on
the low shores of Willey Water from which the water-plants that
Gudrun sketches rise but in which Diana dies, or "the cold-burning
mud—the lotus mystery" in the "Breadalby" chapter (89). The
word *mud* has the same ambivalence in a play by Marinetti, *Le Roi
Bombance (King Revel)*, in which one of the characters is named Sainte
Pourriture (Saint Rot)[29] and also in a text by Helen Saunders published in *Blast* n 2, "A vision of mud": "There is mud all round / This
is favourable to the eclosion of mighty life [...]." Of course, this
brings to mind the mud of the trenches. But what, then, could be
expected from a civilization so deeply stuck in mud? We find a variety of answers among avant-garde artists.

The Inhuman

Some writers, like T. E. Hulme, Pound, and the pre-war Lewis, glorify the nonhuman and the inorganic. Marinetti writes: "we must
acknowledge that we aspire to the creation of an inhuman type."[30]
In *Blast* n 1, Lewis states: "Dehumanization is the chief diagnostic of

the Modern World." For Lawrence, the nonhuman is not exclusively the inorganic. The description of Gerald's career in "The Industrial Magnate" is a violent satire of the new order founded on the destruction of the organic: "There was a new world, a new order, strict, terrible, inhuman, but satisfying in its very destructiveness [. . .] It was pure organic disintegration and pure mechanical organisation" (231). This is what "inhuman" means for the Futurists and industrial society: a satisfying destructiveness. In *Women in Love*, the adjective *inhuman* is polysemic. It applies either to characters who suffer from a patent dissociation of mind and body like Hermione or sensual men who become slaves to industry like Loerke with his hands "like talons, like 'griffes,' inhuman" (423) or the miners in "Coal-Dust." The underworld, "the strong, dangerous underworld, mindless, inhuman" (115) is at once the mine, our subterranean inner world, the dark source of all life or even hell.[31] When the machine dominates man's life, as is the case with Gerald—"*the God of the Machine*"—all humanness is lost. "There is complete ignominy in an unreplenished, mechanised life," Ursula thinks (193). But the inhuman element in the miners or in Birkin may also be fascinating. Ursula thinks: "Something in him, inhuman and unmitigated, disturbed her, and shook her out of her ordinary self" (124). The word *inhuman* takes on a near mystical connotation for her. It becomes synonymous with all that is beyond man, the great mystery of life: "I believe in something inhuman, of which love is only a little part"(438).

As an ironical counterpoint, Gudrun, elated at the sight of the Austrian mountains, exclaims "One really does feel übermenschlich—more than human" (394), thus stressing the Nietzschean theme of the superman which runs through the novel. In the train that takes him to London, Gerald reads an article in *The Daily Telegraph* and sums up what he considers as "newspaper cant": "there must arise a new man who will give new values to things, give us new truths, a new attitude to life, or else we shall be a crumbling nothingness in a few years, a country in ruin—" (54). These lines capture the Zeitgeist of the pre-war period but also parody one of the main themes of the novel: the overcoming of the human.

Common Points and Differences

Gerald is obviously a caricature of the Futurist superman. He is repeatedly associated with images of force, movement, and violence ("he was superhumanly strong" 402), or scientific metaphors ("as if he were soft iron becoming surcharged with her electric life" 331; "his living, radio-active body" [332]). In her most ambitious dreams, Gudrun imagines him as a Napoleon of peace or another Bismarck. But his counterpart, the superman Birkin—who, like Alfred Orage's new man, tries to transcend the human thanks to his "cosmic consciousness"—shares many of the characteristics of the avant-garde groups denounced by Lawrence.

Birkin has the same hope for a new world, the same habit of prophesying, the same interest in primitivism. The Futurists declare: "we are [. . .] the primitives of a new sensitiveness, multiplied hundredfold."[32] While the naïve abstraction of the child's drawing in the "Rabbit" chapter looks grotesque, Birkin appreciates the genuinely primitive art objects that Lawrence's contemporaries admired so much. In his "Technical Manifesto of Futurist Literature," Marinetti recommends his followers to "hate intelligence." Birkin too mistrusts intelligence and education. What he values above all is "knowledge in the blood," just like Marinetti who asserts: "the blood had guessed what the brain had not grasped."[33] Birkin refuses the notion of equality: "We are all different and unequal in spirit [. . .] Your democracy is an absolute lie" (103), he says to Hermione. His individualism ("First person, singular, is enough for me" [56]) is matched only by Ezra Pound's when he declares, 'The Vorticist movement is a movement of individuals, for the protection of individuality."[34] The distinction that Birkin makes between Northern and Southern races is the same that helps Wyndham Lewis justify his rejection of Futurism as being too Mediterranean for the English. Havelock Ellis had already made a similar distinction between Nordic and Celtic races, Worringer between Northern art and classical and Oriental art. But Birkin turns his back on many of these artists and thinkers by refusing any social or political commitment. "Who cares a button for our national ideals?" he exclaims (19). He is content with preaching his personal gospel to a narrow circle of friends. In many ways, he is a kind of dissident avant-gardist.

He seems to obey Marinetti's injunction in the second 1909 "Futurist Manifesto": "Let's Kill the Moonlight!"—a war cry against this hackneyed romantic symbol. Birkin literally tries to kill the moonlight, stoning its reflection on the lake's water in "Moony" to express his rejection of the fusional love offered by Ursula. He wishes to replace this astronomical symbol by another: the "star-equilibrium." Yet, contrary to Marinetti (who could very well manage without women), the new man, according to Lawrence, cannot live without a new form of love. In a letter dated 2 June 1914 to Arthur McLeod, Lawrence analyses very clearly what attracts him and repels him in the Futurists' theories:

> I agree with them about the weary sickness of pedantry and tradition and inertness, but I don't agree with them as to the cure and the escape. They will progress down the purely male or intellectual or scientific line. They will even use their intuition for intellectual and scientific purpose.[35]

Even if he finds their critical outlook on society convincing, he disapproves of the aims and means they use; he cannot accept the enslavement of intuition by intelligence and the utter scorn of the feminine. What comes next is the often-quoted paragraph in which he writes "I think the only re-sourcing of art, re-vivifying it, is to make it more the joint work of man and woman"—which is one of the truths to be discovered in *Women in Love.*

In his novel *Mafarka the Futurist* (1910), Marinetti announces the advent of a mechanical superman who soars up on metallic wings to dethrone the sun. Birkin also sees the future in terms of brutal discontinuity, yet still in the organic order:

> "The eternal creative mystery could dispose of man, and replace him with a finer created being: just as the horse had taken the place of the mastodon [. . .] Human or inhuman mattered

nothing. The perfect pulse throbbed with indescribable being, miraculous unborn species" (478–479).

Only in death does the body return to an inorganic state; Gearld's corpse is a block of ice.

Time is cyclical in *Women in Love* as it was for the early twentieth-century artists and thinkers who had an interest in primitivism and expected the coming of a new man. The African and the Western civilizations, however different, are doomed to the same expansion/reduction cycle. The African and the Jew are much ahead in the process of dissolution.[36] The African statuette that Birkin sees at Halliday's represents for him *"an awful pitch of culture, of a definite sort"* (79), just like the art of the Jane Austen period for which he expresses his admiration in the "Chair" chapter. Alfred Orage, in *The New Age*, and Nietzsche before him had also evoked these ups and downs in the history of civilizations. Though Orage was obsessed with the decadence of modern art, he was the first to publish avant-garde writings in England. He used concepts that were strangely similar to Lawrence's notions of *"reduction-process"* or *"devolution"* (204) as opposed to *"evolution,"* a kind of synonym for entropy. (It is interesting to see that the art critic Herbert Read uses exactly the same vocabulary some fifteen years later when writing about modern art: "I do think we can already discern a difference of kind in the contemporary revolution: it is not so much a revolution, which implies a turning-over, even a turning-back, but rather a break-up, a devolution, some would say a dissolution".)[37] In 1915, Orage writes: "Evolution connotes in this age, not the multiplication and outspread of human faculties but their reduction by assimilation and intensification," and elsewhere: "To go back is to go forward."[38] In "The Crown," Lawrence expresses a similar idea with a certain amount of pessimism: "Whatever act is performed by any man now in this condition, it is an act of reduction, disintegration."[39] The word *reduction* is used quite often in *Women in Love*. It can already be found in the suppressed Prologue to account for Birkin and Hermione's destructive relationship: "there was no hot impulse of growth between them, only this terrible reducing activity of phosphorescent consciousness" (497). Gudrun's statuettes are reductions too.

Where is salvation to be found? In the mystic consciousness man may have of the two streams of life and death that meet in him, this alone can help him to transcend mechanical time. Birkin says to Ursula, "I wanted a man friend, as eternal as you and I are eternal" (481). Thanks to their union, he lives beyond time and knows an eternal now: "This marriage with her was his resurrection and his life" (369). Lawrence frequently invokes some "mystic knowledge" which is, of course, the reverse of the scientific knowledge of the century. There again, he shares the avant-gardists' irrationalist point of view. Even if Marinetti believes in "the complete renewal of man's sensibility brought about by the great scientific discoveries,"[40] he still attaches great value to our instincts, the occult, and the parapsychic. Conversely, Lawrence, who is certainly closer to the expressionists, defends the spiritual in art, keeping at the same time an authentic curiosity for science. Marinetti writes: "Instead of *humanizing* animals, vegetables, and minerals (an outmoded system) we will be able to *animalize, vegetalize, mineralize, electrify, or liquefy* our style, making it live the life of matter."[41] Lawrence mineralizes, vegetalizes, electrifies, and liquefies his style as much as can be done. He both humanizes animals and animalizes human beings: Gerald's eyes are compared to those of a frightened stallion in "Gladiatorial;" Gudrun identifies with the Arab mare. There are innumerable references to science in the novel: electricity, the laws of gravitation, evolutionism, the use of radium and radioactivity, magnetism, astronomy, or physics. In the "Continental" chapter, Gudrun and Gerald are "separate, like opposite poles of one fierce energy" (399). Birkin's meditation over Gerald's corpse includes a presentation of his transformist theories (478–479). It is clear that not all scientific metaphors are associated with Gerald and not all of them are used to parody or implicitly criticize a Futurist discourse. Electricity, for instance, has positive connotations when associated with the idea of a circuit of energy between Ursula and Birkin in "Excurse." "She had established a rich new circuit, a new current of passional electric energy, between the two of them, released from the darkest poles of the body and established in perfect circuit" (314).[42] Whatever his reservations about Marinetti's theories, Lawrence obviously shared his fascination with the mysteries of modern science.

A Modernist Technique

Lawrence was interested in such a would-be scientistic movement as Futurism mostly because he found there something he was after: a modern idiom, freed from "the old forms and sentimentalities," as he says.[43] His reading of the Futurists helped him to define his new approach to characterization while he was working on. "The Wedding Ring." In his June 1914 letter to Edward Garnett, he expounds his new aesthetics, largely basing himself on a quotation from the "Technical Manifesto of Futurist Literature" (1912) that contains a striking mixture of irrational and scientific arguments: "The Deep intuitions of life joined to one another, word for word, according to their illogical birth, will give us the general lines of an intuitive physiology of matter."[44] Lawrence understands the strange word *physicology* as meaning *physic*—i.e., *nonhuman*—which helps him to justify his rejection of anthropocentric literature: "that which is physic—nonhuman in humanity, is more interesting to me than the old-fashioned human element—which causes one to conceive a character in a certain moral scheme and make him consistent."[45] In the novel, Ursula has the same viewpoint: "human beings are boring, painting the universe with their own image. The universe is nonhuman, thank God" (264).

One of Marinetti's precepts is to "Destroy the 'I' in literature, that is all psychology" and to replace [it] "by matter whose essence must be grasped by strokes of intuition, the kind of thing that physicists and chemists can never do". He recommends using "condensed networks of images and analogies" that "keep their astounding force for a long time."[46] Does this account in any way for Lawrence's frequent use of very striking oxymorons like this "universal chill-blazing bonfire of the moonlit night" that we find in the Prologue? In his Supplement to the 1912 Manifesto, Marinetti gives an example of linguistic innovation based on the destruction of syntax, which makes it possible to render the noise, the weight, and the smell of objects (this prefigures Dadaist experiments). Lawrence is aware that he cannot follow the Futurists when their extreme anti-humanism verges on the absurd. He thinks it incoherent to try to render sensations *objectively*, and artificial to destructure language in order to turn it into a kind of scientific formula: "That is where the Futurists are stupid. Instead of looking for the new human phenomenon, they will only look for the phenomena of the science of physics to be found in the human being."[47]

Immediately afterward, he expresses—in scientific terms, nonetheless—his theory of the "allotropic" states of human beings: an individual is like a body that may display different physical characteristics but always keeps similar chemical properties. Birkin seems to comment on the technique at work in the novel when he says: "He was not very much interested in personalities and in people. They were [. . .] variations on a theme" (305). In the first version of "Shortlands,"[48] Birkin asserts: "my Self, my Ego, is an illusion." In the same way, Lawrence calls into question the validity of "the old stable ego of the character" in his letter. To illustrate the notion of "allotropy," he takes the example of diamond and carbon: "The ordinary novel would trace the history of the diamond—but I say 'diamond, what! This is carbon.' And my—diamond might be coal or soot, and my theme is carbon." This carbon or coal, a metaphor for the basic chemical element, refers us back to the mine and the underworld which is at once our origin and the place where we are bound to return. If all the characters only represent allotropic states of the same element, then it becomes easier to understand their apparent contradictions and complexity. The most opposite characters always have something in common. None of them is entirely this or entirely that. Birkin suffers from the same dissociation of the mental and the physical as the people who surround him: "To save himself, he must unite the two halves of himself, spiritual and sensual," he thinks in the Prologue (500). As long as he does not find his female counterpart, he can no more avoid being caught in "the flux of corruption" than the others. At best, "his élan vital" helps him a little to resist decadence.

Lawrence destroys the "I" more radically than Marinetti at the level of narrative technique. The unifying "I" of the omniscient narrator is constantly destabilized. The didacticism of the novel is counterbalanced and partly erased by ironical devices, parody, and self-parody. Birkin's rather pontificating discourse takes up some of the themes developed by Lawrence himself in his essays of the period. Ursula often shows Birkin how incoherent he is—e.g., how can he be an antimaterialist and praise the Jane Austen period? Ursula is not the only one that mocks Birkin; Gerald, Gudrun, and Halliday all jeer at him in turn. Other parodic echoes make for the complexity of the novel. Birkin's words, when repeated more or less faithfully by Hermione, become ridiculous; Gudrun's attempt to frighten the bullocks is a poor retort to Gerald's sadistic attitude toward his Arab mare; the scene where Hermione hits Birkin with a lapis lazuli paperweight foreshadows, in a rather grotesque way, the stoning of the moon by Birkin. The narrator gives us a rather unstable, fluctuating, and perplexing image of his characters. This deconstructing process induces the reader to reflect on the function of these characters rather than to identify with them. It is obvious that one should not look for "the old stable ego of the character" in this novel.

The other idea put forward in this letter to Garnett is that the novel should not follow "the lines of the characters." On the contrary, the characters must fall harmoniously into the rhythmic pattern of the novel. This statement comes as a logical consequence of Lawrence's rejection of anthropocentrism and brings us back to the type of avant-garde aesthetics which is more interested in composition and pure creation than in representational art.

The visual arts play an essential role in the novel, not only at a thematic level, but also in terms of structure. In *Women in Love*, the references to places are of greater significance than the references to time. The novel offers a series of scenes or "tableaux" set in an often discontinuous period of time, with entrances, exits, and changes of place as in the theater, another visual art. These scenes have a very loose chronological link but balance each other in rhythmic fashion, like masses of color on a canvas, around a central explanatory chapter: "The Industrial Magnate." There are echoes and rebounds like those concerning the African statuettes and simple or inverted parallelisms: e.g., between the Arab mare episode and the passage on the equestrian statuette, between the "Man to Man" and "Woman to Woman" chapters; between "Excurse" and "Death and Love," etc.

There are also more elaborate configurations. For instance, Loerke's equestrian statuette refers us back both to another statuette (the African statuette) and to the scene with Gerald on his mare, which, in turn, is echoed in Gudrun's dance in front of the bullocks and the comparison of Gerald with a frightened stallion in "Gladiatorial." The "bullocks" motif reappears in the comparison of the German professor in "Snow" with "a well-seasoned bull," and Gudrun's dance is thematically related to all the other dance scenes. The construction of *Women in Love* is incredibly geometrical in many respects. The story is based on the interaction and evolution of triangular relationships: Birkin/Hermione/Ursula; Birkin/Gerald/Ursula; Gerald/Gudrun/The Pussum; Gerald/Gudrum/Loerke[49] The artist seems to abandon all concern for pure realism and tries to create something more abstract in order to capture "the new human phenomenon" that the Futurists failed to grasp. In "Study of Thomas Hardy," Lawrence asserts: "Geometry, pure mathematics, is very near to art," but what follows may seem confusing when examined out of its cultural context.

> [. . .] when I look at Boccioni's sculpture, and see him trying to state the timeless abstract being of a bottle, the pure geometric abstraction of the bottle, I am fascinated. But then, when I see him driven by his desire for the male complement into portraying motion, simple motion, trying to give expression to the bottle in terms of mechanics, I am confused. It is for science to explain the bottle in terms of force and motion.[50]

This analysis of Boccioni's sculpture reveals how indebted Lawrence was at the time to the Vorticists who accept geometry, hence the creation of autonomous forms, but refuse movement and the study of mechanical forces, hence pseudoscientific schematization.

At the end of "Excurse," Birkin, out of discouragement and derision, thinks to himself:

> "Why not drift on a series of accidents—like a picaresque novel. Why not? Why bother about human relationships? Why take them seriously—male or female? Why form any serious connec-

tions at all? Why not be casual, drifting along, taking all for what
it was worth?" (302)

Early in the novel, Ursula explains that when Gerald killed his
brother by accident when he was a boy, "Perhaps there was an unconscious will behind it" (49). One of Birkin's previous comments
on this notion of accident shows that this "unconscious will" is not
to be understood in Freudian terms:

> Why seek to draw a brand and a curse across the life that had
> caused the accident? A man can live by accident, and die by ac-
> cident. Or can he not? Is every man's life subject to pure acci-
> dent, is it only the race, the genus, the species, that has a uni-
> versal reference? Or is this not true, is there no such thing as
> pure accident? Has everything that happens a universal signifi-
> cance? Has it?
>   He did not believe that there was any such thing as accident. It
> all hung together in the deepest sense. (26)

As a matter of fact, Birkin does not believe in accidents and never
"drifts along." He is not, literally speaking, a *picaro*, and the book is
not really a picaresque novel. The force of desire sets the course of
Birkin's destiny. The failure of his quest is predictable because of his
love for Gerald, who is doomed to destruction and self-destruction.
The few chance meetings which keep the plot going are not sufficient to make us feel that hazard is very important. The story relates
the trajectory of predetermined characters, moved by a great "inhuman" force which somehow testifies to the presence of the cosmic
god in us. The damned, for Lawrence, are those who remain unaware of this presence.

Considering the historical and biographical background of this
work, it is no wonder that the struggle between the dark forces of
the underworld and the electric light of modern civilisation should
result in a semidefeat.

Women in Love is a novelistic construction in the service of a metaphysics. Though it remains close to a certain form of realism, there is
more stylization in it than in *The Rainbow*. Even if Lawrence does not

try to "destroy syntax" or undermine the structure of language, it is definitely an experimental work based on a dialogue with the avant-garde—a dialogue which shows his profound interest in these movements as well as his passionate opposition to some of their excesses. Whatever Lawrence's degree of contamination by modernism (and it was not so unconsiderable), he would certainly have subscribed to this statement of Wyndham Lewis: "It was, after all, a new civilization that I—and a few other people—was making the blueprint for [. . .] It was more than just picture-making: one was manufacturing fresh eyes for the people, and fresh souls to go with the eyes."[51] Only a new artistic language, ideally liberated from conventions and clichés, could, of course, lead to this new awareness.

Notes

1. Wyndham Lewis, *Blasting and Bombardiering.* 1937, quoted by William C. Wees, in *Vorticism and the English Avant-Garde* (University of Toronto Press, 1972,) 11.

2. "Just as the urge to empathy as a pre-assumption of aesthetic experience finds its gratification in the beauty of the organic, so the urge to abstraction finds its beauty in the life-denying inorganic, in the crystalline or, in general terms, in all abstract law and necessity." Wilhelm Worringer, *Abstraction and Empathy*, trans. Michael Bullock (New York: International Universities Press, 1953), VII.

3. Lawrence knew this weekly magazine as a letter to Bertrand Russell dated 1 July 1915 shows: "You *must* work out the idea of a new state. Get anybody and everybody to help Orage, Shaw, anybody, but it must be a *new State*" *The Letters of D. H. Lawrence*, vol. 2, ed. George J. Zytaruk and James T. Boulton (Cambridge University Press, 1981), 366. At the beginning of *Mr. Noon*, Lewie Goddard is reading this magazine.

4. Ezra Pound, "Desideria," *Exile*, spring 1928, 108.

5. He was the founder of the post-impressionist design workshops called "The Omega Workshops."

6. Ezra Pound, "Sculpture" in *Literary Essays*, ed. T. S. Eliot. [New York: New Directions Publishing 1968 (1st pub. 1954], 68.

7. Quoted in *D. H. Lawrence, The Critical Heritage*, ed. R. P. Draper (London and Boston: Routledge and Kegan Paul, 1972), 5.

8. Emile Delaenay, "Lawrence and the Futurists" in *The Modernists*, "Stud-

ies in a Literary Phenomenon" (Rutherford: Fairleigh and Dickinson, Associated University Presses, 1987). Other notable studies of the impact of modernism on Lawrence: Giovanni Cianci, "D. H. Lawrence and Futurism/Vorticism," *Arbeiten Aus Anglistik und Amerikanistik*, 8. 1 (1983); Paul Eggert, "Lawrence and the Futurists: The Breakthrough in His Art." *Meridian 1*, 1982; Nancy Kushigian, *Pictures and Fictions: Visual Modernism and the Pre-War Novels of D. H. Lawrence* (New York, Peter Lang, 1990) Jack Linsay, "The Impact of Modernism on Lawrence" in *Paintings of D. H. Lawrence,* ed. Mervyn Levy, (London: Cory, Adams, and Mackay, 1964) For thematic studies, see notes 12 and 43.

9. *Modernism: A Guide to European Literature, 1890–1930,* eds. Malcolm Bradbury and James Farlane (Harmondsworth: Penguin, 1991), 13.

10. All parenthetic page numbers refer to D. H. Lawrence, *Women in Love,* eds. David Farmer, Lindeth Vasey, and John Worthen [Cambridge University Press, 1987 (1st pub. 1920].

11. In his article "D. H. Lawrence and Sculpture in *Women in Love*" (*The Burlington Magazine*, December 2003); J. B. Bullen asserts that "the roots of [Lawrence's] attitudes to sculpture in this novel are to be found in the pre-War German Werkbund and his chance meeting with Josef Moest on the shores of Lake Garda." He shows the striking similarity between Loerke's statuette and Moest's *Godiva.*

12. *The Letters of D. H. Lawrence,* vol. 1 eds. James T. Boulton (Cambridge University Press, 1979); 548.

13. D. H. Lawrence, *Twilight in Italy and Other Essays*, ed. Paul Eggert (Cambridge University Press, 1994), 43.

14. Cf. "une automobile rugissante, qui a l'air de courir sur de la mitraille, est plus belle que la Victoire de Samothrace." "Manifeste des peintres futuristes" in F. T. Marinetti, *Le Futurisme*, préface de Giovanni Lista (Lausanne: L'Age d'homme, 1980), 172.

15. "Manifeste du futurisme," 1909, ibid., 152. This manifesto was issued simultaneously in French and Italian and was published in the French newspaper *Le Figaro* on 20 February 1909.

16. *Letters*, vol. 2, 180, 182. He had read: *I Poeti Futuristi* con un proclama di F. T. Marinetti e un studio sul verso libero di Paolo Buzzi, Edizione Futuriste di "Poesia." Milano: Corso Venezia, 61, 1912, Ardengo Soffici, *Cubismo e Futurismo*, Firenze, 1914, *Pittura, Scultura Futuriste, Dinamismo plastico*, Edizione Futuriste di "Poesia." (Milano: Corse Venezia, 61, 1914).

17. T. E. Hulme, "A Lecture on Modern Poetry," *Further Speculations,* ed. Sam Hynes, 1955, 75; quoted by John Press, *A Map of Modern English Verse* (Oxford University Press, 1969), 37.

18. *Letters,* vol. 2, 193.

19. Ezra Pound "Vorticism," *Blast* n 1, review of the great English Vortex (London: John Lane Company, 1914).

20. *Letters*, vol. 2, 263.

21. See Edward Nehls, *A Composite Biography* (The University of Wisconsin Press, 1957) 243 *ff*, and 570, note 41.

22. They had borrowed this system of "Blasts" and "Blessings" from Apollinaire who had used it in "L'anti-tradition futuriste" ("Rose aux . . . / Merde aux . . .").

23. Wees, *Vorticism,* 161.

24. Ardengo Soffici, *Primi principi di una Estetica Futurista.* Florence: 1920: "l'art, en tant que produit individuel, n'a plus de raison d'être, uniquement parce que l'expression qui en est la base, est passée des oeuvres particulières dans les actes de la vie." quoted by Ugo Piscopo, "Signification et fonction du groupe dans le futurisme," in *Europe*, 551, March 1975.

25. This manifesto was also published both in French and in Italian. There are facsimiles of the French versions of the Futurist manifestoes in *Marinetti et le Futurisme.* études, documents, iconographie réunis et présentés par Giovanni Lista, Cahiers des avant-gardes (Paris: L'Age d'homme, 1977) no pagination.

26. See the 1909 "Futurist Manifesto." Marinetti also published a manifesto entitled "The World's Only Hygiene" in 1915.

27. *Blast* n 2, 33.

28. D. H. Lawrence, *Reflections on the Death of a Porcupine and Other Essays*, ed. Michael Herbert (Cambridge University Press, 1988) 290.

29. See also in the first "Manifesto of Futurism": "Oh, maternal ditch, half full of muddy water! A factory gutter! I savoured a mouthful of strengthening mud which recalled the holy black teat of my Sudanese nurse!" quoted in F. T. Marinetti, *Le Futurisme, op. cit.* "Oh! maternel fossé, à moitié plein d'une eau vaseuse! Fossé d'usine! J'ai savouré à pleine bouche la boue fortifiante qui me rappelle la sainte mamelle noire de ma nourrice soudanaise," 151.

30. "il faut reconnaître que nous aspirons à la création d'un type inhumain, ibid, 111.

31. "It was all so strange, so extremely desolate, like the underworld, grey, grey, dirt grey, desolate, forlorn, nowhere—grey, dreary nowhere" (390).

32. Umberto Boccioni, Carlo D. Carra, Luigi Russolo, Giacomo Balla, Gino Severini. "Manifeste Technique de la peinture futuriste," *Poesia*. Milan: 11 April 1910, "Nous sommes [. . .] les primitifs d'une nouvelle sensibilité centuplée," *Le futurisme,* op. cit., 174.

33. "Ce que le cerveau n'avait pas compris, le sang l'avait deviné," *Le futurisme,* op. cit., 18.

34. *The Egoist,* 15 August 1915, quoted in Wees, *Vorticism,* 122.

35. *Letters,* vol. 2, 181.

36. While beholding the African statuette, Birkin thinks: "Thousands of years ago, that which was imminent in himself must have taken place in these Africans" (253). Birkin says to Gerald about Loerke: "He is a good many stages further than either you or I can go" (428).

37. *Art Now, a Introduction to the Theory of Modern Painting and Sculpture* [London: Faber and Faber, 1968 (1st pub. 1933)] 44. Herbert Read contributed an article on "Lawrence as a painter" in *Paintings of D. H. Lawrence.*

38. *The New Age,* 17: 6, 10 June 1915, 133–134 et 17: 5, 2 December 1915, 110.

39. D. H. Lawrence, *Reflections on the Death of a Porcupine,* 281.

40. "Le futurisme a pour principe le complet renouvellement de la sensibilité humaine sous l'action des grandes découvertes scientifiques" in "L'imagination sans fils et les mots en liberté," in Lista, *Marinetti et le Futurisme, op. cit.,* facsimile, no pagination.

41. "au lieu d'humaniser animaux, végétaux, minéraux (système dépassé), nous pourrons minéraliser, végétaliser, électriser, ou liquéfier le style, en le faisant vivre de la vie même de la matière." Ibid.

42. For a detailed study of the electricity metaphor, see Andrew Harrison's "Electricity and the Place of Futurism in *Women in Love*" in *The D. H. Lawrence Review,,* vol. 29 n 2, 2000.

43. *Letters,* vol. 2, 180.

44. "Les intuitions profondes de la vie juxtaposées mot à mot, suivant leur naissance illogique nous donneront les lignes générales d'une physicologie intuitive de la matière, Lista, "Manifeste technique de la littérature futuriste" in Lista, *"Marinetti et le futurisme," op. cit.,* fascimile, no pagination.

45. *Letters,* vol. 2, 183.

46. "Détruire le 'Je' dans la littérature, c'est-à-dire toute la psychologie [. . .] [Le] remplacer enfin par la matière, dont il faut atteindre l'essence à coups d'intuition, ce que le physiciens et les chimistes ne pourront jamais faire" / "des filets serrés d'images ou d'analogies" qui "gardent longtemps leur force ahurissante," in "Manifeste technique de la littérature futuriste" in Lista, *"Marinetti et le* Futurisme," facsimile, no pagination.

47. *Letters,* vol. 12, 183.

48. *The Making of Women in Love, A Selection from the Typescripts,* ed. Pierre Vitoux, *Cahiers victoriens et édouardiens* (Montpellier: Université Paul Valéry, 1988), 37.

49. This device is also used systematically in Lawrence's short story "The White Stocking." More recently, Harold Pinter has used the same technique in his early plays.

50. D. H. Lawrence, *Study of Thomas Hardy and Other Essays*, ed. Bruce Steele (Cambridge University Press, 1985), 76.

51. Wyndham Lewis, *Rude Assignment* (London, 1951) 125, quoted in Wees, op. cit. note 2, 211.

Works Cited

Boulton, James, ed. *The Letters of D. H. Lawrence*, vol. I. Cambridge University Press, 1979.

Bradbury, Malcolm and James Farlane, eds. *Modernism, A Guide to European Literature, 1890–1930.* Harmondsworth: Penguin, 1991.

Bullen, J. B. "D. H. Lawrence and Sculpture in *Women in Love.*" *The Burlington Magazine*, cxlv, December 2003.

Delavenay, Emile. "Lawrence and the Futurists" in *The Modernists*, "Studies in a Literary Phenomenon" Rutherford: Fairleigh and Dickinson, Associated University Presses, 1987.

Draper, R. P., ed. *The Critical Heritage*, ed. R. P. Draper. London and Boston: Routledge and Kegan Paul, 1972.

Harrison, Andrew. "Electricity and the Place of Futurism in *Women in Love.*" *The D. H. Lawrence Review*, vol. 29 n 2. State University of New York, 2000.

Lawrence, D. H. *Reflections on the Death of a Porcupine and Other Essays,* ed. Michael Herbert. Cambridge University Press, 1988.

———. *Study of Thomas Hardy and Other Essays*, ed. Bruce Steele. Cambridge University Press, 1985.

———. *Twilight in Italy and Other Essays*, ed. Paul Eggert. Cambridge University Press, 1994.

———. *Women in Love*, eds. David Farmer, Lindeth Vasey, and John Worthen. Cambridge University Press, 1987 (1st pub. 1920).

Lista, Giovanni, ed. *Le futurisme.* Lausanne: L'Age d'homme, 1980.

———, ed. *Marinetti et le futurisme*, Cahiers des avant-gardes, Paris: L'Age d'homme, 1977.

Marinetti, F.T. "Manifeste des peintres Futuristes" in *Le futurisme,* préface de Giovanni Lista. Lausanne: L'Age d'homme, 1980.

Nehls, Edward. *A Composite Biography.* The University of Wisconsin Press, 1957.

Piscopo, Ugo. "Signification et fonction du groupe dans le Futurisme," in *Europe*, n 551, March 1975.

Pound, Ezra. "Desideria," *Exile,* spring 1928.

Pound, Ezra. "Sculpture" in *Literary Essays,* ed. T.S. Eliot. New York: New Directions Publishing 1968 (1st pub. 1954).

Pound, Ezra. "Vorticism," *Blast* n 1, review of the great English vortex. London: John Lane Company, 1914.

Press, John. *A Map of Modern English Verse*. Oxford University Press, 1969.

Read, Herbert. *Art Now, An Introduction to the Theory of Modern Painting and Sculpture.* London: Faber and Faber, 1968 (1st pub. 1933).

Vitoux, Pierre, ed. *The Making of Women in Love, A Selection from the Typescript., Cahiers victoriens et édouardiens.* Montpellier: Université Paul Valéry, 1988.

Wees, William, C. *Vorticism and the English Avant-Garde.* University of Toronto Press, 1972.

Worringer, Wilhelm. *Abstraction and Empathy.* Trans. Michael Bullock. New York: International Universities Press, 1953.

Zytaruk, George J. and James T. Boulton, eds. *The Letters of D. H. Lawrence,* vol. 2. Cambridge University Press, 1981.

Loerke's Statuette

J. B. BULLEN

◆　　◆　　◆

WOMEN IN LOVE is unusual in Lawrence's *oeuvre* in its preoccupation with sculpture. Gudrun Brangwen is a sculptress.
She knows other sculptors in St. Petersburg and Munich. Hermione
Roddice suggests that she teach the techniques of sculpture to Gerald Crich's sister, Winifred, who in her turn wishes to become a
sculptress. "Primitive" or tribal African carving is collected by the
decadent playboy Halliday and images of this same sculpture punc-
tuate the text at significant moments. Loerke is the most prominent
practitioner in the novel and two of his pieces are singled out in the
text: a factory frieze and a bronze statuette of Godiva. The first, Loerke suggests, is a celebration of the mechanical way of life; the second, a naked girl on a horse, he says is "not mechanical." The sculptor shows Gudrun and Ursula a photograph that he carries with
him, and the sight of it elicits divergent reactions from them. In Gudrun it produces "dark homage"[1] while in Ursula it generates profound irritation. Why, asks the latter, is the horse so "stiff" (430)?
The answer she receives is that the sculpture represents, not a real
horse but "a certain *form*": what they see in the photograph, says Lo-

erke, "has no relation with the everyday world" since art and life exist on "distinct planes of existence" (430). Gudrun agrees: "*I* and my art," she says, "have *nothing* to do with one another" (431). The argument comes, of course, from a strain of British aestheticism that Lawrence despised. It received early expression in Roger Fry's 1909 article in the *New Quarterly Magazine*, "An Essay on Aesthetics," where he claimed that art was a function of the imaginative not the practical life and claimed that in "art we have no . . . moral responsibility—it presents a life freed from the binding necessities of our actual existence."[2] He repeated similar views in the catalogue for the second post-impressionist exhibition in 1912 where the post-impressionists "do not seek to imitate form, but to create form," and the idea was taken over by Clive Bell in his book *Art* in 1914. Lawrence would have been familiar with these English adumbrations of European formalism.

Lawrence is very precise about the details of the sculpture. It is:

a naked girl, small, finely made, sitting on a great naked horse. The girl was young and tender, a mere bud. She was sitting sideways on the horse, her face in her hands, as if in shame and grief, in a little abandon. Her hair, which was short and must be flaxen, fell forward, divided, half covering her hands. Her limbs were young and tender. Her legs, scarcely formed yet, the legs of a maiden just passing towards cruel womanhood, dangled childishly over the side of the powerful horse, pathetically, the small feet folded one over the other, as if to hide. But there was no hiding. There she was exposed naked on the naked flank of the horse.

As for the horse itself, it "stood stock-still, stretched in a kind of start. It was a massive, magnificent stallion, rigid with pent-up power. Its neck was arched and terrible, like a sickle, its flanks were pressed back, rigid with power" (429).

Such is the detail that Lawrence supplies there is little doubt about the original of this image. Josef Moest's *Godiva* was first exhibited in 1906.

Several copies were made, some in bronze and some in wood. A bronze version seems to have been bought by Princess Mary of Ro-

Joseph Moest's *Godiva*

mania, and Moest's sister, Rosa Annacker, gave a wooden version to
the Stadtsmuseum in Cologne in 1951. Moest was born in Cologne
in 1873, the son of Richard Moest another sculptor.[3] He studied in
Munich between 1897 and 1902. In 1904 he joined a small group of
four architects, two painters, and two sculptors called the "Kölner
Künstlerervereinigung Stil" dedicated to employing ancient tech-

niques in the context of modern subjects. He travelled extensively in Italy and made regular visits to Davos as part of a cure for tuberculosis. He died young in 1914, at the age of 41. Although Lawrence may not have seen the original statuette, it is clear from his account he must have at least possessed a photograph of it,[4] and there are two pieces of evidence that it was Moest himself who showed it to him. The first comes from a story, "New Eve and Old Adam," that Lawrence wrote in Irschenhausen between May and June 1913 when Lawrence and Frieda were on their way back to England from a long stay at the small village of Gargnano on Lake Garda. The story is set in London and its connection with Moest is solely the surname of the central protagonists. Originally, they had been called "Cyriak,"[5] and then around July 8 Lawrence wrote to Douglas Clayton, his typist, asking him to change the name to "Moest."[6] One of the characters is actually called "Richard Moest"—which was the name of Josef's father, while "Richard" was the middle name of Josef's brother.

If Loerke's *Godiva* is undoubtedly Moest's and the use of this unusual name suggests that the two men knew each other, can we establish how or when they met? I think we can, and the second piece of evidence comes from a postcard that Moest sent his sister from Italy in March 1913.[7] It was from Gargnano on Lake Garda and in it he says that he had arrived in the village on March 3, that he was with a companion, and that he was not sure how long he would remain. His next postcard came from Venice a fortnight later, so we can be fairly sure that he stayed in Gargnano for two weeks. The significance is clear. D. H. Lawrence and Frieda had been renting a house in this same village since September 1912 and they remained there until April 1913. So Moest and the Lawrences were together in the same place for the duration of Moest's stay. Gargnano then had only 1,200 inhabitants;[8] it boasted two hotels—the Hotel Gargnano and the Hotel Cervo—both run by Germans.[9] The wife of the manager of the Cervo, Maria Samuelli, who was also German, befriended Lawrence and Frieda when they first arrived on the lake in September 1912.[10] Had Moest been staying at the Cervo it would hardly be surprising that Maria Samuelli had introduced him to another resident German, Frieda Lawrence,[11] and to her novelist husband who had already begun work on the first version of *Women in Love,* then called *The Sisters.*[12]

There is no evidence whatever that Moest held the views on art that Lawrence attributed to him or that the circumstances in which Loerke produced his *Godiva* were those which led to the production of Moest's sculpture. What is striking, however, is the degree to which Lawrence records the physical appearance of Loerke and the detailed, almost repetitive, attention he gives to his physiognomy. He insists upon his "arresting" and "brown" "quick, full eyes, like a mouse's . . ." (405) and his "fine, thin nostrils" (422). Loerke has "fine, thin, shiny skin, reddish-brown . . . drawn tight over his full temples." His hair was "fine" and black, but "thin . . . on his full, sensitive-looking head, and worn away at his temples" (423). In his brown velvet cap "his head was as round as a chestnut" (468). He had a "thick, coarse, brush-like moustache," which is "cut short about his mobile, rather shapeless mouth" (426). The similarity between this account of Loerke and the portrait of Moest (painted in 1912 by his friend Robert Seuffert and now in Stadtmuseum, Cologne) is very strong. The thin hair indeed outlines the temples; the skin is tightly stretched and distinctly tanned. The eyes in Seuffert's portrait are clearly brown, somewhat murine, and the mouth half-covered by a coarse moustache. Lawrence also has much to say about Loerke's figure, agile and somewhat androgynous. It was, says Lawrence, "slight and unformed" like that of "a boy, almost a street arab" (422); "*chétif* and puny" (468), "smallish" and "odd" (470). The numerous photographs of Moest in the collection of the Cologne Stadtmuseum show a thin, diminutive individual closely resembling Lawrence's account of Loerke.

The character of Lawrence's sculptor Loerke owes a great deal to Lawrence's experiences in pre-war Germany. It would seem that when he met Josef Moest in Gargnano, Moest made a strong, but mainly unpleasant, impression on him and his *Godiva* statuette exemplified for Lawrence something of the emotionally cold aloofness of early twentieth-century aestheticism. Hitherto, it has been thought that that the figure of Loerke and his ideas about sculpture derived mainly from Lawrence's war-time experiences, but we can now see that the roots of his attitudes to sculpture in this novel are

to be found in the pre-war Germany and his chance meeting with Josef Moest on the shores of Lake Garda.

Notes

1. D. H. Lawrence, *Women in Love*, ed. David Farmer, Lindeth Vasey, and John Worthen (Cambridge University Press, 1987), 429; hereafter page numbers cited in brackets after quotations.

2. Roger Fry, "An Essay in Aesthetics," *New Quarterly Magazine*, 2 (1909), 171–90. Reprinted in his *Vision and Design*, 1920.

3. Information from Freya Danhöffer, author of "Joseph Moest (1873–1914)," *Kölner Museums-Bulletin*, 4 (1995), 30–36.

4. In the Moest collection in the Cologne Stadtmuseum there is, amongst the postcards collected by his sister Rosa Annacker, a black-and-white reproduction of the *Godiva*.

5. Possibly, conjectures John Worthen, after Antonia Almgren (née Cyriak) who came to stay with the Lawrences in Gargnano around 1 March 1913. See D. H. Lawrence, *Love Among the Haystacks and Other Stories*, ed. John Worthen (Cambridge University Press, 1987), 247–248.

6. Ibid.

7. This is in an album of such post cards in the Stadtmuseum, Cologne. KSM–G 16795.

8. According to Karl Baedeker, *Northern Italy.* Leipzig, 1913, 285.

9. *Oberitalien mit Ravenna, Florenz und Livorno: Handbuch für Reisende von Karl Baedeker, Achtzehnte Auflage.* Leipzig, 1911, 244. John Worthen kindly supplied this reference.

10. John Worthen, *D. H. Lawrence: The Early Years 1885–1912* (Cambridge University Press, 1991), 431; and information from Worthen himself.

11. On 11 March, Frieda went 'boating with some Germans' on Lake Garda. Letter to Edward Garnett, 11 March 1913. *The Letters of D. H. Lawrence* ed. James T. Boulton, et al. (Cambridge University Press, 1979–2000), i, 572.

12. The editors of *Women in Love* state that Lawrence began *Sisters–1* in the middle of March 1913. See *Women in Love*, 1987, xxi.

Index

❖　❖　❖